As it challenges us to question taken-for-granted assumptions of our discipline, *Embodied Power* urges us to think beyond the constraints of conventional social science. Hawkesworth presents a convincing argument that until political science takes race, class and gender seriously it cannot fully understand contemporary politics. A must-read for scholars in all subfields of political science as well as those seeking more just solutions to today's problems.

J. Ann Tickner, American University

This book is a manifesto for intersectionality as a process-based form of analysis and way of seeing the world. Hawkesworth disposes of the mystifications that constitute the 'standard' methodologies of political science, but goes well beyond mere critique. Her work sets in place a practical alternative to all-too-familiar methodological individualisms and raced-gendered nationalisms.

Terrell Carver, University of Bristol

Once again, Mary Hawkesworth has crafted a lucid and compelling account of racing-gendering processes and the material occlusions and power relations they produce in the United States. *Embodied Power* belongs in the canon of political science and should be required reading for all political scientists. It certainly will be for all of my future students.

Ange-Marie Hancock, University of Southern California

EMBODIED POWER

Embodied Power explores dimensions of politics seldom addressed in political science, illuminating state practices that produce hierarchically organized groups through racialized gendering – despite guarantees of formal equality. Challenging disembodied accounts of citizenship, the book traces how modern science and law produce race, gender, and sexuality as purportedly natural characteristics, masking their political genesis. Taking the United States as a case study, Hawkesworth demonstrates how diverse laws and policies concerning civil and political rights, education, housing, and welfare, immigration and securitization, policing and criminal justice create finely honed hierarchies of difference that structure the life prospects of men and women of particular races and ethnicities within and across borders. In addition to documenting the continuing operation of embodied power across diverse policy terrains, the book investigates complex ways of seeing that render raced-gendered relations of domination and subordination invisible. From common assumptions about individualism and colorblind perception to disciplinary norms such as methodological individualism, methodological nationalism, and abstract universalism, problematic presuppositions sustain mistaken notions concerning formal equality and legal neutrality that allow state practices of racialized gendering to escape detection with profound consequences for the life prospects of privileged and marginalized groups. Through sustained critique of these flawed suppositions, *Embodied Power* challenges central beliefs about the nature of power, the scope of state action, and the practice of liberal democracy and identifies alternative theoretical frameworks that make racialized-gendering visible and actionable.

Mary Hawkesworth is Distinguished Professor of Political Science and Women's and Gender Studies at Rutgers University.

EMBODIED POWER

Demystifying Disembodied Politics

Mary Hawkesworth

Routledge
Taylor & Francis Group
NEW YORK AND LONDON

First published 2016
by Routledge
711 Third Avenue, New York, NY 10017

and by Routledge
2 Park Square, Milton Park, Abingdon, Oxon OX14 4RN

Routledge is an imprint of the Taylor & Francis Group, an informa business

© 2016 Taylor & Francis

The right of Mary Hawkesworth to be identified as author of this work has been asserted by her in accordance with sections 77 and 78 of the Copyright, Designs and Patents Act 1988.

All rights reserved. No part of this book may be reprinted or reproduced or utilised in any form or by any electronic, mechanical, or other means, now known or hereafter invented, including photocopying and recording, or in any information storage or retrieval system, without permission in writing from the publishers.

Trademark notice: Product or corporate names may be trademarks or registered trademarks, and are used only for identification and explanation without intent to infringe.

Library of Congress Cataloging in Publication Data
Names: Hawkesworth, M. E., 1952- author.
  Title: Embodied power : demystifying disembodied politics / Mary Hawkesworth, Rutgers University.
  Description: New York, NY : Routledge, 2016. | Includes bibliographical references.
  Identifiers: LCCN 2015046406| ISBN 9781138667297 (hardback) | ISBN 9781138667310 (pbk.) | ISBN 9781315618968 (ebook)
  Subjects: LCSH: Power (Social sciences)–United States. | Sexism in political culture–United States. | Racism–Political aspects–United States.
  Classification: LCC HN90.P6 H38 2016 | DDC 303.30973–dc23
LC record available at http://lccn.loc.gov/2015046406

ISBN: 9781138667297 (hbk)
ISBN: 9781138667310 (pbk)
ISBN: 9781315618968 (ebk)

Typeset in Bembo
by Taylor & Francis Books

CONTENTS

Acknowledgments ix

1 Embodied Power 1
   Alternative Frameworks 6
      Intersectionality 6
      Postcolonial and De-colonial Theory 10
      Gendered Racialization, Racialized Gendering 14
   Chapter Overview 17

2 Conceptual Practices of Power 25
   A Critical History of American Political Science 33
   Conceptual Practices of Power 41
      Classification 41
      Methodological Individualism 43
      Methodological Nationalism 44
      Abstract Universalism 45
      White Androcentrism 45
   Conclusion 46

3 The Science and Politics of Bodies 50
   Biologizing Race 52
   Biologizing Sex 58
   Biologism Resurrected 66

Resurrecting Biological Race 68
Conclusion 72

4 From Race and Sex to Racialization, Gendering, and Sexualization   73

Constructing the Boundaries of Belonging 74
The Transnational Politics of Racialization 81
Racialization under the Guise of Race Neutrality 83
Constructing Racialized-Gendered Tiers of Citizenship 85
Protecting the Nation from Internal and External Threats 96
Conclusion 105

5 Ways of Seeing, Modes of Being   110

Individualism 112
Colorblind Perception 117
Methodological Individualism 123
Methodological Nationalism 128
Conclusion 135

6 Revisioning Power, Reclaiming Politics   140

Intersectionality as an Analytical Frame 143
    Recognizing Racialized-Gendering 143
    Displacing White Androcentrism as the
      Unmarked Norm 144
    De-naturalizing Difference 145
    Investigating Processes 146
    Engaging Multi-level Analysis 147
    Intersectionality's Methodological Precepts 148
Whiteness: From Historical Artefact to Discursive Formation 149
Correcting Contorted Causality 152
Expanding the Contours of the Political 159
Conclusion 164

Bibliography   *166*
Index   *182*

ACKNOWLEDGMENTS

Training in an academic field involves intensive socialization to discipline-based norms concerning the objects of study, the nature of knowledge, the appropriate means of intellectual inquiry, and the scope of investigation suitable to the profession. As a graduate student in the 1970s, I was required to pass qualifying exams in four fields: American politics, comparative politics, international relations, and political theory. My training was rigorous and demanding and equipped me well to teach a wide range of courses as I launched my academic career. To the best of my recollection, however, none of my courses seriously addressed race or gender. My constitutional law classes covered "the incorporation controversy," which explored when and under what conditions the equality clause of the 14th Amendment was binding on the states, but the focus was jurisprudence not racial and gender equality. When we discussed the use of the Commerce Clause to extend federal jurisdiction on civil rights, we marveled at the political ingenuity of certain members of Congress to outmaneuver Southern Democrats, but did not dwell on the depredations of segregation or the profound consequences of continuing racism for the lives of citizens of color.

Thus, my path to an understanding of embodied power – state practices that produce hierarchically organized groups through racialized gendering – has been long and painfully slow. Certain aspects of my dis-identification with disciplinary norms concerning disembodied politics can be traced to my involvement with feminist activism and the development of women's and gender studies as an interdisciplinary field. Addressing racism and white privilege have been central concerns of U.S. feminism since the 1970s, however imperfectly realized. During my 19 years at the University of Louisville, the "Difficult Dialogues" organized by Dr. Judi Jennings, then director of the University Women's Center, created a space to confront racism, racialization, and white indifference. The urgency of racial inequality was brought home by work with the interracial coalition built by Ann Braden to combat persistent residential segregation, under-representation of Blacks in the university despite the existence of court-ordered desegregation, Klan activity, and the reorganization of local politics (merging county and city governments) to dilute the Black vote.

The opportunity to work with outstanding scholars of color and to witness their struggles in the academy proved equally powerful as a transformative force. I owe a great debt of thanks to colleagues who shared their scholarship with me and who pressed me to begin reading the rich literature in African American philosophy, Black history, and critical race theory. Donna Eaves, Carol Cummings, Eric Hill, Blane Hudson, Yvonne Jones, Stephen Houston Marshall, and Victor Olorunsola introduced me to African American Studies and shared their time and their expertise generously in discussing this path-breaking work.

Within APSA circuits, I have had the privilege of working with feminist scholars in the Black Caucus and the Latino/a Caucus who were determined to expand the agenda of the Women's Caucus for Political Science to address the needs of women of color in the profession. I am particularly grateful to Julia Jordan-Zachery, Anna Sampaio, Ange-Marie Hancock, and Cristina Beltran for their organizational genius and for sharing their works-in-progress, which have profoundly influenced my thinking.

I owe a special debt to Breny Mendoza who introduced me to post-occidental scholarship and whose brilliant critiques of U.S. politics and policy have stimulated enormously productive conversations. At the instigation and with the help of Jane Bayes, we have moved these discussions from restaurants and dinner tables to panels at the APSA, IPSA, ISA, and WPSA.

At Rutgers, I have also been extremely fortunate to have colleagues whose innovative research challenges me to see the world in far more complex and sophisticated ways. Nikol Alexander Floyd, Abena Busia, Carlos Decena, Judith Gerson, Angelique Haugerud, Zenzele Isoke, Marisa Fuentes, Zakia Salime, Shatema Threadcraft, Brittney Cooper, and Melanye Price have enriched my intellectual world, as well as departmental and university politics.

Two journals have also figured prominently in reshaping my thinking beyond the traditional boundaries fixed in political science. *The International Feminist Journal of Politics* has broken new ground, demonstrating how racialized gendering and gendered racialization operate in the international arena and in transnational organizations and activism. My work with *Signs: Journal of Women in Culture and Society* has also been transformative. The insights of interdisciplinary scholars have illuminated dimensions of politics seldom discussed in political science. Reading the probing works of authors and reviewers has afforded me splendid insights about how to use interdisciplinary knowledge production to open new modes of inquiry in a traditional discipline such as political science.

It is no exaggeration to say that this book owes its existence to Jennifer Knerr, whose editorial encouragement, insight, patience, and assistance have been extraordinary. No expression of thanks can possibly repay my debt to Jennifer for her continuous support over the past five years. Thanks also to Ze'ev Sudry for all his expert assistance in moving the manuscript through final review and production processes.

My final unpayable debt of thanks is to Philip Alperson, whose support and gentle ministrations have enabled the research and writing of this book despite medical emergencies, work crises, and monumental commutes.

September 7, 2015

1
EMBODIED POWER

> Ignorance is not just a black space on a person's mental map. It has contours and coherence, and for all I know rules of operation as well.
>
> *(Thomas Pynchon 1984, 15)*

Politics in the 21st-century United States has deviated rather dramatically from established notions about rule of law, stable institutions, and predictable outcomes of conventional practices. In the first presidential election of the new millennium, for example, the winner was determined not by a plurality of votes or by the Electoral College but by the U.S. Supreme Court, an institution bound by the Constitution and judicial precedent not to decide "political" questions. The polling results from Florida, which generated *Bush v. Gore* (531 U.S. 98 [2000]) were tied to voting lists riddled with errors and mistaken entries that purged more than 12,000 qualified Black voters from registration rolls during the 2000 election cycle. If the fates of the most powerful political actors in the nation were affected by embodied power, so too were the fates of some of the least advantaged members of the polity. Federal welfare legislation passed in 1996, which replaced welfare entitlements (AFDC) with "Temporary Assistance to Needy Families" (TANF), allowed states to severely restrict poor women citizens' autonomy, privacy rights, reproductive freedom, and bodily integrity, subjecting them to unwaged labor ("workfare"), interrogation about their sexual histories, and mandatory paternity identification through genetic testing (Smith 2004). In the aftermath of the terrorist bombings of the World Trade Center and the Pentagon, more than 5,000 men – predominantly Muslims and Arabs – were held in detention, many in solitary confinement for 23 hours per day, subjected to recurrent strip searches without being charged with a crime and without having access to legal counsel (Sampaio 2015). Beyond the borders of the United States, "detainees," held in "black sites" without being formally charged, were subjected to brutal interrogation techniques condoned by the CIA, the Department of Defense and the Department of Justice – techniques designed to "feminize" and "dehumanize" by destroying personality, individuality, agency, and resistance (Kaufman-Osborn 2005). "Sovereign citizens," proclaiming themselves contemporary "Minute Men," patrolled the increasingly militarized southern border of the United States as vigilante and state "securitization" measures operated to bar Latino/as from undocumented entry. To protect its citizens from "perceived" threats, 23 US states passed "stand-your-ground laws" that allow use of deadly force in "self-defense" without the duty to retreat, laws that inspired the murder of 17-year-old Trayvon Martin, and subsequently sustained the acquittal of his murderer. Recent deaths of multiple Black men while in police custody, which were captured on videotape and circulated on social media, put a spotlight on extrajudicial violence and raised important questions about the conversion of misdemeanor offenses into crimes punished by death. In the aftermath of political unrest in Ferguson, Missouri, on the first anniversary of the fatal police shooting of Michael Brown, armed white vigilantes, who called themselves "Oath Keepers," began patrolling the streets of this majority-Black community.

Each of these examples involves a form of embodied power that does not fit well with conceptions of politics advanced within the discipline of political science. Whether invoking the classical Aristotelian conception of participating in the activities of ruling and being ruled, a Weberian conception of rational-legal bureaucratic decision-making, a new institutionalist focus on the official institutions of state, a pluralist emphasis on interest accommodation, a functionalist understanding of the central challenges of political systems (e.g., state building, nation building, participation, allocation of values, redistribution, systems integration), or a sustained examination of "political behavior," political science offers an abstract account of equal citizens, and a disembodied account of politics in which race, gender, ethnicity, nationality and sexuality play no central political role. Although overt instances of racist or sexist oppression may on occasion be acknowledged, they are treated as anomalies that reveal nothing about politics or political power *per se*. Adhering to liberal assumptions about equal citizenship, national belonging, human rights embedded in national constitutions and international conventions, and exercises of power circumscribed by law, disembodied politics pays no heed to scripted practices of subordination associated with racialization and gendering.

The central thesis of this book is that inattention to embodied power severely limits contemporary understandings of the political. Disembodied politics fails to account for mechanisms of power that operate epistemically and ontologically, shaping perceptions, understandings, ways of being and ways of interacting with others. Indeed, disembodied politics renders invisible state policies and practices that create particular raced-gendered-sexualized identities situated in relations of domination and subordination. Through criteria for citizenship and naturalization, census categories, manifold classification systems created by statute and bureaucratic decisions, state practices of policing, surveillance and securitization, distributive and redistributive policies, health and employment regulations, states engage in racialization and gendering, creating forms of inequality "written on the body," producing women and men as members of particular races, classes, ethnicities, nationalities, and sexualities. The state does far more than "manage" a diverse population, its produces *group* identities in and through exclusionary political processes and substantive policies.

Embodied power refers to the production of hierarchically organized groups through racialization and gendering, and to practices that situate raced-classed-sexed individuals within particular groups, which profoundly affects the kinds of public persona and political action possible for them. Racialization and gendering simultaneously create the dominant and the subordinate by means of laws, norms, policies, and practices that categorize, separate, assign places in the social order, and seep into individual consciousness in ways that try to ensure the individual knows his/her place.

Embodied power is manifested in multiple ways:

- Categories of race and sex produce "group" membership. Women and men from diverse cultures, traditions, and regions, who may have little if anything in common, are deemed "the same" by virtue of their placement within one category. For example, hundreds of ethnic groups in South Asia, the Caribbean, and in South, Central, and North America were subsumed under the rubric "Indian" in the context of colonization. From 1882 through 1965, the Asian Exclusion Acts homogenized half the world's population into one – "Asian" – category, a group excluded from immigration and naturalization in the United States.
- Racist and sexist ideas provide rationales for and legitimate practices of state-sanctioned oppression. For example, the African slave trade, the conversion of indentured servitude to chattel slavery, the exploitation of indigenous labor through *encomiendas*, and extermination of indigenous peoples were integral to European colonization of the "new world" in the 16th through 19th centuries. Just as declarations about the rights of Afghan women, and the feminization of Muslim men at Abu Ghraib and Guantanamo were integral to the "War on Terror."
- Racist and sexist practices require and produce performances of servility, subservience, and subjection. As Frantz Fanon (1952) demonstrated in *Black Skin, White Masks*, scripted practices of subordination associated with colonialism were often internalized by the colonized, resulting not only in the conviction of inferiority, but internalized self-hatred – a phenomenon familiar to racialized and sexual minorities in contemporary nations.
- Racialization is integral to war-making through the construction of "the enemy" and the partition of the world into stable nation-states and "peripheral" zones in which proxy wars exacerbate local conflicts. Both the

depiction of these so-called peripheral wars and accounts of their causes (boundary disputes, irredentist claims, ethnic and tribal divisions, religious clashes, local war lords, rogue states) depend upon and re-inscribe racial hierarchies. The extreme violence – expulsion of populations, seizure of land, rape, ethnic cleansing, and genocide – involved in wars in the former Yugoslavia, Rwanda, and Darfur make the dynamics and consequences of racialization and gendering visible. Situating these horrors in a discourse of "failed states," however, masks the role of racialization and gendering in these conflicts, appealing instead to a civilized/barbaric binary that rests upon racist presuppositions.

- Gendered racialization produces modes of invisibility and hypervisibility. As white men are positioned as the unmarked norm – the citizen, the humanitarian, the cosmopolitan – their race becomes invisible. By contrast, black women are made hyper-visible in relation to putative welfare dependency and black men are criminalized both in terms of popular expectations and in terms of police surveillance.
- Racialized gendering also eclipses individuality as "whites" are positioned in stark opposition to "Blacks" and "men" to "women." Commonalities and idiosyncrasies, privileges and constraints, are occluded as dichotomous categorization masks intricate relations of co-constitution and complex differentiation within and across races and genders.

Embodied power may also engender mobilizations by the marginalized to contest imposed identities and unwarranted constraints on freedom, and to disrupt conventions that do psychic damage as well as impairing economic, social, and political survival. As decades of struggle against apartheid in South Africa, for civil rights in the USA, and to create a Muslim *Ummah* (community) in multiple Middle East and North African states demonstrate, mass mobilization, grassroots protest, and violent confrontation are triggered by oppressive practices associated with racialization and gendering. Contestations over dominant social beliefs and values, entrenched or recently cultivated prejudices and hatreds, as well as modes of social organization that concentrate privilege and disadvantage on different sectors of the population can generate transformed self-understandings and social relations. Consciousness raising, dis-identification from hegemonic norms, construction of collective identities and allegiances, and, sometimes, armed conflict can be manifestations of embodied power – when those who have been marginalized struggle to craft new identities and new polities, freed from stigma and insult.

Whether examined in historical context or in contemporary affairs, embodied power manifests in state action and in political mobilization against raced-gendered practices of the state. Racialization and gendering are apparent in domestic policy (e.g., education, health, social services, criminal justice, military recruitment, securitization, immigration) and in international relations (e.g., characterizations of "rogue" states and "humanitarian" interventions, distributions of foreign aid and development initiatives, operations of state terror, and armed insurrections). The mechanisms of embodied power are diverse. They include stereotyping and construction of target populations; differential treatment, marginalization, and exclusion of particular racialized groups; silencing; withholding epistemic authority and political recognition; surveillance; detention; death and collective extermination. Given its pervasive presence, why is embodied power so neglected by the discipline of political science?

In their fascinating work *Agnotology: The Making and Unmaking of Ignorance*, Robert Proctor and Londa Schiebinger (2008, 2) suggest that "ignorance has a history and a complex political and sexual geography." Far from being a "natural absence or a void where knowledge has not yet spread," "unknowing" is produced and maintained in diverse settings. Proctor and Schiebinger advocate the study of ignorance and the development of tools for understanding how and why various forms of knowing "have not come to be" or have disappeared, or have been delayed or neglected. And they emphasize that in contrast to deliberate efforts to suppress information through secrecy or the destruction of documents, unknowing is often inadvertent, the result of adherence to unquestioned tradition or a "culturopolitical selectivity," which relegates some things to the realm of the invisible, illegible, or unintelligible.

In a sense, *Embodied Power: Demystifying Disembodied Politics* is an exercise in agnotology, an effort to explain why pervasive practices of racialization and gendering remain unrecognized and unstudied in the context of mainstream political science.[1] I suggest that certain disciplinary assumptions about the nature of politics and the requirements for scientific study of the political world have rendered embodied power particularly difficult to perceive. A way of seeing embodiment as pre-political, a way of naturalizing the nation-state, and a way of privileging institutional analysis and methodological individualism contribute to a way of *not seeing* processes of racialization and gendering as integral to state enactments of embodied power. Reworking Pynchon's insight in the epigraph to this chapter, one might say that ignorance is indeed a "black spot" on the discipline's mental map, which excludes certain kinds of evidence, and privileges particular kinds of explanation, thereby rendering embodied power beyond the threshold of visibility. Indeed, processes of racialization and gendering developed over the past five centuries under the auspices of "science" have been embedded in law, custom, accredited knowledge, and diverse social practices, lending coherence to forms of unknowing that continue to haunt political science in particular and public life more generally.

As Banu Bargu (2015) has noted, political thinkers from Hobbes to Foucault have contributed to discourses that conceal the state's recourse to embodied power. Bargu suggests that political analysts "abstract from the materiality of human bodies, transform relations of force between bodies into a formal discourse of rights and obligations, and fail to attend to the material agency of subjugation insofar as it constitutes subjects" (Bargu 2015, 12). This "disembodiment" shifts attention away from bodies toward a conception of "legal persons" (12). Indeed, "decorporealization" erases the bodies of individuals who are incorporated into "the body politic" as abstract, rights-bearing juridical subjects. Decorporealization also "erases actual conflict that lies at the foundations of sovereignty, eliminat[ing] the historical reality of war, elid[ing] history" (13).

Contemporary political science replicates the decorporealization characteristic of modern political thought, contributing to the erasure of embodied power in historical practices and ongoing social and political conflicts. Later chapters explore various mechanics of erasure, tracing the construction of raced and gendered bodies as biological entities to the long eighteenth century. By attributing relations of superiority and inferiority to nature, proponents of empirical scientific inquiry and modern political thinkers position racial and gendered hierarchies beyond the reach of the state. To the extent that race and gender are construed as biologically given, whether as individual attributes or population characteristics, racialization and gendering are effectively removed from the realm of the political. But as Chapters 2 and 3 demonstrate, the de-politicization of embodiment coincided with the expansion of European empires through brutal conquest, labor exploitation and enslavement and the emergence of new republics that barred women from political participation. As the blatant violence of conquest, colonization, and dispossession of indigenous people by settler societies was rendered invisible, a peculiar inversion of causality surfaced in political analyses. The colonized, enslaved, and disenfranchised – the raced and the gendered – were said to be responsible for their own condition. Their physical subjugation was attributed not to defeat by European colonizers or laws declaring them subordinate or dependent, but to their inherent inferiority. Characterized as childlike, primitive, or savage, lacking the discipline required for self-governance, those deemed less than fully human were condemned to paternalist rule "for their own good."

In recent decades, several innovative approaches to the study of politics have helped to make visible processes of racialization, gendering, and sexualization long neglected by mainstream political science. Critical race theory, feminist theory, postcolonial theory, post-occidental theory, and the theorization of intersectionality advanced by Black feminist scholars and feminist scholars of color offer analytical frameworks that foreground the centrality of racialization and gendering in political life. Moreover, they identify patterns of unknowing, misrecognition, and inverted notions of causality that erase embodied power. The central tenets of these innovative approaches are sketched in the next section.

Alternative Frameworks

Intersectionality

Theorizing embodied power is one of the most distinctive contributions of the concept of *intersectionality* developed by Black feminist theorists (Crenshaw 1989,

1991; Roberts 1999, 2011; Hancock 2007a, 2007b, 2011, 2016; Simien 2007; Alexander-Floyd 2012; Cooper 2016). Intersectionality challenges the presumption of "sexual dimorphism" – the belief that there are two and only two sexes; the notion that race is a biological phenomenon; and the view that sexual desire follows automatically from possession of particular male and female genitalia. Rather than acquiescing in the normalization of a political order stratified by race, sex, heterosexuality, and the geopolitics of North/South, intersectionality scholars conceptualize racialization and gendering as political processes that create and sustain divisions of labor, social stratifications, modes of subjection, and structures of desire. Moreover, they trace the historical emergence of – and the political work done by – beliefs concerning biological determinism to European epistemic regimes that were themselves intricately tied to practices of enslavement, colonization and the invention of "modernity."

Rather than accepting the naturalization of race, sex, and sexuality, intersectionality thoroughly "denaturalizes" embodiment, demonstrating how racialized notions of maleness and femaleness are constructed in relation to conquest, Middle Passage, waged, unwaged and coerced labor, legal constraints, and political status – and then consolidated into national orders and international regimes of finely honed hierarchies of difference. Far from reflecting a "natural condition," intersectional analyses demonstrate how biological determinist accounts of race and sex are themselves mechanisms of racialization and gendering that mask violent modes of domination.

Contemporary Black feminist scholars have traced the roots of intersectional analyses to nineteenth century African American women's analyses of the simultaneity of oppression that structured their lives (Sheftall 1995; Cooper 2016; Hancock 2016). Two centuries of writing by and about Black women analyze multiple hierarchies of power that weave race, gender, class, and sexuality into a potent mode of "multiple jeopardy" (King 1988). These insightful analyses illuminate the multiple vectors of power that interact in practices such as enslavement, economic exploitation, coerced reproduction, Black Codes, lynching, eugenics, sterilization abuse, poverty, denial and infringement of constitutional rights, political repression, institutional, attitudinal, and cultural racism.

Critical race and feminist legal theory scholar, Kimberlé Crenshaw (1989, 140) coined the term *intersectionality* to counter the pervasive tendency in jurisprudence and social science "to treat race and gender as mutually exclusive categories of experience and analysis." As an intellectual practice, categorization creates order by distinguishing among "kinds" or "types," subsuming individual cases under a particular kind within a system of categories that are purported to be mutually exclusive and cumulatively exhaustive. Crenshaw pointed out that the fundamental assumptions underlying "single-axis" categorization made the experiences of Black women invisible. Indeed, as exemplified by U.S. court decisions pertaining to racial discrimination and sex discrimination, single-axis analysis made it impossible for Black women to gain redress for the intermingling and co-constituting modes of raced-gendered discrimination they experienced in daily life. Because the modes of racial discrimination Black women faced were not shared by Black men and the modes of sex discrimination they faced were not shared by white women, the courts consistently ruled that the harms Black women experienced counted as neither racial nor sexual discrimination. The analytic tools used by the courts rendered invisible the complex "systems of oppression, namely racism, classism, sexism, and heterosexism [that] worked together to create a set of social conditions under which Black women and other women of color lived and labored, always in a kind of invisible but ever-present, social jeopardy" (King 1988, 47). By placing the simultaneous and interacting oppressions experienced by women of color not only beyond legal redress, but beyond the threshold of intelligibility, the U.S. courts enacted a potent form of embodied power. Crenshaw (1989, 140) argued that both legal reasoning and policy frameworks must be rethought and recast to counter "this single-axis framework [that] erases Black women in the conceptualization, identification and remediation of race and sex discrimination by limiting inquiry to the experiences of otherwise-privileged members of the group."

Over the past four decades, intersectionality scholarship has proliferated.[2] As a research paradigm, intersectionality offers a heuristic rather than a unified genre or a single intellectual or political project (Roshanravan 2014; Mendoza 2016). As European feminist theorist Kathy Davis (2008, 79) has suggested, at a minimum, "intersectionality initiates a process of discovery, alerting us to the fact that the world around us is always more complicated and contradictory than we ever could have anticipated. It compels us to grapple with complexity in our scholarship." Yet many scholars suggest that intersectionality research necessarily goes well beyond an analysis of complexity. "As analytical technique," Julia Jordan-Zachery (2007, 256) has noted, "intersectionality allows us to stop essentializing differences ... [it] illuminates structural dimensions of inequality ... how they play out in individual lives ... [and their] relevance ... to political strategies." In the words of Evelyn Simien (2007, 266), "intersectional analysis attends to power relations between groups, rendering visible invisible norms that privilege some and disadvantage others." Confounding binary thinking, "the simultaneity of oppression makes it clear that race and gender cannot be reduced to individual attributes to be measured and assessed for their separate contributions in explaining political outcomes, from vote choice to policy preferences ... Race and gender cannot be defined in terms of strict dichotomies – either black or white or male or female – when race is gendered and gender is racialized in such a way that it creates distinct advantages and disadvantages for particular raced-gendered configurations" (Simien 2007, 266).

In a series of articles and essays, Ange-Marie Hancock (2007a, 2007b, 2009, 2011, 2016) has noted the transformation of intersectionality from "a content specialization: the study of women of color ... [whose] goal is political inclusion, increasing knowledge about groups previously excluded from study" to "a research paradigm [that] can answer new questions, inconceivable within traditional models – questions about distributive justice, power, and government function central to the discipline of political science (Hancock 2007a, 249–50). In the context of political science research, Hancock (2007b, 67) suggests that intersectionality as a research paradigm makes at least two important methodological interventions: it "changes the relationship between the categories of investigation from one that is determined a priori to one of empirical investigation ... Additionally, intersectionality posits an interactive, mutually constituted relationship among these categories and the way in which race (or ethnicity) and gender (or other relevant categories) play a role in the shaping of political institutions, political actors, the relationships between institutions and actors and the relevant categories themselves." In contrast to notions of colorblind and value-free research, Hancock (2009, 97) emphasizes that intersectionality "interrogates power relations that constitute race as a category of political difference in the United States at either the institutional or the individual level."

Linking innovative research to social transformation, Nikol Alexander-Floyd (2012, 9) defines intersectionality "as the commitment to centering research and analysis on the lived experiences of women of color for the purpose of making visible and addressing their marginalization ... challenging business as usual in mainstream disciplines' habits of knowledge production." In contrast to the purported value-neutrality of social science research, Breny Mendoza (2016, 106) notes that "emphasizing the multidimensional vectors of power that structure both lived identities and social reality, intersectionality illuminate[s] ties between epistemic location and knowledge production, and offer[s] analytic strategies that link the material, the discursive, and the structural." Indeed, "as a conceptual and analytic tool for thinking about the operations of power," Brittney Cooper (2016, 405) notes that intersectionality "can illuminate the diverse ways in which relations of domination and subordination are produced":

> Challenging the ever-shifting machinations of systems that seek to reinstantiate and reinscribe dominance ... intersectionality's primary concern is to expose the way that circulations of power enable or disable articulations of identity. Intersectionality makes visible the disciplinary apparatus of the state – census, demography, racial profiling, surveillance – [which] is already interpellating identities in violent ways ... and theorizes how legal constructions continually produce categories of bodies that exist outside the limits of legal protection. In other words, the ways in which juridical structures affix narratives of criminality to black male bodies (or brown bodies), for instance Trayvon Martin and Jordan Davis, on the basis of a very particular race-gender schema.
> *(Cooper 2016, 392, 396, 367)*

By "exposing the operations of power in places where a single axis approach might render those operations invisible," Cooper emphasizes that "intersectionality has a teleological aim to … dismantle dominant systems of power, to promote the inclusion of Black women and other women of color, and transform the epistemological grounds upon which these institutions conceive of and understand themselves" (2016, 404). Intersectionality provides an invaluable analytical tool for the investigation of embodied power precisely because it calls attention to state action that enabled and authorized practices of enslavement, dispossession, economic exploitation, reproductive violence, *de jure* segregation, discrimination in employment and education, disenfranchisement and second-class citizenship, which coexist with constitutional guarantees of formal rights.

Postcolonial and De-colonial Theory

Anti-colonial theory offers a second important analytical framework for the illumination of the deficiencies of disembodied politics. Crafted by theorists in the global South, postcolonial and de-colonial theory challenge the hegemonic accounts of modernity and development that originated in Europe and North America, contesting the narrative of progress associated with modernity as an "unfolding of reason and freedom" (Hegel 1807) that legitimated European colonialism and imperialism. Articulating "epistemologies of the South" (Mignolo 2000; Santos 2014), the South Asian *Subaltern Studies Group*, typically associated with postcolonial scholarship, and the Latin American Modernity/Coloniality Group, originators of de-colonial or post-occidental scholarship, advance radical reinterpretations of capitalism, modernity, and colonialism that demonstrate the centrality of race and racialization to these processes. Although there are many differences between the substantive arguments of the Subaltern Studies Group, which focuses on the British colonization of India and other parts of Asia, and the Modernity/Coloniality Group, which analyzes the earlier Spanish and Portuguese colonization of the Americas, postcolonial and de-colonial scholarship offer key insights for the investigation of embodied power and the dynamics of disembodied politics.[3] Rather than isolating colonialism in the distant past, or casting it as an aberration in the progressive unfolding of "modern" civilization, they illuminate the integral connections between "modernity" and "coloniality." They analyze racialization and gendering as strategies of power essential to the colonial project. They make visible the epistemic violence central to the suppression of indigenous knowledges and cultures. And they document the production of homogeneous national citizenship through the violent suppression, expulsion, or extermination of "heterogeneous" elements in the population. By insisting on historical specificity, they challenge "two founding myths of Eurocentrism: first, the history of human civilization as a trajectory from *state of nature to liberal democratic* Europe (present in evolution, modernization); and that, second, *differences between Europe and non-Europe are biological,* not a consequence of particular history of power" (Quijano 2000, 542, emphasis in original). By tracing continuities in ways of seeing, modes of thinking, accredited knowing, and systems of signification cultivated during centuries of colonial domination with pervasive lingering effects, they demonstrate how a particular Eurocentric intersubjective universe became the foundation for a global model of power that persists in the 21st century.

Frantz Fanon (1952) was one of the first anti-colonial thinkers to recognize the fundamental continuity in and devastating effects of colonial social, economic, cultural, ethical, sexual, and epistemological relations. In *Black Skin, White Masks*, Fanon traces the process by which colonizers produce the colonized as an inferior racial group. He coins the term "epidermalization" to capture the reduction of rich cultures, knowledge systems, and ways of being to a demonized and denigrated "blackness." Beyond conquest and exploitation, colonial racialization contributes to internalized oppression. The colonized lose their cultural bearings, adopt the language of the colonizer, and accept the premise that European culture is inherently superior. Inured to the civilizational discourses of the colonizer, the colonized develop a potent self-hatred as the embodiment of an inferior race. According to Fanon, one pernicious aspect of racialization is that the colonized are required "not only to be black but to be black in relation to the white man." Judging oneself and one's culture by the standard of white civilization, the colonized develop a conviction of their own inferiority, suffering a profound loss of self-respect, cultural pride, and self-confidence.

Fanon suggests that academic disciplines, most notably philosophy, psychology, anthropology, biology, and political science are deeply implicated in the project of epidermalization. They accredit Eurocentric claims concerning evolution, modernization, and development that posit white models of civilization as the telos of humanity. Through the educational system, these disciplines inculcate aspirations to emulate European norms that saturate the consciousness of the colonized, shoring up white structural domination. To overcome such internalized oppression is a demanding process that cannot be accomplished at the level of thought alone. Indeed, Fanon argues that to reassert their humanity, the colonized must participate in revolutionary violence.

Following Fanon, Peruvian sociologist Anibal Quijano theorized the coloniality of power as a process of racialization integral to colonization. Where Fanon had focused on French colonialism in the 19th and twentieth century, Quijano examined a much older form of Spanish and Portuguese colonization of the Americas dating to the fifteenth century. According to Quijano (2000), Iberian colonialism involved a "new politics of population reorganization" (538), "a model of power characterized by codification of differences between conquerors and conquered under rubric of 'race'" (533). In contrast to differences grounded in culture and tradition, race connoted a "different *biological* structure that placed some in a situation of inferiority to others. Conquistadors made race constitutive of a new form of domination" (533). As they articulated a purportedly "natural" hierarchy that positioned "Indians," "Blacks," and "Mestizos" as lower orders of humanity than the Spanish and Portuguese, the conquistadors produced the differences they claimed merely to describe through discursive homogenization of populations accompanied by physical violence, dispossession, and exploitation.

Quijano suggests that homogenization was a key technology of coloniality. The European colonizers "found a great number of different peoples, each with its own history, language, discoveries and cultural products, memory and identity. The most developed and sophisticated of them were the Aztecs, Mayas, Chimus, Aymaras, Incas, Chibchas, and so on. Three hundred years later, all of them had become merged into a single identity: Indians. This new identity was racial, colonial, and negative. The same happened with the peoples forcefully brought from Africa as slaves: Ashantis, Yorubas, Zulus, Congos, Bacongos, and others. In the span of three hundred years, all of them were Negroes or Blacks" (Quijano 2000, 551–52).

The mechanics of homogenization were brutal. As peoples were dispossessed of their singular historical identities and their modes of subsistence, they were forced into a stratified labor regime that became a defining feature of racial difference. Beginning in 1503, the Spanish crown issued *encomiendas* that granted land to soldiers and colonists, along with a right to demand tribute and extract forced labor from the Indigenous ("Indian") population who lived on that land. When the encomienda system was ended in 1551, the Indigenous were assigned the status of unpaid serfs; but in contrast to the feudal system in Europe, serfs in the new world were afforded neither the protection of a feudal lord nor a piece of land upon which to work. "Africans" who survived the Middle Passage were consigned to forced labor and often worked to death. Resuscitating Aristotelian claims about "natural slaves," the colonizers claimed that "Indians" and "Africans" were unworthy of waged labor, a privilege reserved to "Europeans" and their descendants. The inferior races were obliged to work for the profit of their owners. Indeed, the obligation to work was deemed by some colonizers to be fit punishment for indigenous practices that the Christian conquistadors characterized as crimes that offend nature. Mestizos, the offspring of European sexual exploitation of Indigenous and African women, were assigned to artisanal and urban clerical positions in colonial society. Only the Spanish and Portuguese, pure in Christian "blood" and ancestry, were granted land ownership by the monarchy, according them control over human and material resources, as well as education, and culture in the colonies (Quijano 2000, 538–40).

According to Quijano, as a technology central to the coloniality of power, race did far more than function as a mechanism of social classification. "In America, the idea of race was a way of granting legitimacy to relations of domination imposed by conquest" (534). It situated the conquered in a "natural" position of inferiority and distributed the human population by ranks, places, and roles. It produced new social identities, as it justified "extraction of wealth, and suppression of indigenous knowledge production, systems of meaning making, cultural life, symbolic systems, and modes of self-understanding" (541). Moreover, it condemned the conquered to illiteracy, offering "conversion" to Christianity as the only vehicle for learning (541). Indeed, Quijano suggests that "Since the 16th Century, race has proven to be the most effective and long-lasting instrument of universal social domination, encroaching upon the much older principle of gender domination" (535).

Both postcolonial and de-colonial theorists have also noted that racialization introduced a new sense of time, a temporality that did more than simply contrast "the modern" to the "traditional." Envisioning Europe as the telos of historical development, colonizers relocated the colonized, along with their respective histories and cultures, in the past — as "primitives," "savages," or "barbarians" (Mignolo 2000). Whether ensconced in discourses on modernization or evolution, the colonized were situated on a historical trajectory whose culmination was Europe, posited as the pinnacle of civilization. Although there were intensive debates over whether the civilizing mission could be accomplished in the course of one lifetime — or whether it required centuries or millennia — modernization discourses suggested that human intervention could shape the course of history. The "future was not simply a natural unfolding or a divine plan but something produced by the action of individuals, their calculations, their intentions, decisions" (Quijano 2000, 547). Part of the colonizing project, then, was to inculcate modernizing mentalities, to implant a desire on the part of the colonized to idealize and aspire to modernity — that is, to "Europeanness."

Racialization reordered all aspects of Indigenous life, from intimate relations to labor practices, from the complexion of the population to structures of authority, and in so doing, it sought to engender forms of subjective consciousness resigned to hierarchical social relations:

> Race designated who would become a slave, an indentured laborer, or a free wage laborer. Race determined political status during the colonial era, and subsequently dictated who would have access to full citizenship in the nation-state. As the foundation of Eurocentrism, race defined what counted as history and knowledge, and condemned the colonized to live as peoples without history, without the rights of man, and without human rights. As European knowledge production was accredited as the only valid knowledge, indigenous epistemologies were relegated to the status of primitive superstition or destroyed. Eurocentrism locked intersubjective relations between the European and the non-European in a temporal frame that always positioned the European as more advanced. Whether the opposition pitted the civilized against the barbarians, wage workers against slaves, the modern against the premodern, or the developed against the underdeveloped, the superiority of the European was never questioned.
>
> *(Mendoza 2016, 113–114)*

Postcolonial and de-colonial theorists characterize the destruction of Indigenous knowledge, spirituality, and worldviews as *epistemic violence*. As colonizers produced "Indians," whether in the context of the Americas or later in South Asia, they silenced the peoples of the global South, substituting Occidentalist and Orientalist views for the lived realities of Indigenous and subaltern existence. Systems of representation that celebrated the civilizing mission asserted European superiority as it consigned the colonized to enslavement, indenture, and cultural annihilation. Mystification was integral to the epistemic violence of Eurocentrism. For the system of representation circulated by the colonizers masked the brutal violence of colonization. The rhetoric of civilization, modernization, evolution, and progress masked the brutal technologies of embodied power that subjugated the colonized and the enslaved.

As non-Europeans were envisioned as "pre-Europeans, who would in time be Europeanized, civilized" (Quijano 2000, 556), the colonists consolidated a regime of rights restricted to white, property owning men. Color was used to organize "natural" divisions of the human population within settler societies that crafted constitutions proclaiming popular sovereignty. "Modern institutions of citizenship and political democracy" established "legal, civil, and political equality for socially unequal people. As a structure of power, the nation state articulates specific democratic ways to address disputes over control of labor and its resources and products, sex and its resources and products, authority and its specific violence, inter-subjectivity, and knowledge" (Quijano 2000, 557). Depicted as an advance over European feudalism, the liberal republics of the new world pioneered a space of domination in which the newly created status hierarchies grounded in race and gender were rendered invisible. The homogeneity envisioned by Rousseau as a requirement for a democratic republic was produced by the extermination of some and the exclusion of others. In Spain and France, the first centralized states in Europe, racial homogenization resulted from the expulsion of Muslims and Jews. Across the Atlantic, laws disenfranchised those epidermalized as "Black," "Red," "Yellow" and "Mestiza/Mulatto/Metis," as well as those gendered female.

Gendered Racialization, Racialized Gendering

Feminist scholars have pointed out that racialization was gendered in the colonial era – Indigenous and enslaved men and women suffered different modes of subordination at the hands of colonizers. And gender was racialized, norms of masculinity and femininity varied markedly across "race." Indeed, as Sally Markowitz (2001, 391) has demonstrated, "strong sex/gender dimorphism," which is associated with contemporary versions of biological determinism was conceived as an achievement of civilization, perfected only by the European bourgeoisie. "Sex/gender difference [wa]s imagined to increase as various races 'advance' … the ideology of the sex/gender difference itself turns out to rest not on a simple binary opposition between male and female but rather on a scale of racially coded degrees of sex/gender difference culminating in the manly European man and the feminine European woman" (391).

In "Heterosexualism and the Colonial Modern Gender System," Maria Lugones (2007) suggests that colonized women and men were both racialized and sexualized by the conquistadors. Gendering provided a powerful means to destroy the social relations of Indigenous men and women, as men were feminized and sexually abused and women were appropriated for sexual and reproductive labor. Europeans introduced sexual hierarchies that broke down solidarity among men and women grounded in norms of complementarity and reciprocity. "In place of harmonious collaboration, European colonizers positioned [Indigenous] men and women as antagonists. Through sexual violence, exploitation, and systems of concubinage, the colonizers used gender to break the will of Indigenous men and women, imposing new hierarchies that were institutionalized with colonialism. The bodies of women became the terrain on which Indigenous men negotiated survival under new colonial conditions. Sacrificing Indigenous women to the lust of the conquerors, perversely, became the only means of cultural survival" (Mendoza 2016, 116).

As Breny Mendoza (2014, 2016) has pointed out, the exact contours of racialized gendering hve been a subject of intensive debate among de-colonial feminist scholars in Latin America. Although there is disagreement about how to characterize the nature of patriarchy in Indigenous and enslaved communities prior to colonization, de-colonial feminist scholars agree that gender inequality was exacerbated under colonization. Focusing on the Yoruba from Nigeria, Benin, and Togo who were imported as slaves to Brazil beginning in 1549, for example, Rita Segato (2001) has noted that low intensity patriarchies became more hierarchical when subjected to the gendered logics imposed under colonization – with devastating consequences for women. As public and private spheres were separated and gendered, Yoruba women were domesticated and privatized, losing the power they once held in the community. Although Yoruba men retained some communal authority, they were humiliated and symbolically emasculated by the depredations of enslavement to such an extent that even their discourses on emancipation adopted a hierarchically gendered logic. Demands for freedom and political rights were cast as claims to restore their "manhood" (Segato, 2011).

Examining gender relations in pre-colonized Andean societies, Silvia Rivera Cusicanqui (2004) notes that complementarity within the normative heterosexual couple afforded a measure of equality and reciprocity in private as well as public spheres. Full membership in the community presupposed involvement in a conjugal couple, and power and respect grew with age. Both men and women were entitled to inherit. According to Cusicanqui, the system of complementarity was weakened and eventually destroyed – not at the moment of colonization, however, but later with the advent of republican systems of governance, modernization, and development. A gradual process of patriarchalization accompanied the encroachment of the modern nation-state upon Andean communities. Over time, the imposition of the European gender system did indeed undermine egalitarian relations between men and women, as the "civilizing" process encouraged heightened manifestation of gender difference.

The gender system developed by European colonizers involved multiple hierarchies of gender difference, altering the lives of European women living in the new world as well as Indigenous and enslaved women. The combination of European superiority, male supremacy, and racial degradation that played out in the process of colonization produced complex gradations of raced-gendered hierarchy. The superiority of Europeans over "Indians" and "African" slaves was codified in law, and manifested in all aspects of colonial political, economic, social and cultural life. But the principle of male supremacy embraced by colonizers had to be mitigated in the colonial context to reinforce European superiority. No Indigenous man or enslaved African male could be acknowledged to be superior to a European woman. Thus, racialized gendering required that European women be subordinated to European men, yet celebrated as more "civilized" than colonized men and women. Toward that end, they were domesticated, ensconced within the private sphere, extolled for their maternal sentiments, yet excluded by their purportedly "natural" inferiority from property ownership and political participation. By contrast, the Indigenous and the enslaved were dehumanized, which entailed a measure of "de-gendering." Taking egalitarian relations between colonized and enslaved men and women as evidence of barbarity, Europeans suggested that "savages" manifested biological difference in their relations to reproduction (sex), but they lacked a gender system (Lugones 2010). The European colonizers shored up that "lack" by treating the colonized and the enslaved as beasts of burden, subjecting them to grueling physical labor. Thus Lugones adds a gendered dimension to the central tenet of the coloniality of power: not only does race demarcate human from sub-human (rather than one kind of human from another), but race distinguishes those who have achieved the civilizational project of gender difference from those ungendered animal-like sub-humans. "Gender hierarchy marks the civilized status of European women and men; its absence defines the non-human, racialized, naturalized non-Europeans, who are sexed but genderless" (Mendoza 2016, 117). Whether cast as hypersexualized animals or beasts of burden, the colonized were fit for breeding, brutal labor, or extermination and the colonizers treated them as such.

Both intersectionality and the conceptualization of the coloniality of gender make it clear that dichotomous constructions of sex (i.e., men/women) fail to account for dimensions of embodied power central to racialized gendering and gendered racialization. The racializing logic introduced by European colonization created multiple categories of raced-genders that are rendered invisible by universal claims about "men" and "women." Thus, universal claims constitute one dimension of Enlightenment thought that actively misleads. Universal claims render invisible explicit political practices from conquest and colonization to legislation that dehumanize and disenfranchise, which propertied European men have devised to ensure that individuality is their exclusive preserve. Discourses about natural rights, the rights of Man, and individual liberty emerged at the same time that European thinkers were inventing race and sex as biological categories.

By eliminating the ethnic specificity of hundreds of peoples, subsuming them under geographic designations ("Africans," "Caucasians," "Indians," "Orientals") or colors ("Black," "Red," "Yellow," "White"), European scientists created racialized collectives. By overriding manifold cultural differences among women and masking human similarities, as well as blatant systems of social advantage and disadvantage, Enlightenment thinkers defined "sex" exclusively in relation to reproductive biology. Within Enlightenment thought, men proclaimed their humanity, defined in terms of individuality and rights, while relegating the less-than-fully human – the racialized and sexualized – to undifferentiated collectives, unentitled to the rights of man. As analytical frameworks, intersectionality and de-coloniality block the erasure of embodied power. They insist that individuality as a realm of freedom, choice, interest maximization, and self-determination be investigated in relation to its contradictory twin – biological determinism, which condemns those racialized and sexualized to subservience, marginalization, and domination – all construed as pre-political.

Chapter Overview

The following chapters map the contours of embodied power and trace modes of thinking that render it invisible. Chapter 2, "Conceptual Practices of Power," examines the occlusion of embodied power in the discipline of political science, a discipline that identifies the study of power as its central mission. As a social science discipline profoundly shaped by the behavioral revolution of the 1960s, political science claims merely to observe, describe and explain the political world. But the conceptual apparatus developed by the discipline does more than just describe the world. It shapes perceptions of the political and influences how political actors make sense of themselves, their choices, their options, and their environment. By investigating both the history and the contemporary practice of political science, I show how a conception of disembodied politics has been produced and sustained, making it extremely difficult to perceive embodied power in disciplinary practices or in the political world.

Chapter 2 explores various explanations for the lack of attention to race, gender, and sexuality in a discipline that claims power as a central analytical concept. Taking the American Political Science Association (APSA) Task Force *Report on Political Science in the 21st Century* as my point of departure, I examine historical, methodological, and theoretical accounts of the discipline's inattention to embodied power. Finding these explanations unsatisfactory, I offer a critical history of American political science to show that racialization and gendering have been constitutive of knowledge production within the discipline. Classic works by founders of the discipline such as James Bryce, John W. Burgess, Theodore Roosevelt, and Edward Ross define democracy as a white-male endeavor, conceptualize the nation-state as a racially homogeneous entity, and justify policing membership and imperial expansion as defensive measures to safeguard the white democratic nation from the threat of those "lesser races" unfit for self-government. Rather than interpreting these explicitly racist and sexist views as artefacts of a fleeting historical moment, I suggest that these field-forming works established analytical frameworks that have shaped and continue to shape the objects and methods of political inquiry. Indeed, I argue that the conceptual practices of power envisioned in these early works laid the foundation for and accredited disembodied politics. Disciplinary norms pertaining to classification, methodological individualism, methodological nationalism, abstract universalism, and white androcentrism structure research in political science in the ways they depoliticize embodied power. The final section of this chapter sketches how each of these analytical frames introduce ways of seeing and ways of thinking that render invisible state practices of racialization and gendering. As methodological strictures, these conceptual practices of power make it nearly impossible for mainstream political science to take intersectionality and de-coloniality seriously. By masking embodied power, these conceptual practices sustain notions of disembodied politics that perpetuate raced-gendered systems of privilege and disadvantage.

To challenge presumptions that race and sex are physical characteristics that bear no relation to state action or political power, Chapter 3, "The Science and Politics of Bodies," traces the historical development of biological determinism. Through an examination of scientific discourses and political instruments such as laws, policies, and constitutional rights, I demonstrate that the conceptualization of determinate biological races and dichotomous sexes is a product of modernity, elaborated and consolidated from the 15th to 19th centuries. Both science and politics were intimately intertwined in the production of "race" and "sex" as biological categories. In contrast to the naturalizing claims of biological determinism, gendered racialization is a political division of the population that masquerades as natural order. In exploring several scientific taxonomies that biologize race, I show that from its earliest conceptualization race was never limited to claims about physiology, morphology, or skin color. On the contrary, theorizations of race characterized "natural" varieties of humanity by combining "observations" about geographical region and pigmentation with opinions about cultural traits, physical appearance, intellectual potential, aesthetic value, and political capacity. Similarly, sexual dimorphism was never simply an account of reproductive anatomy. From their emergence in the long eighteenth century, claims about "opposite sexes" involved arguments about intellect, maturity, educability, sexual appetites, and ability for self-governance.

Drawing upon the insights of intersectionality theorists, Chapter 3 also shows how the mutual constitution of race/gender/sexuality challenges universalizing claims about "men" and "women." Within the racialized taxonomies of Enlightenment science and philosophy, fine gradations were drawn among men and women of various races. Attributes and capabilities assigned to elite white men and women were markedly different from those credited to "lower" races and classes – so different that the very humanity of the "lower" orders was called into question. These putative differences were encoded in laws that denied rights to self-governance, mobility, property, marriage, education, professional employment, and citizenship to those relegated to the bottom of the social hierarchy. By barring those condemned to subordination from education, denying them opportunities for self-development and independence, and prohibiting their full participation in political life, states produced "inferiority" that was labeled natural.

Although the intellectual and moral defects of "scientific" claims about race and sex as biological categories have been repeatedly debunked, biologism continues to haunt the popular imagination and the discipline of political science. The chapter catalogues the fallacies associated with biological determinism, but also traces the resurrection of these defective views in sociobiology, evolutionary psychology, cognitive science, neuroscience, and genomics. Suffering from vicious circularity, and theoretical and empirical shoddiness, biological determinism nonetheless circulates widely to shore up claims about the "natural" superiority of white Euro-American men. Within political science, persistent assumptions about biological determinism mask the historical role of the state in producing raced-gendered social orders and contemporary practices of embodied power. Notions of natural difference sustain vibrant "unknowing" about major political phenomena such as the brutality of colonization, conquest, displacement, dispossession, and enslavement. By placing embodied power beyond the scope of political inquiry, biological determinism consolidates a known world that legitimates hierarchies of difference.

To escape the grip of biological determinism, Chapter 4 explicates a necessary shift in conceptual terrain from notions of race and sex as physical attributes or population characteristics to an understanding of processes of racialized gendering and gendered racialization. Rather than viewing race and sex as discrete systems, processes of racialized gendering involve the simultaneous production of relations of domination and subordination as women and men are positioned as members of particular races, classes, ethnicities, and nationalities. The state has been a key player in the production of finely honed hierarchies of difference, developing laws, policies, regulatory codes, and distributive mechanisms that differentiate subsections of the population by physically separating them, diminishing the status of some and aggrandizing the status of others, and selectively imposing constraints on freedom, participation, education and labor opportunities, and rights. To take embodied power seriously, then, political scientists must investigate the complex technologies of racialized gendering that produce material differences in the everyday lives of citizens, while also interrogating the symbolic systems created to justify disparate treatment.

To concretize gendered racialization, this chapter traces various policy instruments used in the United States from the earliest days of the republic to create a white race nation, which accorded full citizenship only to white men. It contrasts the treatment of enslaved and free Blacks with that of the sovereign Indigenous peoples who populated the continent at the time of white settlement and with that of Chinese and Japanese migrants who attempted to establish livelihoods in the USA. By exploring the specific racialization of men and women within these groups, the chapter illuminates the varied repertoire of embodied power, while also demonstrating how abstract universal claims about race or sex necessarily go astray. The chapter also shows how Anglo-Americans forge a shared identity of "whiteness" over time – in and through the process of racializing Black, Indigenous, Mexican, and Asian "others."

To challenge the notion that gendered racialization is an historical anachronism typical of an earlier era of U.S. nation-building long since transcended, the second section of the chapter examines the construction of racialized-gendered tiers of citizenship within the recent past. It explores racial segregation in relation to state practices pertaining to housing, education, urban renewal, highway construction, gentrification, policing, welfare, and child protective services. By analyzing the disparate effects of the "war on drugs," it attempts to make sense of the exponential growth of the prison population at a time when crime rates were falling. It explores various explanations of the transformation of the prison population from 70 percent white in 1950 to 70 percent Black and Latino in 2002, a period in which ethnic patterns of criminal activity had not fundamentally changed. The final section of the chapter investigates racialized gendering in the "war on terror" both within the borders of the United States and in the international context. In dramatic contrast to notions about equal citizenship and the rule of law, the chapter analyzes racial profiling of Latino, Middle-Eastern and South Asian men. From the suspension of the right of *habeas corpus* and the arrest and detention – without charge – of several thousand men on U.S. soil, to the indefinite detention and torture of men presumed to be enemy combatants, racialized gendering in the 21st century has been particularly brutal. It has not been only suspected "Muslim terrorists" who have been racialized and feminized through strip searches and gendering interrogation techniques, Latino/a migrants and citizens in the United States have been subjected to heightened surveillance, arrest, detention, and deportation as immigration and securitization policies have forged new cooperation among local, state, and federal law enforcement authorities.

Chapter 4, "From Race and Sex to Racialization, Gendering, and Sexualization," demonstrates that embodied power operates in complex ways in the contemporary United States, affecting domestic and foreign policy. Despite formal guarantees of equal citizenship, racialized gendering is used by local, state, and federal governments to produce and maintain asymmetries with respect to individual liberties and immunities, educational and employment opportunities, income and wealth disparities, prospects for upward mobility, as well as civil and political rights. Far from marking natural attributes, racialization and gendering are political processes with palpable effects on livelihoods, citizenship, physical integrity, and even life itself.

Chapter 5, "Ways of Seeing, Modes of Being," returns to the puzzle of "unseeing" and "non-knowing" that haunts embodied power. The examples of state practices of racialized gendering explored in Chapter 4 are far from subtle. Yet, neither mainstream political science nor popular media discuss these phenomena in terms of racialization and gendering. On the contrary, over the past two decades claims concerning a "post-racial," "postfeminist" era suggest that embodied power is no longer an issue in the contemporary world. To dispel such erroneous notions, this chapter explores certain theoretical presuppositions that structure political research and popular understandings in ways that render embodied power invisible. Presumptions about individualism, colorblind perception, methodological individualism, and methodological nationalism singly and in combination make it exceptionally difficult to perceive racialization, gendering, and sexualization. These assumptions sustain "ways of seeing" that determine the meaning of observed events, identify significant issues worth probing, indicate sensible problem-solving mechanisms, and accredit particular explanatory accounts, which push embodied power below the threshold of visibility.

The chapter excavates the tacit presuppositions that inform individualism, colorblind perception, methodological individualism and methodological nationalism. In each case, it shows how problematic assumptions skew perceptions in ways that occlude the relevance of gendered racialization. Assumptions about formal equality, equal opportunity, and legal neutrality, for example, make it near impossible to see state practices that produce and sustain hierarchies of difference. By masking state deployment of embodied power, these problematic assumptions support alternative explanatory frames that naturalize unequal outcomes, and individualize responsibility for success and failure to succeed. Presumptions about colorblindness in conjunction with assumptions about equal opportunity, for example, attribute differences in health, wealth, income, and mortality to the genetic lottery, or worse to cultural depravity or individual irresponsibility. Holding the worst-off responsible for their plight, convictions about colorblind perception rule out discrimination as an explanation for inequality, falling back on racialized and gendered stereotypes to account for disparate outcomes. The policy consequences of presumptions about individualism and colorblindness are examined in the context of U.S. Supreme Court decisions concerning "reverse discrimination" and voting rights.

Within political science methodological individualism involves ontological, epistemological, psychological, and ethical assumptions that structure mainstream research practices. Claims that the individual should be the primary unit of political analysis are grounded in presumptions about individuals as the fundamental constituents of the social world and the only valid source of knowledge about that world. Yet, the conception of the individual at the heart of this framework is not neutral. Informed by the Scottish Enlightenment, the individual is conceived as a self-interested agent who acts to maximize preferred outcomes. Thus, methodological individualism construes politics in terms very much like those embraced by economists. Politics is an activity in which self-interested individuals engage in voluntary transactions to improve their condition. Within this narrow frame, votes and decisions are the principle political currency; a group is nothing more than an aggregate of individuals; and political outcomes simply reflect the aggregate choices of individuals. Such a narrow construal of politics has many limitations, which are outlined in the chapter. Most importantly in the context of embodied power, the reduction of the state to an aggregation of individuals completely misses the intricate ways in which states produce raced-gendered-sexualized hierarchies that structure individual self-understandings, social relations, and life prospects. To demonstrate the inadequacy of methodological individualism as an explanatory framework, I contrast the individualist approach to sexual trafficking embedded in the Victims of Trafficking and Violence Protection Act passed by the federal government in 2000 with the far more nuanced and sophisticated accounts advanced by Jennifer Suchland (2015) and Saskia Sassen (2001, 2002), who analyze sex trafficking in the complex economic, political, and social context of neoliberal marketization.

Methodological nationalism is the final "way of seeing" examined in Chapter 5. In contrast to methodological individualism, methodological nationalism takes the nation-state as the fundamental unit of analysis in political research. Yet the conception of the nation that informs this approach suggests a "people" with intricate ties to the land quite independently of the power politics of state formation. The romanticized assumptions about "blood," origins, ancestry, language, culture, and history that underlie methodological nationalism obscure the historical origins of nations in war, conquest, and colonization, just as they hide diversity within populations and the political work expended by the state to suture the nation together – from subduing dissent, expelling non-conformers, quelling riots, and breaking strikes to civil war. To show how methodological nationalism can distort understandings of contemporary politics, the chapter concludes with two examples drawn from the second Iraq War (2003–2011). I contrast the construction of the U.S. as a nation whose mission is to protect freedom, democracy, and pluralist civil society, advanced by the G. W. Bush Administration to legitimize the invasion of Iraq and the overthrow of the Saddam Hussein regime, with the construction of the authentic Islamic nation of Iraq by the Moqtadda al-Sadr's Mahdi Army, which was advanced to justify the murder of Iraqi men and women who were "corrupted by the West" and collaborated with the U.S. occupiers. To demonstrate that methodological nationalism plays out well beyond the rhetoric of a sitting government (the G. W. Bush Administration) and an aspiring political force (the Mahdi Militia), I analyze the presuppositions that inform the 2009 Human Rights Watch report *'They Want Us Exterminated': Murder, Torture, Sexual Orientation and Gender in Iraq*. By comparing these recent examples, it is possible to see the seductive power of methodological nationalism, which converts sustained practices of racialization, gendering, and sexualization into claims about national defense and deploys invented pasts and fictive futures to mask virulent forms of embodied power.

The final chapter of the book, "Revisioning Power, Reclaiming Politics" explores how intersectional analysis can enrich the study of politics, both by overcoming specific blind spots associated with mainstream political science and by expanding the conception of politics at the heart of contemporary political inquiry. Chapter 6 begins by analyzing the constitutive elements of intersectionality as an analytical framework:

1. recognizing racialized gendering;
2. displacing white androcentrism as the unmarked norm;
3. denaturalizing difference;
4. investigating processes; and
5. engaging multilevel analysis.

In explicating each of these analytic dimensions, I show how it challenges existing methodological strictures in political science and requires significant intellectual reorientation if the discipline is to move beyond problematic reductionism and acknowledge both embodied power and the messiness of complexity in the political world.

Displacing white androcentrism is particularly challenging because it has operated not only as the unmarked norm in political science, but as modernity's unmarked norm. To counter its effects, then, it is helpful to consider how "whiteness" informs a system of knowing, shaping perceptions, historical archives, public memories, and modes of explanation. Toward this end, I draw upon Rebecca Clark-Mane's (2012) analysis of the "grammars of whiteness," exploring three rhetorical tropes – a temporality that places raced-gendered inequalities in the past rather than the present, a flattening of difference that precludes recognition of the distinctive dimensions of racialized-gendered oppression, and a consistent failure to engage contradictory claims about racialized-gendered others – that help entrench white privilege even among those who believe themselves to be antiracist. Once these rhetorical moves have been made visible, it becomes easier to perceive embodied power.

When state practices of embodied power operate below the threshold of visibility, explanatory accounts of the effects of gendered racialization can be markedly contorted. Whether appealing to notions of reverse discrimination, assessing the source of terrorist threats in contemporary polities, or offering accounts of urban riots, explanations can be seriously skewed when they ignore systemic gendered racialization. Chapter 6 examines two particular explanatory frames – cultural pathology and deficits in moral character – that circulate widely in social science to explain social inequalities. Surfacing in optimistic claims about ethnic assimilation, multiculturalism, cultural pluralism, and cosmopolitanism, these flawed causal accounts seriously misconstrue the nature and effects of racism, sexism, and heteronormativity. Failing to comprehend the role of the state in producing and marginalizing "unassimilable" groups, contorted causal accounts sustain policy prescriptions that are far from progressive. They deny the racialized any legitimate claim on society for redress. They depoliticize race by eviscerating investigations into its causes and consequences. They de-legitimize mobilizations for collective justice, and they entrench social injustice, placing it beyond the possibility of political remedy.

When race, ethnicity, gender, class and sexuality are included in the study of politics, they challenge central concepts and beliefs concerning the nature of power, the scope of state action, and the practice of liberal democracy. When the majority of the world population becomes the subject of political inquiry, numerous received views in political science are called into question and new issues are opened for investigation. For the majority comprise women and men who have been racialized within the context of specific nations and within transnational geopolitical formations. The final section of the chapter explores dimensions of politics made visible by intersectional analysis. These include the politics of embodiment, the politics of exclusion, the politics of diversity, the politics of intimacy, the politics of identity, identity politics as a mode of resistance, the politics of raced-gendered institutions within nation-states and in international regimes, and the politics of knowledge.

As an analytical tool, intersectionality raises new questions about traditional approaches in political science – whether the focus is the official institutions of state, the struggle for power, the authoritative allocation of values, or comparative political behavior. Yet is also expands the scope of political inquiry to encompass robust forms of power operating in the 21st century. By demonstrating how conceptions of disembodied politics mask embodied power, reinforce relations of domination and subordination, and place systemic injustice beyond political redress, this book seeks to persuade readers of the importance of intersectionality as an analytical framework. Far more than a content specialization, an understanding of gendered racialization and racialized gendering should be an "obligatory point of passage" for all scholars who seek to understand politics fully (Latour 1988, 43–49).[4]

Notes

1. By referring to "mainstream" political science, I refer to the paradigms accredited within the discipline that dominate graduate training and contemporary research practices. The discipline of political science is, of course, a multifaceted enterprise. Critical race scholars, feminist scholars, certain proponents of a "new" political science, and political scientists who specialize in the study of gender, race, and ethnicity have devoted their intellectual energies to demonstrating the scope and effects of racialization and gendering. This important research, however, continues to remain peripheral to the mainstream discipline. For an analysis of this problem, see the Report of the APSA Task Force on *Political Science in the 21st Century* (American Political Science Association 2011).
2. As intersectionality scholarship has grown, so too have its critics. For helpful overviews of these debates, see Davis (2008), Cooper (2016), and Hancock (2016).
3. For a detailed discussion of differences in these two approaches to coloniality, modernity, and capitalism, see Mendoza (2016) and Chibber (2013).
4. I am indebted to Lisa Disch for this conceptualization.

2
CONCEPTUAL PRACTICES OF POWER

> To address the effects of power, one must first render power visible.
> (Chantal Mouffe 1996, 254)

In their introduction to *A New Handbook of Political Science*, Robert Goodin and Hans Dieter Klingemann (1996, 7) define politics and political science in a manner altogether compatible with embodied power: "Politics is the constrained use of power. The study of politics examines the nature and source of those constraints and the techniques for the use of social power within those constraints." Yet, racialization and gendering are largely absent from this comprehensive guide to the discipline.[1] Although "the concept of power is at the heart of political enquiry; indeed, it is probably the central concept of both descriptive and normative analysis" (Isaac 2003, 54), embodied power has been markedly absent from the manifold forms of power studied within political science. Indeed, the American Political Science Association (2011, 14) task force *Report on Political Science in the 21st Century* notes that "studies conducted since the 1980s have consistently shown a bias against the study of race and inequality within political science as compared to most other social science disciplines ... Flagship journals have, on the whole, rarely addressed issues of race, ethnicity, and gender (Walton, Miller, and McCormick 1995; Orr and Johnson 2007; Smith 2004) ... [and] text books treat race, ethnicity, and gender ... as marginal aspects of the political system, rather than as woven into the fabric of American politics (Aoki and Takeda 2004; Wallace and Allen 2008; Lavariega Monforti and McGlynn 2010; Novkov and Barclay 2010)."[2] As a consequence of such sustained neglect, the task force report concludes that the discipline is "ill-equipped to address in a sustained way why many of the most marginal members of political communities around the world are often unable to have their needs effectively addressed by governments ... [and] ill-equipped to develop explanations for the social, political and economic processes that lead to groups' marginalization" (1).

Feminist scholars, critical race scholars, and scholars from the global South have long challenged omissions and distortions associated with disembodied conceptions of politics.[3] They have noted that the classification of women and people of color as "minorities" marginalizes the majority of the world population, creating the false impression that white residents of Europe and North America constitute far more than 16 percent of the global populace. As Marianne Githens (1983, 475) noted more than three decades ago, "the orientation of political science as a field, the concepts used, and the questions asked treat gender research as an addendum to the discipline or worse, women's political behavior is subsumed under a framework of deviance ... fail[ing] to see that study of half the human population might change understandings of power, politics and political life." In a sweeping indictment of the discipline's lack of attention to race and gender, Charles Mills (2015, 6) characterized contemporary political science "as a monologue coming from the European West, the white West, with little or no thought being given to the possible need to consider the replies to these diktats from the West's non-white 'Others' – or indeed, whether the very geography of the 'West' may need to be remapped." In an earlier work, Mills (2007, 238) had pointed out that taking the "Euro-American reference group as the constitutive norm skews perception both in terms of geographic misrepresentation (Europe is depicted as larger than Africa on maps) and historical misrepresentation (Europe is elevated into a self-creating entity unto itself)."

Over the past few decades, several hypotheses have been advanced to explain the discipline's failure to engage embodied power. Some emphasize the pervasive assumption that race and sex are biological phenomena, and as such altogether beyond the reach of the political. Others note that whether understood as a biological given or as a social construct, race and gender are taken to be determined by forces that have nothing to do with the state or the dynamics of politics. Jane Junn (2007, 126) has noted that within political science, "gender and race are taken as given, as exogenously determined, hence they can be aggregated into static and unidimensional categories." Speaking specifically of the absence of race from political studies, Rogers Smith (2004, 41) suggested that "political scientists have tended to think of racial identities as things generated at root from biology and/or economics and/or culture and/or history and/or often unconscious or at least informal social psychological processes and social activities" – all domains that fall within the purview of other social sciences, and therefore, legitimately excluded from the study of politics.

Reflecting larger belief systems circulating in the United States, Charles Mills (2007, 232) links the shortsightedness of political science to cultural values: "Mainstream theorizing in political science frames American sexism and racism as 'anomalies' – U.S. culture is conceptualized as essentially egalitarian and inclusive, with the long actual history of systemic gender and racial subordination relegated to the status of minor 'deviation' from the norm ... turn[ing] things upside down: sexism, racism, patriarchy and white supremacy have not been the exception but the *norm*." In *American Exceptionalism and the Remains of Race*, Edmund Fong (2015, 10) suggests that inattention to race is integrally related to the myth of self-making that has structured the "American" imagination: "Both racism and the reaffirmation of racial difference lay outside an enduring American ethos of self-transformative possibility." Precisely because "politicized racial identification" is taken to be "anachronistic and suspect," political scientists may reject racial classification in an effort to avoid reinforcing group identities that are deemed to be "divisive and 'balkanizing'" (Fong 2015, 10).

In contrast to explanations rooted in presuppositions concerning biology or culture, some scholars have connected the absence of attention to embodied power to methodological constraints of the field. When political actors are conceived as abstract individuals or self-maximizing rational actors, there is no need to take race, sex or sexuality into account. In the words of Joni Lovenduski (2000), the "persistent assumption that the same factors are influential for women and men" constitutes a "methodological battle" confronting gender researchers. Where biological and cultural assumptions may admit the possibility of racial and sexual "difference" that is pre-political, insistence on the individual as the unit of analysis imposes a norm of sameness. "Methodological presuppositions about the individual as the unit of analysis combined with a normative position on political action that assumes equality of agency among individuals make it extremely difficult to accommodate a politicized context of gender [or race] when working with individual-level data" (Junn 2007, 125). Within this analytical framework, as "individuals," women and raced "others" are the same as white men, hence there is no reason to study them. Indeed, as Nancy Burns (2007, 464–65) pointed out, positing the individual as the unit of analysis has made political science "an odd melding of individualism and essentialism ... One standard approach has been to adopt gender as a rather content-free dichotomous variable dropped into a regression, on the idea that that will offer evidence about whether, by chance, gender matters" (464). By treating gender as a dichotomous variable, political science invariably ignores differences among women and among men, masking intra-group differences and replicating the problem of "single axis analysis" criticized by intersectionality theorists. By reducing gender to a notion of biological sex, quantitative approaches to political science "reduce the visibility of the subtle causes and effects of gender differences" (Lovenduski 2000).

Rogers Smith (2004, 44) has suggested that certain methodological constraints may stem from a history of exclusionary political practices: "political scientists may acknowledge that "race sometimes affects politics as an exogenously generated independent variable." Yet, this acknowledgment results in diminished attention to the study of race. Political scientists "bring race into study of politics only when it is likely to explain political behavior ... When all decision-makers are racially homogeneous, there is no point in 'controlling' for race, since there are no variations to correlate with variances in other dimensions of political life ... If Blacks are not present as office holders or voters, [then] political scientists do not see them as relevant" (44). This explanation could be extended to sex — in part: if women are not present in elective offices, then political scientists do not see them as relevant. Yet women have been the majority of voters in the United States since 1980. Thus their neglect by the discipline remains puzzling. A methodological framework that positions race and sex as potential independent variables, appears to make it an empirical question when and under what conditions embodied power has political effects — even as it ignores historical practices of embodied power such as disenfranchisement, exclusion from citizenship, or neglect in scholarship.

In their *Report on Political Science in the 21st Century*, the APSA task force also offer a number of possible explanations for the discipline's lack of attention to embodied power. Concentrating on the failure to study race, the task force recast Rogers Smith's analysis, attributing the discipline's myopia to "political science's emphasis on elites, and, therefore, its concomitant lack of focus on those 'outside' the traditional halls of power" (American Political Science Association 2011, 17). They also draw Cold War politics into the frame, suggesting that "during the Cold War American political science saw its role as helping to defend American democracy and, for that reason, the discipline as a whole was less willing to address topics that could be seen as leading to a critique of that democracy" (17).

The report also calls attention to methodological reasons for the neglect of embodied power. "The discipline tends not to use 'identity' as a core analytical category for understanding important aspects of political behavior, social movements, and the development of public policies. It tends to treat identity as given and outside of analysis. This limits the extent to which groups, both those that are marginalized and those that are privileged, and especially the relationship between the two, can be fundamental to understanding political processes and their consequences" (17). By treating race and sex as issues of "identity," rather than as the effects of political processes, this explanation shifts the terrain from questions of power to matters of subjective identification. While taking the important step of calling attention to group advantage and disadvantage, this account nonetheless reinforces the view that race and sex are not inherently political; they can at best be treated as exogenous independent variables that *might* influence political processes.

In developing its final hypothesis about the systemic absence of the study of race and sex in political science, the APSA task force turns to the conception of science that informs the discipline. "Political science tends not to be self-reflective about the analytical limitations of many of its traditional methodological approaches. The tendency to accept its approaches as 'objective' science, for example, tends to inhibit the development of a more critical debate about the potential phenomenological bases of much empirical social science" (18). The language of the report as it attempts to grapple with "political science's lack of epistemological self-critique and awareness about the role of 'science' in driving research questions and answers" (17, 18) is itself revealing – as it manifests the very tensions it seeks to analyze. The task force characterizes the explanatory hypothesis about the lack of critical reflexivity concerning the limitations of scientific methodology as "controversial." Rather than speaking unanimously as it does throughout the report, the task force breaks ranks in articulating this hypothesis, noting that "some members of our task force *felt* strongly about the need to point out the way that an uncritical emphasis on 'science' allows the discipline to engage in research that is fundamentally exclusive, but still maintain the illusion of 'objectivity'" (18, emphasis added). By alluding to the feelings of an indefinite "some" (a numerical minority or a minority of minority scholars on the task force?), the report not only signals lack of complete agreement about this hypothesis, it introduces some doubt about the validity of this hypothesis. The task force attempts to rule out some reasons for the lack of unanimity on this point, assuring readers that "This is not an argument about quantitative versus qualitative data, or one about empiricism versus its critics." Yet, the report's discussion of the limitations imposed by the scientific nature of the discipline reveals how difficult it is to attain the critical reflexivity about scientific methodology that the task force endorses.

For an explication of the "science" of politics, the report turns to an essay about the history of the discipline crafted in 1996 by Gabriel Almond, a past president of the APSA. In contrast to positivist conceptions of science that shaped the discipline post-World War II, which were grounded in the fact/value dichotomy, Almond's essay blurs the boundaries between the empirical and the normative. Where mainstream political science insists that its central tasks involve description, explanation and prediction, relegating evaluation or normative analysis to a domain beyond the sphere of science, Almond offers a very soft and inclusive version of political science. According to the task force report:

> In his history of the discipline, Almond argues that political science has focused on two fundamental questions: (1) the properties of political institutions and (2) the criteria used in evaluating them. He states that the essential object of political science is the creation of knowledge, deriving inferences or generalizations about politics drawn from evidence, inferences based on empirical information. For Almond, "objective, rigorous scholarship is indeed the privileged thread in our disciplinary history" (1996). Clearly, the idea of objective science is embedded within the language he uses to describe the discipline's focus.
>
> *(American Political Science Association 2011, 18)*

Rather than examining the kinds of scientific inquiry associated with statistical analysis, formal modeling, and rational choice (the mainstream), the task force offers a selective reading of science, embracing a capacious account that can accommodate a host of different methodological approaches, harking back to the nineteenth century. The historical account extrapolated by the task force from Almond's essay is itself instructive:

> Almond delineates the history of the discipline's development during the late 19th and early 20th centuries. According to his timeline, during the nineteenth century political science focused on issues of development and modernization, and scholars began focusing on defining, operationalizing, and measuring political phenomena. Concurrent with those in other scientific movements around the world, political scientists in the nineteenth century moved toward historical induction rather than writing about human nature. By the turn of the twentieth century, political science was largely legal, philosophical, and historical in its methodology.
>
> That changed in the early twentieth century with the Chicago School. Almond credits Charles Merriam with ushering in modern political science. Through an interdisciplinary research strategy, the introduction of quantitative research methodologies, and organized research support, Merriam and his students were able to show that understanding of the political world could be significantly enhanced. Merriam and his colleagues were among the first to adopt statistical sampling techniques and use experimental research to study political activity. Political science was not alone in this movement, however; the shift within the discipline coincided with the development of survey research in general, which began with the Middletown studies, which examined life in a small Midwestern town, and exploded after World War II (Ito 2007). Within political science, this "behavioral revolution" intensified in the late 1950s and 1960s with the creation of the Institute of Social Research and establishment of the National Election Studies at the University of Michigan. Almond sees this behavioral revolution as a break from the legalism and historical approaches of the past. For him, political science's history is one of eclectic inclusion, rather than methodological absolutism or epistemological infighting.
>
> *(American Political Science Association 2011, 18–19)*

Characterized as eclectic, interdisciplinary, inductive, part of the transformation of knowledge production around the world, the scientific study of politics is said to enhance understanding. With such a benign depiction of the discipline, concerns about the exclusionary nature of political science seem out of place. And yet, the task force has suggested that something about the discipline's practice of scientific inquiry has contributed to the neglect of "race" and "inequality" more generally.[4] To home in on that issue, the report offers a post-behavioral interpretation of political science:

> Modern science is not value-neutral. It is, in fact, a product and reflection of the cultures and societies that produced it. Thus, science does not begin with

the objective collection of data. Instead, science begins first with the perception of a problem, and then with a decision about the kinds of information that might be appropriate to solving it. Both constrain and channel the collection of data. They also constrain who becomes (and does not become) the object of inquiry. For example, most quantitative approaches tend to focus on the norm, or "average," within a population. Sarah Ito, in *The Averaged American*, documents how the Middletown studies constituted a break from previous social scientific approaches precisely in their focus on "normal" Americans rather than "deviant" or "problem" populations. Ironically, the researchers chose Middletown because it was not the norm in terms of racial/ethnic diversity. It was, in fact, significantly whiter than most Midwestern towns at that time.

Within political science, this tendency to focus on explaining average populations and/or events is reflected in discourses of "expected value," "maximizing sum of squared deviations from the mean," and "predicted probabilities, holding all other factors at their mean values." It is also reflected in the assumption that any phenomena, even those about which little is known, can be defined by a normal distribution. This focus, unfortunately, *excludes groups that lie outside that norm*, which can include racial/ethnic minorities, religious minorities, and any other movement or population that *deviates in significant ways* from the rest of the population. Ignoring these sectors of society has left political scientists ill-equipped to explain – or even to anticipate – non-average events like the fall of the Berlin Wall in 1980, the terrorist attacks on September 11, 2001, or Obama's election in 2008, or smaller events like the groundswell of protest in Iran that occurred in 2009.

(American Political Science Association 2011, 18–19, emphasis added)

Even as it struggles to provide a lucid account of the dramatic failure to engage embodied power, the task force report replicates central problematics of the discipline. White citizens are positioned as "normal," unspecified "others" as deviant outliers. Whereas it is "unfortunate" that those who exist "outside the norm" are excluded, it hardly seems fair to blame political science for neglecting those who "deviate in significant ways from the rest of the population." Like the discipline that it seeks to call to account, the report lacks critical reflexivity in its most basic reckoning of the "population." Women constitute 52 percent of the world population; people of color comprise near 80 percent. On a global scale, it is white men, the unmarked norm, who deviate from the rest of the population. Even in the United States, when women and people of color are tallied, white men make up less than 25 percent of the adult population. Yet it is this white male minority who have been and continue to be the focus of mainstream political science.

In summarizing the consequences for political science of neglecting women and people of color, that is, the *majority* of the population, the task force report emphasizes the inability to predict or explain "non-average events," such as the collapse of the Soviet system. But again the report seems to miss the mark, for the real toll of failing to study the majority of the population lies in constructing a conception of politics in which brutal forms of power are rendered invisible. At issue is not failure to predict singular events, but failure to investigate modal practices. Rogers Smith (2004, 41) noted this consequence: "Precisely because racial identities have been politically constructed in ways that served to legitimate racial inequalities, by making them seem natural and pre-political, even students of politics did not treat racial identities as substantially created by formal laws and political institutions ... We still may be failing to explore fully the role of politics in creating racial identities and racial conflicts, which in turn may mean that we are also failing to explore fully the role of racial politics in shaping many political patterns, identities and institutions." Although the task force report cites Smith's essay repeatedly, it seems to have missed that critical point.

By shifting attention to failure to predict singular events, the report allows the adequacy of the discipline's generalizations to escape scrutiny. But it is the patent inadequacy of generalizations based on a fraction of the population that feminist and critical race scholars have called into question. Attention to the experiences of the majority – women and people of color – may undermine the validity of "truths" long established by the discipline. Consider, for example, the correlation between higher education levels and enhanced political participation – a correlation that is acclaimed as as close to a "law-like generalization" as political science has to offer. As Jane Junn (2007) has carefully documented, women's rising education levels have not resulted in the increases in public office that the correlation predicts, precisely because the correlation was based exclusively on white men's experience. "The most important explanatory variable for political action at the individual level is SES, a mix of educational attainment and income ... despite higher levels of education among women compared to men, inequality in the political sphere will likely persist for the same reasons that income inequality remains between men and women of equal educational attainment and credentials" (Junn 2007, 126–27). What has been, and continues to be, advanced as scientific truth about the factors that contribute to political participation is "contrary to observed phenomena when women's experience is considered" (Junn 2007, 126–27). Similarly, when the experiences of the people of the global South are made central to political investigation, a host of settled truths are called into question from understandings of the causes of conflict and explanations of poverty to accounts of terrorism, and the cartography of the political (Mills 2015, 6–7).

By allowing the dynamics of embodied power to remain invisible, the discipline offers a distorted account of politics that both masks and perpetuates raced and gendered inequities. Mistaken understandings of race and gender occlude dimensions of power that operate at the micro, meso, and macro levels. To avoid perpetuation of oppressive power relations, it is important to analyze conceptual practices of power within political science. Toward that end, the next section of the chapter offers a critical history of the discipline that moves beyond benign descriptions of disembodied politics (e.g., "development and modernization") to explicate the raced and gendered political world envisioned and consolidated by political science.

A Critical History of American Political Science

In the last few decades of the nineteenth century, academic field formation involved a process of differentiation as science was delineated from natural philosophy, humanities from philology, history from philosophy, sociology from history, and political science from sociology. This intensive differentiation was intimately tied to the project of intellectual legitimation. Each new intellectual field offered a framework for organizing social relations and naturalizing certain power relations. Each offered an ensemble of ideas, concepts, and categories to give meaning to the phenomena it placed within its universe, and to sustain the boundaries it constructed to distinguish itself from other scholarly discourses. In the words of Nikolas Rose and Peter Miller (1992, 6–7), political science offered a "system of thought" that specified particular problems for government to address, along with "systems of action" through which those problems could be resolved. Within this frame, "political discourse" can be understood as "a domain for the formulation and justification of idealized schemata for representing reality, analyzing it, and rectifying it" (Rose and Miller 1992, 7).

In developing accounts of their origins, academic disciplines often tend toward the "Whiggish" (Butterfield 1931), offering a selective account that takes the present not only as the culmination of the past, but its telos. Referring to this approach as "recurrent histories," Nikolas Rose (1996, 3) notes that recurrent histories distinguish sanctioned from lapsed ideas, influences, and thinkers in order to "police the present" and "shape the future":

> The sanctioned past is arranged in chronological sequence, as that which led to the present, anticipated it, the virtuous tradition of which the present is the inheritor. It is the past of geniuses, precursors, influences, obstacles overcome, crucial experiments, discoveries. Opposed to this sanctioned account is lapsed history of false paths, errors and illusions, prejudice and mystification. Consigned to the lapsed past are all books, theories, arguments, explanations associated with systems of thought incongruous with the present. Recurrent histories take the present as both the culmination of the past and the standpoint from which its historicity can be displayed … play[ing] a constitutive role in scientific discourses … they help demarcate the regime of truth which is contemporary for the discipline.
>
> *(Rose 1996, 3)*

In contrast to the teleology of recurrent histories, Rose characterizes critical history as an effort "to open space for analytical judgment, us[ing] investigation of the past to enable one to think differently about the present, through an examination of the conditions under which our current forms of truth have been made possible ... Critique seeks to delegitimate the present of the discipline by exposing its past to write a different future" (3).

By contesting the terms in which political science recounts its past, it is possible to take a second look at disembodied politics. In contrast to the benign construction of race and sex as pre-political or exogenous to the political, the early works of American political science actively constructed a conception of the nation-state as white men's domain and advocated a "civilizing" mission that justified empire building as beneficial to the "backward" races and paternal rule as necessary for the "inferior" sex.

Both James Farr (2004) and Rogers Smith (2004) have offered brief accounts of this troubling past. In a symposium in *PS: Political Science and Politics*, Farr drew attention to "nineteenth-century political scientists who promoted notions of civic engagement [that] were silent about women and issues of gender, as well as about race and colonial government" (38). Noting that these scholars sought "to stabilize and moderate the American experiment with democracy," Farr suggests that they invented a conception of "civic education [that] consisted mainly in learning about how to exercise duties and rights in light of the actual state ... Women had duties and rights but among them was not to be counted voting or holding elective office, some of the most famous political scientists argued against suffrage." Claiming that women "lacked the practical training and knowledge needed to cast the vote intelligently," political scientists envisioned "differential civic education ... or 'special training' for women's unique role [as] the 'natural consequence of the distributed class of duties' to the State" (38). The goal of stabilizing the experiment with democracy also necessitated "differential duties and rights dependent upon race." Treating the very presence of Blacks on U.S. soil as the "fundamental tragic fact in the Life of the South," eminent scholars lamented the error of enfranchising Black men during Reconstruction as "the great bulk of negroes were not fit for the suffrage" (James Bryce cited in Farr 2004, 39). To capture the intensity of the conception of differential duties and rights, Farr cites Westel Willoughby's treatise, *Social Justice* (1900, 266):

> The proper attitude of the so-called higher nations to the lower, less civilized races is obvious. It cannot but be held that, just as there is a duty on the part of a parent or guardian to educate, even with the collateral use of compulsion if necessary, the undeveloped faculties of the child, so it lies within the legitimate province of an enlightened nation to compel – if compulsion be the only and the best means available – the less civilized races to enter into that better social and political life the advantage of which their own ignorance either prevents them from seeing, or securing if seen.

Smith (2004, 41) also draws attention to "a great deal of explicit racism in the writings of many key figures of the discipline." From accounts of racial struggles cast in terms of social Darwinist notions of the survival of the fittest to claims about constitutional liberty as the achievement of the "bearers of the Teutonic germ," scholars, who were also notable statesmen, advocated a rigid racial hierarchy. Woodrow Wilson championed segregation. Henry Cabot Lodge proposed race-based immigration restrictions. Theodore Roosevelt supported Black disenfranchisement. John W. Burgess vindicated imperialism, claiming that "the Teutonic nations are called to carry the political civilization of the modern world into those parts of the world inhabited by unpolitical and barbaric races" (1890, 45; cited in Smith 2004, 41). Smith notes that from 1906 to 1990, only "2% of over 6000 articles published in the *American Political Science Review* (APSR) and the *Political Science Quarterly* addressed the experiences of African Americans and nearly two-thirds of these fell within a race-relations politics which sought to manage the black problem to the benefit of whites" (42). As an example, Smith cites Harold Gosnell's "condescending studies in the 1930s designed to investigate whether blacks could rise from a lower to higher cultural level, which is the standard for the modern world" (Gosnell 1935, 11 cited in Smith 2004, 42).

Although both Farr and Smith are rightly critical of this blatant racism and sexism, neither suggests that these early views systematically shaped the discipline of political science. In contrast to overt racialization, Farr notes that "silence or relative inattention ... became a disciplinary heritage when dealing with race" (39). Smith mentions that "studies by black political scientists of black experience are never read by whites" and he is unequivocal in stating that "our profession has contributed *historically* to the political construction of race in America as a vast system of unjust inequalities" (45, emphasis added). Yet, he remains tentative in his conclusions about the effects of such past practices and continuing segregation in disciplinary knowledge production, fearing that "we *may* still be failing to explore fully the role of racial politics in shaping many political patterns, identities, and institutions" (41).

In tracing the transnational circulation of racialized conceptions of the nation-state, Australian scholars Marilyn Lake and Henry Reynolds (2008) offer a far less sanguine account of the long-term effects of late 19th- and early 20th-century political science. In *Drawing the Global Colour Line: White Men's Countries and the International Challenge of Racial Equality*, they suggest that the discipline cultivated ways of thinking and acting that profoundly shaped the political world. Political science developed detailed analyses that accredited certain practices of power, racializing and gendering techniques, forms of calculation, modes of exclusion, and administrative routines and procedures that vindicated a hierarchical racial and gender order. Moreover, in their movement from scholarly treatise to the halls of government, these early political scientists became policy-makers who shaped laws, policies, and analytic practices both within and across nations. Through their racializing interpretations of the past, they helped institutionalize notions of racial and gender "order" that continue to haunt contemporary thinking with profound consequences for the world and the people who inhabit it.

James Bryce, for example, was a distinguished scholar, statesman, and diplomat who served as the British ambassador to the United States from 1907 to 1913. His three volume tome *The American Commonwealth* (1888) became an instant "classic," gaining "Biblical authority" in Britain, North America, South Africa and Australasia (Lake and Reynolds 2008, 50). In celebrating the U.S experiment with democracy, Bryce called particular attention to the institutional structures created in the design of the Constitution. This work set a pattern in subsequent political science of deploying the term, "democracy," to characterize political systems that restricted citizenship to white men, thereby legitimating forms of racial and gender exclusion. The logic informing *The American Commonwealth* was shaped by Bryce's award-winning essay, *Holy Roman Empire* (1864), which purported to trace "Aryan development" across the millennia. From Rome to Britain to the USA, the "Teutonic Branch" of humanity had manifested a unique capacity for power and influence, which, according to Bryce, cemented its destiny to conquer and occupy the world (Horsman 1981). Convinced that "Anglo-Saxon genius" was embedded in "democratic" institutions, Bryce advanced an account of Reconstruction (1865–1877) that depicted the enfranchisement of newly freed Black men as a danger to democracy. According to Bryce (1888, 92), Reconstruction's ill-fated experiment entrusted the responsibilities of democratic citizenship to unqualified people: "Emancipation found them utterly ignorant; and the grant of suffrage found them as unfit for political rights as any population could be." Articulating a conception of a temporal continuum that contrasted the modern achievements of the Teutonic Branch with the primitivism of other races, Bryce infantilized "Negro intelligence," characterizing it "[a]s rather quick than solid, and though not wanting in a sort of shrewdness ... show[ing] the childishness as well as lack of control which belongs to primitive peoples" (496). For this reason, Bryce argued that Blacks should be accorded civil rights but not political rights, a distinction that came to play a central role in post-Reconstruction practices to disenfranchise African Americans.

In "Thoughts on the Negro Problem," published in the *North American Review* in 1891, Bryce described African Americans as "an alien element, unabsorbed, unabsorbable" (652). And he noted that they should be deported back to Africa – except that their labor was needed to sustain the economy of the American South. In 1902, in *The Relations of the Advanced and the Backward Races of Mankind*, Bryce further elaborated his notion of the "natural" racial order, expanding his analysis of "the risks a democracy runs when the suffrage is granted to a large mass of half-civilized men" to encompass "Asiatics" as well as "Negroes" (38). In this work and in his third edition of *The American Commonwealth* (1900), Bryce adopted the language of evolution to position the "Caucasian" at the "pinnacle of modern wisdom and knowledge," with lesser races lagging far behind. And he weighed-in against the proposition that citizenship skills could be learned with proper educational opportunity. "History and science tell us that social and moral advancement is an extremely slow process, because it issues from a change in the physical as well as mental nature of a race" (Bryce 1888, 643). Because the "Negro" trailed so far behind the Caucasian in evolutionary development, Bryce argued that it would take many thousands of years before Blacks could be entrusted with the franchise. Keenly aware of the restrictions upon racial exclusion created by the 14th and 15th Amendments to the U.S. Constitution, Bryce suggested that states would have to be creative in devising mechanisms that were racially neutral but that could be used to exclude Blacks from voting. Toward that end, he mentioned literacy tests and property or poll taxes as race-neutral devices that could circumvent constitutional mandates concerning nondiscrimination on basis of color or prior condition of servitude.[5]

Bryce lamented the negative consequences that the failed experiment of Reconstruction had on U.S. political institutions and on the character of white men. Among the destructive consequences of Black enfranchisement, Bryce counted electoral corruption and a "deterioration of national character" resulting from widespread violence. In a perverse inversion of causal relations, however, Bryce blamed Black voting and office holding for the "coarsening" of white men. Determined to resist "Negro domination," whites turned to force and fraud to reassert their mastery. "Such a Saturnalia of robbery and jobbery has seldom been seen in any civilized country and certainly never before under the forms of free self-government" associated with the Teutonic Branch (Bryce 1902, 484). White men's recourse to violence generated a spirit of lawlessness "which tells for evil on every branch of government and public life" (507). In addition to the corrosive effects on democratic institutions, Black freedom also gave rise to "race repulsion" that motivated white men to implement Jim Crow segregation, which had negative consequences for any future interracial democracy (505). "So complete a system of separation" made it impossible to cultivate "the spirit of fellow feeling and public security essential to the workings of democracy and civil society" (507). In blaming African Americans for having exercised the rights of citizenship secured by the Civil War Amendments and attributing responsibility to them for unlawful action by white men to restore white supremacy, Bryce established an explanatory trope that became the received view in political science, echoed by eminent scholars such as John W. Burgess, W.A. Dunning, Theodore Roosevelt, and Woodrow Wilson (Tulloch 1988).[6] By assessing political developments exclusively from the perspective of white men and rendering invisible the extraordinary suffering of those constructed as "lower" races, disembodied politics diverted attention away from brutal historical practices of racial and gender oppression.

Bryce's conception of racial order also positioned "Asiatics" as backward peoples who posed a formidable threat to the standard of life and the standard of leisure in white settler societies. The second half of the nineteenth century was an era of mass migration: 50 million Europeans, 50 million Chinese and 30 million

Indians migrated to the Americas, Australasia, and South Africa (Lake and Reynolds 2008, 6). Although these migrants all set out in search of better lives, not all were "equally suited" to the demands of democratic citizenship. According to Bryce, white men possessed the capacity for self-governance; others did not. "Coolies, Islanders, Asiatics, and Blacks were cast not simply as deficient workers, colonists and citizens but also as men. They were docile, servile, dependent, unfree" (Lake and Reynolds 2008, 7). Bryce praised the spirit of the Chinese Exclusion Act (1882) and the efforts of California and Australia in the 1890s to "avert race contact" through immigration restriction. Indeed, he praised immigration control on the grounds that it preserved the possibility for democracy. According to Bryce, democracy required equal citizenship. Excluding those who could never be equal from the national territory was thus an important means to preserve democratic institutions. Bryce saw no contradiction in proclaiming that individual liberty and freedom of movement were universal rights that could be exercised only by civilized Anglo-Saxon men. Nor did he find it unreasonable to assert that many peoples were "unfit" for liberty or self-government. In 1898, Bryce told Theodore Roosevelt that "healthy despotism" was required for the Philippines and Cuba, "No talk of suffrage or any such constitutional privileges for them; but steady government by the firmest, honestest men you can find, and no interference if possible by Congress when the firm and honest men have been found" (quoted in Tulloch 1988, 205).

Founder and Dean of the School of Political Science at Columbia and founder of the *Political Science Quarterly* in 1886, John W. Burgess has been hailed as the "father" of American political science. In their history of the discipline, *The Development of American Political Science*, Albert Somit and Joseph Tanenhaus (1967) note that "on reexamination, Burgess ranks not only as the 'father' of American political science, but among the truly great figures in history. His aspirations for a scientific politics, grasp of scientific method, insistence upon broad interdisciplinary training, and concern with systematic theory set a standard rarely surpassed from his day to the present." Like Bryce, Burgess believed that democratic institutions were a world historical achievement, unique to the Teutonic genius of northern Europe and the United States. Borrowing language from Hegel's *Philosophy of Right*, Burgess conceptualized the modern state as the progressive realization of human reason through history. And he defined political science as the science of the state. In *Political Science and Comparative Constitutional Law* (1890), Burgess argued that the state must be grounded in a homogeneous nation – a people unified by language, custom, and culture. As a sovereign entity, a fundamental responsibility of the modern nation state was to secure its physical boundaries and preserve homogeneity within its borders. Thus, Burgess argued not only that racial homogeneity was a prerequisite for a successful state, but that "the highest duty of the state is to preserve, strengthen, and develop its national character" (1890, 42). Toward that end, Burgess stipulated that a nation-state could "righteously deport the ethnically hostile element in order to shield the vitals of the state from the forces of dissolution and in order to create room for a population in sufficient numbers, in loyalty and capacity to administer the Empire and protect it against foreign powers" (42–3). Like Bryce, Burgess moved quickly from a conception of democratic governance as the preserve of the Teutonic race to a claim that modern nation-states had a duty to "civilize" other nations and races. Also following Bryce's lead, Burgess devoted considerable study to Reconstruction, which he depicted as "the most soul-sickening spectacle Americans have ever been called on to behold." In *Reconstruction and the Constitution* (1902), Burgess constructed a racial order that positioned African Americans as the least advanced of all peoples: "A Black skin means membership in a race of men which has never of itself succeeded in subjecting passion to reason, has never, therefore, created any civilization of any kind" (cited in Lake and Reynolds 2008, 69). Given such "vast differences in political capacity between the races," Burgess concluded that "it is the white man's mission, his duty, and his right, to hold the reins of political power in his hands for the civilization of the world and the welfare of mankind" (Lake and Reynolds 2008, 69). For Burgess, as for Bryce, the science of politics was deeply invested in white nationalism, Teutonic supremacy, and imperial rule.[7]

Arguments advanced by political scientists that deployed the rhetoric of reason, freedom, and democratic governance to justify racial subordination, immigration restrictions, and imperial rule had palpable effects on U.S. domestic and foreign policy. Theodore Roosevelt provides a prime example of the institutionalization of the racialized and gendered logic of early political science in public policy. In his essay, "National Life and Character" (1897, 289), Roosevelt asserted that "nineteenth century democracy needs no more complete vindication for its existence than the fact that it has kept for the white race the best portions of the new world's surface, temperate America and Australia" (289).[8] But the victory secured by the "white race" was not secure. On the contrary, Roosevelt argued that it was under dire threat from the proliferating population and migration of "inferior" races. With the introduction of the census as a new administrative technology, states had documented that population growth was not evenly distributed: the "lower races of men" were increasing faster than the "higher." Anticipating a clash that pitted "East" against "West" and "South" against "North," Roosevelt noted with alarm that "the dark races are gaining on us, as they have already done in Haiti and are doing throughout the West Indies and our Southern States" (quoted in Lake and Reynolds 2008, 97). Characterizing this emerging global racial competition as "the warfare of the cradle," Roosevelt insisted that "no race has any chance to win a great place unless it consists of good breeders and good fighters" (1897, 293–294). Thus, Roosevelt wed pro-natalism to U.S. imperialism as the key to ensuring the survival of the white nation: "The woman must be the housewife, the helpmeet, the homemaker, the wise and fearless mother of many healthy children … when men fear righteous war, when women fear motherhood, they tremble at the brink of doom" (1902, 2).

In a 1901 address to the American Academy of Political and Social Science entitled "The Causes of Race Superiority," Edward Ross (1901, 88) discussed the falling birth rate among educated white Americans as a form of "race suicide," attributable to the selfishness of women (159).[9] Roosevelt was convinced that U.S. "national character" was altogether incompatible with such an unsavory end and he dedicated himself to the imperative of overseas expansion – and war if need be – as an appropriate national response to the challenges posed by inferior races. Echoing Hegel's argument that war could be a stimulus to moral development, a means to unify the nation by mobilizing them against an external enemy, Roosevelt characterized the Spanish-American war as a means of overcoming the divisions created by the Civil War. Responding to the nation's call for defenders, white American soldiers from north and south, cities and rural areas, Republicans and Democrats forged bonds as they fought together against "half-caste and native Christians, warlike Moslems and wild pagans … utterly unfit for self-government [who] show no signs of becoming fit" (Roosevelt 1902, 9). In his zeal to secure the Anglo-Saxon destiny of domination over the "lower" races, Roosevelt railed against the corrosive influence of Spanish "aristocratic" rule, yet failed to recognize the freedom dreams of Cubans and Filipinos who sought independence in order to build democratic institutions.

These early works structured the objects of political inquiry within a particular system of race and gender relations. The nation state was an achievement of Anglo-Saxon civilization. It emerged through a process of development or "modernization" only under the tutelage of white men who understood their duty to the "lower" races. From its earliest conceptualization as an object of study, the nation-state was a raced and gendered concept. It afforded the opportunity for self-governance to white men and actively excluded women and people of color. Indeed, within the framework established by political science, exclusions from citizenship were required for the sake of democracy itself. By vindicating a specific racial and gender order in relation to the unfolding of reason and freedom, the founders of political science performed what Charles Mills (2015, 10) has called "a double mystification." They masked the brutal practices of white settler societies ranging from slaughter of indigenous populations and centuries of exploitation of slave labor to *de jure* exclusions from schooling and rights of citizenship of large segments of the population born on "American" soil. They invented a past in which founding violence was cast as an independence struggle against the British Crown, while violence against the indigenous and enslaved populations was masked by claims about inherently backward races. The reliance on "race" to explain the civilizational genius of the Teutonic Branch and the child-like primitivism of the "less civilized" also provided a justification for coercive control of "inferiors" within national borders and imperial expansion overseas.

Following Foucault, Nikolas Rose (1996, 6) has suggested that "political objects cannot be understood as something given, independent, preexisting political knowledge, discovered by investigation… Social science constitutes the object in the process of knowing it." The authoritative knowledge generated by the founding generation of American political science constituted "democracy" as a white male endeavor, the "nation-state" as a racially homogeneous entity, and "imperial expansion" as a defensive move to safeguard the achievement of democracy from the threat of "lesser races" unfit for the demands of self-government. Although the discipline of political science has moved beyond the explicit racism of these early works, it continues to rely on an analytical framework that signifies and condenses the world by encoding objects, situations, events, experiences, and sequences of action within systems of thought envisioned and accredited by these early works. Norms pertaining to classification, statistical regularities, methodological nationalism, methodological individualism, scientific rigor in relation to abstract universalism and white androcentrism continue to define the discipline in ways that mask embodied power. Disembodied politics is shored up by these conceptual practices of power, which do more than "neglect" the experiences of the majority population. They make state involvement in racialization and gendering invisible. The next section briefly explicates these conceptual practices of power; their persistence in political science is documented in Chapters 3, 4 and 5.

Conceptual Practices of Power

Academic disciplines make the world knowable through precise techniques for framing research questions, organizing and analyzing data, accrediting forms of explanation and modes of argument. Training within a discipline involves learning to perceive the world through accredited categories and studying phenomena through routinized research procedures. Although specific research paradigms change over time (e.g., structural functionalism gives way to new institutionalism, political culture studies are supplanted by rational choice models), certain fundamental research heuristics persist. Providing concepts, definitions, and hypotheses to guide research, a fundamental research "heuristic" or frame involves a shared set of assumptions so central to a mode of analysis that they cannot be jettisoned (Lakatos 1970, 132). As a social science that seeks to discern patterns in the political world that reveal more than statistical frequencies, political science encourages systematic observation and subsequent classification of observed phenomena on the basis of similarities and differences. Disciplinary norms pertaining to classification, methodological individualism, methodological nationalism, abstract universalism, and white androcentrism structure knowledge production in political science in ways that depoliticize embodied power. Rather than innocent assumptions or neutral analytical techniques, they are best understood as conceptual practices of power.

Classification

Methods texts suggest that classification is a descriptive technique that organizes phenomena accorded to perceived differences. The key to successful classification is the construction of categories that are mutually exclusive and cumulatively exhaustive. When a system of categories is constructed according to these principles, each observation will fit within only one category and there will be no remainders once categorization is complete. The organization of the human population into "higher" and "lower" races and superior and inferior sexes was a hallmark of scientific classification from the eighteenth through the twentieth centuries (see Chapter 3 for a fuller account). As the works discussed above demonstrate, however, classification is a normative as well as a descriptive process. Categories organize perception and naturalize differences, structuring hierarchies that are taken for granted.

Intersectionality theorists have pointed out that dichotomous variables developed within parsimonious systems of categorization distort what they claim merely to describe. Classification uncouples phenomena from their contexts and streamlines them in ways that sacrifice the messiness of complexity. As is evident in Roosevelt's mandate, noted above, that the "woman must be the housewife, the helpmeet, and the homemaker," Black women were not included in the category "woman." Few Black women had the luxury of restricting their energies to homemaking during this era and rather than being encouraged to procreate, they were constructed as profligate reproducers who threatened the white race-nation, and as such were targeted for "eugenic" sterilization. As intersectionality scholars emphasize, the point is not simply that Roosevelt did not have Black women in mind when he issued his sweeping mandate. The point is that assumptions about mutually exclusive categories based on sex or race cannot recognize cases that appropriately fit more than one category. The system of categorization itself situates some below the threshold of intelligibility.

When classifications suggest continuous rather than dichotomous variables, their descriptive claims often exude a normative dimension. Although the blatant racism of the early civilizational discourses affirmed by political science has been left behind, classification schemes that circulate in contemporary political science still structure the world according to a racial order that implies teleological development culminating in the liberal democratic nation-state. Consider, for example, locutions such as "developing" nations, "democratizing" states, or "advanced" economies, which situate the majority of countries in the world on a trajectory towards neoliberal capitalism, as if that were the only form of "modernity." As Pinar Bílgín and Lili Ling (2014) have pointed out, under the guise of descriptive classification, political science imposes subaltern politics on the rest of the world.

Some might argue that contemporary classification in political science simply captures statistical regularities. Yet, such a claim overlooks the way in which quantitative approaches must first operationalize concepts in order to be able to count the object under investigation. And by constructing mean and modal categories, statistics creates "averages" and "outliers." As pioneers in statistical analysis such as Francis Galton, Karl Pearson, and Charles Spearman made clear, to "reveal" regularities, technical devices must be constructed to calculate correlation and to normalize distributions. As the APSA *Report on Political Science in the 21st Century* demonstrates, assumptions about white men as the modal category can skew even the most rigorous statistical claims about the empirical world. Thus the presumptions of neutral description and value-free classification constitute conceptual practices that mask certain power relations.

Methodological Individualism

Early works in political science celebrated the individual's capacity for self-governance as a hallmark of advanced civilization, then made it clear that only certain political subjects (white men) were individuals *per se*, capable of participating in democratic governance. Yet as a neutral and inclusive term, the "individual" appears to include precisely those who have been barred from political participation. Thus, individualist discourses mask state practices of embodied power. Similarly, methodological individualism masks group membership, practices of subordination, and the tendency to posit white men as the unmarked norm.

As a methodological premise, individualism both reflects the formal equality established in democratic constitutions (e.g., one person, one vote) and posits the equality of the value preferences that inform individual actions. But the analytical assumption of the equality of persons is false both historically and in contemporary societies. Women and people of color were not and are not now the equals of modal (much less elite) white men. Thus, methodological individualism has the unsavory effect of masking both group inequalities and the political production of raced and gendered subordination. Individualist assumptions can also have adverse policy consequences. By downplaying the role of the state in producing and sustaining inequality, erroneous presumptions about equality can individualize blame for unequal social conditions. When those disadvantaged by racism and sexism are "assimilated as putative equals to the status and situation of white [men]," it negates "the need for any measures to repair the inequities of the past" (Mills 2007, 237).

By insisting that the individual is the basic unit of analysis, methodological individualism masks embodied power. It makes it difficult to see that what is taken as true for the dominant group, seldom holds for those who are constructed as racialized and gendered others. As Jane Junn has noted, the assumption that individuals have equal agency would hold if and only if the political system itself were neutral, not favoring any particular race, class, or gender. Yet, in contemporary systems marked by pervasive social, economic, and political inequalities, the presumption of equal agency only serves "to block empirical and theoretical work to illuminate more precisely when and how power and hierarchy structure opportunities and incentives to act in politics" (Junn 2007, 130).

Methodological Nationalism

The early works in political science laid the foundation for methodological nationalism, framing the nation-state as the fundamental object of political inquiry. At the same time that they framed democratic government as a civilizational achievement of Anglo-Saxon nations, they naturalized the "nation" as a racially homogeneous, bounded social group, replete with culture, politics, and economy (Wimmer and Glick Schiller 2003), and argued that some "nations" were far more advanced than others. Some were suited to democratic self-government, others were not.

By naturalizing the nation as a people bound by blood, and long-established ties to the land, early political science masked the fairly recent invention of the "modern" nation state, consolidated in the eighteenth century as part of the Westphalian system established by the Treaty of Westphalia (1648). Emphasizing the nation as a home to a homogeneous population, political science also masked the fundamental nature of white settler societies that gained access to land through conquest and colonization. Whether invoking the language of Anglo-Saxons, Aryans, Teutons, or Caucasians, political science discourses racialized whites, constructing them as one race on the basis of skin color and European heritage. Through such racialized rhetoric, the discipline itself helped produce a sense of racialized national identity on the part of settlers who until that time had understood themselves in far different terms related to religion, period of arrival in the Americas, state of residence, country of origin, or Union or Confederate supporters. By naturalizing the nation, they rendered invisible the arduous work of nation building – of forging "the one from the many" – along with the exclusions of the "unassimilable" that historically entailed. And they de-emphasized certain political cleavages (e.g., region, religion and class) that had fueled a great deal of political violence since the founding of the United States of America.

Methodological nationalism is systemically entrenched in the research heuristics of political science. Whether the field is comparative politics (institutions, behavior, law, processes, culture) or international relations, the nation-state is taken as the fundamental unit of analysis. Even those who try to challenge the premises of nationalism through the study of the transnational or the cosmopolitan take the nation-state as their point of departure and their unavoidable comparator. But methodological nationalism obscures certain forms of political power, most notably embodied power. Organizing knowledge around certain kinds of difference (e.g., unitary versus federal states, democratic versus authoritarian regimes), it masks the production of embodied difference through racialization and gender- as the discipline moves toward a recognition of pluralist democracies, is about homogeneity as a precondition of democracy, it of formal equality as a defining characteristic of members of the ich renders state complicity in the production of racial and e near impossible to see.

Abstract: Universalism

Seeking to identify law-like generalizations about political life, political science necessarily abstracts from particular cases to provide explanations and predictions that hold across specificities. The authority of science turns on the capacity to distinguish between the universal and the particular, the idiosyncratic, the anomalous. But precisely because the majority of the human population has been excluded from political studies, the discipline has allowed the elite white male to masquerade as the unmarked norm, the instantiation of the universal. As a consequence, whites appear to be raceless as racial characteristics are attributed only to others; and white men appear to be unencumbered by gender as women carry the burden of "the sex." Only a presumption about the importance of abstract universal explanation can account for the pervasive and persistent tendency within political science to treat the fields of gender and politics, and race/ethnicity and politics as content specializations of little interest to the discipline at large. Only convictions concerning abstract universalism can explain why cutting-edge research that foregrounds experiences of the majority population and challenges the received view in political science remain unread, uncited, and untaught.[10]

Michelle Le Doeuff (2007, 42–43) has pointed out that abstract universalism involves a sleight of hand. "Work, which while claiming to be exhaustive, forgets about women's existence and concerns itself only with the position of men, should be described as particularist, a form of masculinism. In practice, work 'on women' … still meets indifference, that formidable form of resistance … To choose to ignore this type of work, or to consider it as 'specialist' and of interest only to the equally specialized audience of women … betrays an intellectual block, as surely as expounding the idea that women are not part of history" (43). Research that neglects people of color manifests a comparable form of particularism. By allowing the particular to masquerade as the universal, abstract universalism narrows the sphere of the political and operates as a technology of exclusion. Thus abstract universalism is a form of white androcentrism.

White Androcentrism

Founding works in American political science explicitly declared democratic politics the prerogative of white men. They were unabashed in their stances against women's suffrage and for "race-neutral" mechanisms to disenfranchise African American men. In a sense, then, they were heirs to the mythos of the American Revolution, which purported to build a system of governance on the principle of equality even as it sustained the legal practice of chattel slavery and exclusion of all but propertied white men from the practice of politics. The mythos of "American exceptionalism" circulated the notion that the United States was free from the ascriptive hierarchies of "the Old World" even as race and sex were deployed to exclude citizens born on U.S. soil from the full privilege of birthright citizenship.[11] White androcentrism underlies these profound contradictions. Only when the privilege of white men provides the vantage point for understanding politics, is it possible to perceive the exclusion of the majority of the population from political rights as inconsequential to the meaning or practice of democracy. Only white androcentrism enables the construction of the white race-nation as the progressive unfolding of reason and freedom. Only white androcentrism erases colonial domination of indigenous peoples, chattel slavery, and centuries of disenfranchisement from official histories of the nation. Only white androcentrism can construct imperialism as a form of benign paternal rule.

Although many would like to claim that white androcentrism was purged long ago from the research heuristics of political science, it continues to surface in multiple paradigms from "realist" approaches to international relations and rational choice models of political behavior to claims about the "clash of civilizations." White androcentrism surfaces in methodological individualism that remains oblivious to institutional contexts that enable and constrain individual action and to structural forces that ensure that individuals are not equally unfettered subjects. White androcentrism is also constitutive of "strategic color-blindness" that assimilates marginalized people of color as putative equals to privileged whites in ways that negate the need for any measures to address or redress the inequities of the past (Mills 2007, 239). By letting myths of self-making mask advantages that accrued from laws that barred women and people of color from education, professional employment, and political participation, white androcentrism precludes perception of embodied power. It sustains notions of disembodied politics that insist that racial and gender neutrality are the limit in contemporary public policy. Remaining blind to ongoing racial and gender discrimination, white androcentrism suggests that efforts to redress inequalities are unwise and even counter-productive for they constitute "reverse discrimination" that further entrenches misguided racial identifications (Haney Lopez 2014, 203). White androcentrism informs claims that color no longer matters in this post-racial era, trumping the evidence from repeated studies that document "how racism continues to function systematically and comprehensively across all significant social institutions ... function[ing] formally and informally on multiple social levels and that the impact is cumulative, reinforced by law, policy, and by public narrative" (Rose 2013).

Conclusion

To discuss recurrent histories of the discipline along with mechanisms of classification, statistical analysis, methodological individualism, methodological nationalism, abstract universalism, and white androcentrism as conceptual practices of power is to situate political science in relation to complex ways of seeing and thinking that advantage some and disadvantage others. By calling attention not only to what is foregrounded in political analysis, but also to what is pushed below the threshold of visibility, it is possible to consider how embodied power operates in and through knowledge production.

Thirty-five years ago, Cynthia Cockburn (1981, 41) suggested that the "difficulty of analyzing multiple hierarchical categories simultaneously (class, gender, race) stems in part from seeing structures as independent and static, bearing no relations to one another." To overcome these difficulties, Cockburn recommended that scholars "attend instead to processes, the details of historical events, and changes that illuminate the connections between power systems ... [in order to] see the formation of people as raced, gendered, classed simultaneously" (41–42). As proponents of intersectionality and post-occidental approaches have argued, systems of advantage and disadvantage are mutually constitutive; they exist only in relation to each other. To investigate that mutual constitution requires interrogation of conceptual practices of power as well as material relations and institutional processes. Rather than resting content with the limitations of disembodied politics, it is imperative to investigate how racialized and gendered advantage and disadvantage are produced across physical, economic, and sociopolitical domains. Toward that end, political studies must take up questions concerning racialization and gendering within organizations and systems of solidarity, and they must attend to the critical role of political institutions in skilling and deskilling bodies, structuring aspirations and opportunities, and producing subjectivities that are engaged with or alienated from political life.

When racialized gendering and gendered racialization are conceived as practices of political power, mainstream categories in political science necessarily shift. Articulating the views of feminist and critical race scholars, Kate Bedford (2004, 612) suggested that "there is no doubt that existing research on voting behavior, political elites, representation, social movements, democratization, political economy, globalization, and state-society relations would be enhanced ... [if] taken-for-granted categories of analysis received greater critical attention, [and] researchers recognized the [raced] gendered nature of their inquiries into 'citizenship,' 'participation,' 'independence,' 'self-interest,' and the like. Perhaps the boundaries of politics would expand, as concerns with social reproduction, dependence, and subsistence received greater attention. Social policies might be designed differently; international economic policies might change; research priorities might shift. The next three chapters explore these possibilities.

Notes

1 Three of the 24 chapters are written by feminist scholars who draw attention to issues pertaining to race and gender (Ann Tichner in the field of international relations; Iris Young in political theory; and Barbara Nelson in the study of public policy).
2 Although the task force report's title *Political Science in the 21st Century* suggests a comprehensive frame, it would be more apt to characterize the focus as "American political science." American political science is but one of many approaches to the

study of politics, government, and international relations in the contemporary world, but it is often considered the hegemonic approach. It emphasizes the scientific study of political life to identify "law-like" generalizations that enable the discipline to move from observation and description to explanation, and prediction, analytical tasks that can be isolated from evaluation or normative concerns. It endorses quantitative approaches, and "positive" theory, most notably rational choice models, for political analysis. For critiques of this hegemonic model, see Kristen Monroe (2005) and Schram and Caterino (2006).

3 Although critical race scholars have focused on omissions and distortions in disciplinary claims associated with race and feminist scholars have focused on the absence of women, prior to recent work by intersectionality scholars, very few studies have examined the complex interplay of these hierarchies of difference. Many of the studies examined in this chapter fall far short of the research norms established by intersectional analysis. For an elaboration of those norms, see Chapter 6.

4 Although a few passages in the report mention sex, the discipline's neglect of race is the central focus of the analysis. Sex, gender, and sexuality tend to be subsumed under a generic "inequality."

5 Lake and Reynolds (2008) note that Connecticut and Massachusetts were the first states to impose literacy tests in 1850s; Mississippi's constitutional convention recommended the establishment of a literacy test in 1890, and was quickly followed in the USA by South Carolina (1895), Louisiana (1898), North Carolina (1900), Alabama and Virginia (1901), and Georgia (1908). Following developments in the United States carefully, the Cape Colony in South Africa adopted literacy tests in 1892.

6 Tulloch points out that this orthodox interpretation of Reconstruction was challenged only in 1935 with the publication of W. E. B. Du Bois's *Black Reconstruction in America* (New York: Atheneum). But due to the tendency of white political scientists to ignore works written by Black scholars, it took much longer to displace this view of the post-Civil War era.

7 According to the history compiled by Columbia University in honor of its 250th anniversary, Burgess was also chiefly responsible for keeping women out of Columbia during his tenure (http://c250.columbia.edu/c250_celebrates/remarkable_columbians/john_burgess.html).

8 Roosevelt's essay was both a review of and a response to Charles H. Pearson's *National Life and Character: A Forecast* (London: Macmillan 1893). Pearson emphasized that space in temperate zones – the territories in which Anglo Saxons flourished – was in short supply, threatened in particular by mass migration from China and South Asia. Because birth rates for these "lower races" surpassed those of whites, Pearson forecast a growing rivalry between East and West for world domination. Pearson was pessimistic about the capacity of "civilized" white societies to triumph in the emerging global competition. Rejecting Pearson's pessimism, Teddy Roosevelt endorsed vigorous measures in relation to white population growth and empire building to secure white supremacy.

9 Ross was a political economist whose expertise spanned politics, economics, and sociology. He held academic appointments at Indiana, Cornell, Stanford, Nebraska, and Wisconsin over the course of his distinguished career and served both as secretary to the American Economics Association and as president of the American Sociological Association. His diatribes against Chinese and Japanese migrant laborers in California, however, led to his firing from Stanford.

10 As part of its study of *Political Science in the 21st Century*, the APSA task force (American Political Science Association 2011, 15–16) sampled the curriculum at 15 "highly ranked" departments and at 3 historically Black universities that offer the PhD. Their findings suggest that "four of the eighteen – about one in five – of the programs have subfields that include race/ethnicity or gender … Our analysis suggests that issues of race in American politics, for example, are not considered an essential part of what a

student specializing in that subfield needs to know ... Not surprisingly, those programs with faculty who have race/ethnicity or gender as areas of focus in their research also tend to have more course offerings that included these topics. Those universities, of which there are many, that have only one or no faculty whose scholarship focused on difference and inequality are much less likely to provide this type of content to their graduate students."

11 In *The New American Exceptionalism*, Donald Pease (2009, 28) points out that American exceptionalism has been retroactively assigned to the distant origins of the British colonies in North America. But the term did not in fact emerge into common usage until the late 1920s when Joseph Stalin invented it to accuse the Lovestonite faction of the American Communist Party of a heretical deviation from party orthodoxies. "Extracting 'exceptionalism' from Communist Party jargon, scholars moving centerward from the anti-Stalinist left injected it into the central vocabulary of American social and political science. An absence – the relative failure of socialism in the United States – became the defining point of the nation's history, a ratification of the special dispensation of the United States in a revolutionary world where Marx still tempted."

3
THE SCIENCE AND POLITICS OF BODIES

> Rigid adherence to particular understandings of politics and power can seriously impede our ability to recognize and comprehend new political phenomena.
> *(True and Mintrom 2001, 29)*

In the sciences (natural and social) and in the popular imagination, sex, like race, is typically construed as a biological or physical characteristic. Indeed, race and sex are perceived as matters of biological self-evidence. Whether white or black, man or woman, the senses "perceive" these incontestable identity markers as objectively designated biological embodiment. Taken as "given" or "natural," race and sex are deemed to exist outside of politics and culture. As fixed and immutable features of the human population, race and sex are believed to lie altogether beyond the reach of the state.

Thus, the characterization of race and sex as political constructs intimately tied to practices of domination and subordination may at first appear to defy credulity. The challenge of this chapter is to demonstrate that *biologization* is an historical phenomenon – to show that "the private, enclosed, stable body that seems to lie at the basis of modern notions of sexual and racial difference is also the product of particular, historical, cultural moments" (Laqueur 1990, 13). Over the past few centuries, biological determinism has become "the conceptual structure that organizes social experience on the basis of shared understandings" (Devor 1989, 45–46). To denaturalize such settled opinions about race and sex, this chapter traces the emergence of biological determinism as an integral part of modernity's struggle to supersede theological and metaphysical ontologies. In this effort to throw off medieval modes of thinking and feudal hierarchies that entrenched religion in imperial rule, the projects of science and politics often converged. Scientific language offered a way of organizing the species altogether compatible with transformative political ideas circulating in the age of republican revolutions. Claims about inherent abilities of particular kinds of people were readily appropriated as a basis for restrictions on citizenship and political participation, forms of employment, and educational opportunities. But science was not simply a neutral tool appropriated for good or ill by political actors. It was a thoroughly political endeavor: classifications developed by naturalists slipped between the natural world and the social to establish not only the expertise of the naturalists over the natural, but also the dominance of the natural over the social (Laqueur 2009). By claiming the authority of science, biological determinists could promote their own social ideals ostensibly grounded in their scientific discoveries, cautioning skeptics against the cataclysmic consequences of systems and policies that contravened the limits of physical possibility.

Science and politics are intricately intermeshed in the history of modern forms of embodied power, generating and accrediting claims about population differences that haunt individuals from cradle to grave. They work together to create and sustain divisions within the population that are dubbed "organic" and then used to consolidate national and imperial orders structured by finely honed hierarchies of difference. Far from capturing an inherent truth about embodiment, claims about race and sex are products of social thought and relations. they are historical entities invented by particular cultures, but their global circulation over the past few centuries has afforded them transnational purchase and impressive resilience.

Critical race theorists conceptualize race as "a political division … a system of governing people that classifies them into social hierarchy based on invented biological demarcations" (Roberts 2011, x). Feminist theorists conceptualize sex as a dichotomous demarcation of the human species solely in relation to reproductive function (Connell 1987). Intersectionality theorists insist that separate systems of categorization grounded in race and sex render invisible the mutual constitution of these complex systems of embodied power. Sally Markowitz (2001, 390), for example, has noted that "'scientific' classifications of race and sex have long been associated with each other: in temperament, intelligence and physiology, so-called 'lower races' have often provided a metaphor for the female type of humankind and females a metaphor for the 'lower race' … while 'lower races' are often represented as feminine and men of these races as less than masculine, the femininity of non-white women … is likely to be denied (the better no doubt to justify their hard physical labor or sexual exploitation)." Tracing racialized genders and gendered racializations is important because "in dominant Western ideology, a strong sex/gender dimorphism often serves as a human ideal against which different races may be measured and all but white Europeans found wanting. This ideal then functions as a measure of racial advancement that admits of degrees determined by the (alleged) character of the relationship between men and women within a particular race … Sex/gender difference is imagined to increase as various races 'advance' … Thus, the ideology of the sex/gender difference itself turns out to rest not on a simple binary opposition between male and female but rather on a scale of racially coded degrees of sex/gender difference culminating in the manly European man and the feminine European woman" (Markowitz 2001, 390–91).

In contrast to static notions of race and sex, racialization and gendering are multidimensional political processes that produce, consolidate, reproduce and amend intricate relations of domination and subordination. Through scientific discourses and political instruments such as laws, policies, and rights, racialized gendering and gendered racialization create divisions of labor and power, differentiated forms of embodied existence, social stratifications, modes of subjectivity, and structures of desire. This chapter sketches the complex interplay of science and politics in the production of "race" and "sex" as biological categories since the 16th century. The next chapter explores the mutually constituting dynamics of racialization and gendering in contemporary politics and policy.

Biologizing Race

Biological determinism or biologism, the view that there are fundamental, innate physiological differences among kinds of humans, manifested in the incontrovertible evidence of race and sex, has been called the "dominant cognitive schema in North America" (Devor 1989, 45–46). Biological explanations for differences in physiognomy, health, inclination, outlook, behavior and ambition surface regularly in popular media and in arguments advanced by socio-biologists, evolutionary psychologists, and cognitive scientists. Because nature is often imagined as constant in contrast to the dynamic and ongoing changes in history, it may seem surprising that biological accounts of embodiment have a history – and a fairly short one at that. Conceptions of race as a biological category are a product of modernity, integrally tied to European practices of exploration, trade, and colonization. To grasp the distinctive features of the biologization of race, it is important to note that biological "race" is not coterminous with slavery, ethnocentrism, xenophobia, or all hierarchical taxonomies of humans.

Slavery existed in many parts of the ancient world as the fate of those conquered in war. As Sally Kitch (2009, 48) has noted, slavery was a matter of "ill fortune not an inherent or necessarily life-long status." Ethnocentrism, a conviction about the superiority of one's own people, and xenophobia, a suspicion of and hostility toward strangers, may be characteristic of many cultures, but as Dorothy Roberts (2011, 6–7) points out, neither ethnocentrism nor xenophobia is equivalent to a biological conception of race. Neither entails the "partition of all humans into a small number of types ... or treats visible difference as a marker of immutable distinction that determines each group's permanent social value." Nor does either "read moral and intellectual ability into physical difference" (Roberts 2011, 7).

Taxonomies that situate humans within a hierarchical system also have ancient provenance. A.O. Lovejoy (1936) has argued that ancient and medieval European thought shared a theology of the natural world as a well-ordered hierarchy ordained by God. Within the "Chain of Being" or *Scala Natura* (scale of nature), all forms of life could be classified on a continuum from the lowest (minerals, vegetables, animals) to the highest (humans, angels, God). The scale privileged spirit over matter and positioned all living things according to their proximity to an omniscient, omnipotent, and immortal deity. Placement within the great chain of being entailed authority: higher beings could legitimately rule over lower forms of existence, but the power they exercised was bounded by moral principles also believed to be ordained by God.

The moral boundaries of the great chain of being began to shift by papal dispensation. In 1455, Pope Nicholas V issued a directive authorizing the Portuguese to "attack, subject, and reduce to perpetual slavery all enemies of Christ along the west coast of Africa" (Roberts 2011, 6). This license for the slave trade was initially grounded in religion, as the Roman Catholic Church envisioned enslavement as punishment for heathens, encouraging forms of punishment that were sufficiently severe to motivate conversion (Morgan 1997). The Church stipulated that captives who converted to Christianity were to be set free. Salvation of the eternal soul warranted a life of freedom in God's earthly kingdom.

As European exploration accelerated in the 17th century, revealing a proliferation of nations and tribes, French traveler and physician François Bernier (1684) published an essay suggesting "A New Division of the Earth" based on physical appearance and geopolitical location. Bernier used the term "race" to capture five observable forms of human variety:

1. Europeans, North Africans, Near Easterners, and Indians;
2. sub-Saharan Africans;
3. Blacks of the Cape of Good Hope;
4. Asians; and
5. the Lapps of Norway.

Refusing to rank these "kinds" of humans, Bernier suggested that his classification scheme was compatible with the abstract, "theoretical" equality of humanity, while also sensitive to differences noted through empirical observation (Stuurman 2000). While Bernier insisted that the similarities among sentient beings outweighed observed differences, he nonetheless thought it worthwhile to begin to catalogue certain physical variations among men, such as presence or absence of facial hair and relative intensity of perspiration. Thus Bernier launched a precedent in studying the different "species" or "races" of men, attending primarily to the males of the species. And by focusing on beards and sweat, observables that ancient thinkers had associated with men's greater ability to process heat, Bernier also established a pattern of comparing some men with characteristics associated with women (absence of beards, lesser heat) (Kitch 2009, 37).

The great Swedish taxonomist Carl Linnaeus (1707–1778) set out to classify all living things into classes, orders, genera, species, and varieties, publishing 12 editions of *Systema Naturae* during his lifetime. Breaking with the divinely-ordained order of the great chain of being, Linnaeus identified similarities between primates and humans, while also suggesting that there was a discernible hierarchy among humans. Linnaeus divided the genus *Homo* into two species: *Homo sapiens* (man) and *Homo troglodytes* (ape). He then divided *Homo sapiens* into four natural varieties, which combined observations about geographical region and skin color with opinions about cultural traits, physical appearance, intellectual potential, and aesthetic value. As Dorothy Roberts has summarized:

> At the pinnacle of beauty and intelligence, Linnaeus placed *H. sapiens europaeus*: "Vigorous, muscular. Flowing blond hair. Blue eyes. Very smart. Inventive. Covered by tight clothing. Ruled by law."
>
> *H. sapiens americanus*, according to Linnaeus, was "ill-tempered, impassive. Thick straight black hair; wide nostrils; harsh face; beardless. Stubborn, contented, free. Paints himself with red lines. Ruled by custom."
>
> Linnaeus described *H. sapiens asiaticus* as "Melancholy, stern. Black hair; dark eyes. Strict, haughty, greedy. Covered by loose garments. Ruled by opinion."
>
> And at the bottom, he placed *H. sapiens afer*: "Sluggish, lazy. Black kinky hair; silky skin; flat nose; thick lips; females with genital flap and elongated breasts. Crafty, slow, careless. Covered by grease. Ruled by caprice."
>
> (Roberts 2011, 29–30)

Biologization as an account of purportedly natural "racial" difference entered the European imagination in the late 17th century and flowered fully over the course of the eighteenth century (Banton 1998). From the outset, scientific taxonomies of race linked observations about pigment and hair with geography and racializing stereotypes about intellect and social organization. In the same era that "the individual" was being conceptualized as an autonomous entity, unfettered by membership in a line of descent or kinship ties, and the scientific valorization of empirical investigation was according "Nature" an unprecedented authority, science was inventing hierarchical racial value. In marked contrast to the putative freedom of the abstract individual, science created racial "types" – persons who ostensibly exhibited the characteristic qualities of a class. With the invention of race, European science claimed for itself the prerogative to set the standards by which all humans were to be measured; to position themselves as the pinnacle of human development against which all others must be measured; and to extrapolate from a few observations "universal" claims about dimensions of life that are not empirically observable (i.e., intellect, attitudes, moral inclinations).

The exact number of races advanced to demarcate humanity varied according to the scientific investigator. Focusing on comparative anatomy, German physician and professor of medicine Johann Friedrich Blumenbach (1752–1840) introduced a system of racial classification that identified five races. In the second edition of *On the Natural Variety of Mankind* (1779), Blumenbach suggested that physical morphology (a comparison of the shapes of skulls and faces, along with skin color and hair texture) indicated five racial types: Caucasian (or "Georgian"), the white race; Mongolian, the yellow race; Malayan, the brown race; Ethiopian, the black race; and American, the red race. As a proponent of monogenesis (the belief that all humans descended from Adam and Eve – the original "Georgian" type), Blumenbach suggested that because they had been favored by climate and personality, Caucasians had preserved the beauty and excellence of the first humans. Other races had "degenerated" from that level of perfection due to environmental factors such as the sun and poor diet. In contrast to later race scientists, however, Blumenbach argued that degeneration could be reversed in a proper environment. And he noted the boundaries of his racial categories were indistinct and overlapping, which precluded an absolute hierarchy of races.

In contrast to Blumenbach, French anatomist Georges Cuvier (1769–1832) included only three categories in his racial typology (Caucasian, Mongolian, and Ethiopian), divisions derived from the "beauty or ugliness" of their skulls and the "quality" of their civilizations. Like Blumenbach, he traced the origin of all races to Adam and Eve, but where the Caucasian race had preserved the beauty of God's first humans, changes in the physiognomy of Mongolians and Ethiopians had been caused by an environmental catastrophe some 5000 years earlier, the kind of catastrophe that could account for the extinction of many life forms. A critic of early theories of evolution advanced by Lamarck, Cuvier considered the order of the racial hierarchy fixed, arguing that distinctive anatomical features, intelligence, and social organization of the various races reflected proximity to animal existence. In Cuvier's racial typology, the Ethiopian was characterized as "the most degraded of human races, whose form approaches that of the beast and whose intelligence is nowhere great enough to arrive at regular government ... marked by black complexion, crisped or woolly hair, compressed cranium, and a flat nose. The projection of the lower parts of the face, and the thick lips, evidently approximate it to the monkey tribe: the hordes of which it consists have always remained in the most complete state of barbarism" (Cuvier 1817, 50). By contrast, with its "oval face, straight hair and nose, the Caucasian race – to which the civilized people of Europe belong – is the most beautiful of all ... superior to all others by its genius, courage, and activity" (71). With his emphasis on the fixity of the three races, and his insistence that anatomical and cranial measurements revealed inherent intellectual differences that held profound implications for social and political life, Cuvier anticipated both proponents of polygenesis and key features of racial science consolidated over the next two centuries.

As the works of Linnaeus, Blumenbach, and Cuvier make clear, the biologization of race included claims about superiority and inferiority that go well beyond discussions of physical traits. Intelligence, moral capability, political structures, and levels of civilizational accomplishment were all critical elements in the "natural order" purportedly discerned by empirical observation. As critical race, de-colonial, and postcolonial theorists have noted, the science of race elaborated in Europe emerged at a time when European colonists were using law to create a new racial order. Ian Haney Lopez (1996, 19) notes that "law translates ideas about race into material and societal conditions that entrench those ideas." In the British colonies in North America, for example, the earliest male settlers used legislative assemblies to create a social hierarchy that accorded different powers, rights, and responsibilities to propertied white men. As science theorized a gendered racialized order, colonial law institutionalized it.

Carole Pateman (1998, 248) has suggested that within the Anglo-American community free white men defined their status in terms of three dimensions of "self-protection: the capacity to bear arms, the capacity to own property and the capacity for self-government." Colonial laws mandated militia duty for white men. They passed laws governing freedom of contract, according white men property in their own person and in their labor power. They established criteria for citizenship that afforded free white men rights of participation and immunities from certain kinds of state intervention. From the earliest days of settlement in North America, British colonists used the law to draw lines of inclusion and exclusion based on a racial conception of membership. In 1662, ten years before the British government awarded the Royal Africa Company the sole privilege of supplying African labor to the colonies, Virginia passed legislation to alter the common law practice of patrilineal descent, through which citizenship was passed down as a birthright from father to children. Instead, the Virginia House of Burgesses (or freemen of the borough) decreed that enslaved women passed their lifetime bondage to their offspring (Mills and Pateman 2007). Thus, this early experiment in democratic governance stripped citizenship from the progeny of free white men who procreated with enslaved women. In so doing, it established a racial regime that defined slaves – including the sons and daughters of free white men – as "chattel" or personal property of their masters. It suspended the principle of *ius soli*, which established citizenship by birth within a geographical territory.

Prior to 1700, many Blacks and whites entered the British colonies as indentured servants, who promised a fixed number of years of service in return for passage to North America. In 1705, Virginia passed a statute that guaranteed white indentured servants "a musket, money, and bushels of corn when they completed service," while converting Black indenture into enslavement (Roberts 2011, 9). Black servants were deemed ineligible for freedom; they were banned from carrying fire arms; their mobility was restricted; and their life-long bondage was passed on to their children. As a form of property, slaves were excluded from civil law altogether: they could not marry, own property, or testify in court. Categorized by law as property, they were subject to the arbitrary will of their owners. A South Carolina statute accorded white masters "absolute power and authority over Negro slaves" (Roberts 2011, 9).

In her systemic examination of marriage practices in the new world, *Public Vows: A History of Marriage and the Nation*, Nancy Cott (2000) notes that the British colonies in North America were the first secular authorities to criminalize and nullify intermarriage among people of different "races" or colors. In 1664, Maryland enacted the first criminal law against "freeborn English women who made shamefull Matches" with African slaves. Six of the original colonies prohibited marriage between whites and Blacks and between whites and Mulattoes; three banned interracial sex outside of marriage (Cott 2000, 44). Anti-miscegenation laws prohibited marriage not only between people of different legal statuses, freeborn and enslaved, but also across color lines, prohibiting unions between free Blacks and free whites. Indeed, as the number of free Blacks increased in the decades following the American Revolution – as enterprising Blacks purchased their freedom, conscience-stricken masters freed their slaves, and northern states began to abolish slavery – the number of states passing miscegenation laws increased. Although Pennsylvania repealed its anti-miscegenation law in 1780 as did Massachusetts in 1843, the numbers of states prohibiting interracial marriage grew throughout the nineteenth century.

Through legal statute, then, a racial order was created that denied Blacks birthright citizenship, freedom of movement, freedom to marry, the right to dispose of their labor power, the right to bear arms, and entitlement to civil and political liberties. Enslaved Blacks were not only barred from education, literacy was criminalized. In 1723, Virginia passed a series of laws designed to subordinate free people of color to Englishmen. These statutes "excluded free Black, Mulatto, and Indian men from militia and sanctioned them if they appeared armed for muster; mandated that free children of Mulatto female servants be indentured for a period of 30 years; and denied the franchise to free Negro, Mulatto and Indian men" (Kitch 2009, 66). When the British Crown objected that it could not "see why one freeman should be used worse than another merely upon account of his Complexion," the colonists responded that these constraints were required to prevent free men of color from conspiring with the enslaved to overthrow the social order through armed insurrection (Kitch 2009, 67). Law was the mechanism by which Blacks, Mulattoes, and Indigenous Americans were dehumanized and reduced to the "degraded and degenerate state" that white scientists claimed to discover in nature.[1] Although science theorized racial difference, "the very first step of creating race, dividing human beings into racial categories, [wa]s a political practice" (Roberts 2011, 4).

The legal construction of race attempted to accomplish what nature could not. Human beings do not conform to the definition of a "natural kind." Within scientific and philosophical discourses, a natural kind refers to a "type" that exists independent of the observer, which is defined in terms of a set of properties common to all members of the kind and possessed only by members of the kind. No subset of the human population possesses absolutely unique properties; nor do all members of any subset of the population share exactly the same properties. As the Human Genome Project painstakingly documented, human beings are 99.9 percent identical and there is far more variation within a "race" than there is across "races." Scripted practices of subordination such as those encoded in colonial and settler society law and enacted in brutal physical and sexual exploitation may produce certain commonalities, but these are social distinctions not natural proclivities.

The science and politics of race "transformed not only what it meant to be enslaved [and] what it meant to be free" (Roberts 2011, 12), but also profoundly shaped physical embodiment, perceptions of shared fate, notions of entitlement, and distributions of property and wealth. In the words of Dorothy Roberts (2011, 24), "the diabolical genius of making this political system seem biological is that the very unequal conditions it produces become the excuse for racial injustice."

Biologizing Sex

As Gayle Rubin (1975, 179–180) noted in her path-breaking essay "The Traffic in Women: Notes on the Political Economy of Sex," "From the standpoint of nature, men and women are closer to each other than either is to anything else ... The idea that men and women are two mutually exclusive categories must arise out of something other than a non-existent 'natural' opposition." Feminist scholars have demonstrated that until the long eighteenth century the tendency to convert human commonalities into "sexual difference" was far more typical of philosophers and theologians than scientists and had far more to do with souls than with bodies.

Aristotle was perhaps the first to suggest a fundamental opposition between the sexes. In the *Metaphysics*, he notes that "Female and male are contrary and their difference is a contrariety" (1058a30). In explicating this notion, however, Aristotle advanced arguments concerning the sexed nature of the soul as well as difference in reproductive function to depict the female as the "privation" of the male. In keeping with tenets of the great chain of being, Aristotle conceptualized the soul as a complex of nutritive, sensitive, and rational elements – all of which women possessed in lesser degrees than men. According to Aristotle, women have diminished nutritive requirements and therefore need less nourishment than men. Women are deficient in desire – as evidenced by women's "passive" role in copulation. And women are defective in rationality – the deliberative faculty that enables individuals to regulate their actions is inoperative in women; it exists but it lacks "authority." With respect to reproduction, Aristotle suggests that women play a relatively minor role, providing the soil that nourishes the seed, the nutrients, and the matter from which life is generated. Men contribute the greater part in reproduction by giving life its form, essence, or soul. If women are the material cause of life, men do far more by providing both formal and efficient cause. "The female always provides the material, the male that which fashions it, for this is the power that we say they each possess, and this is what is meant by calling them male and female" (*Metaphysics* 738b20). In recognition of their lesser role in the generation of life, indeed of their inability to engender life, Aristotle dubs women "impotent males" (*Metaphysics* 728a17–22).

Aristotle certainly suggested that being male *manqué* carried political consequences. As "misbegotten males," women could not be expected to assume the same social and political responsibilities as those free of defect. According to Aristotle's construal, "Nature" has lessons that humans must heed in developing a sound social order. Those whose deliberative faculties have full authority must be granted the power to act freely according to their best judgment; those unfit for such tasks should be placed under their command and trained in the art of compliance: "Although there may be exceptions to the order of nature, the male is by nature fitter for command than the female, just as the elder and full grown is superior to the younger and immature" (Aristotle, *Politics* 1259b). Thus, Aristotle helped launch the trope of appealing to nature to legitimate the social and political order, but his arguments were grounded in what Thomas Laqueur has called the "one sex" model of embodiment.

In *Making Sex: Body and Gender from the Greeks to Freud*, Laqueur (1990) examines the textual and visual representations of bodies in medical discourses from the ancient world to the twentieth century. His research suggests that premodern medical thinking conceived embodiment in very different terms than those developed in modernity. What modern medicine posits as self-evident marks of opposition in sexual embodiment – penis versus vagina, ovary versus testicle, menstruation versus absence of monthly bleeding, was construed quite differently under the "one sex" model. According to Galenic and humoral theory, genitalia were morphologically identical in women and men but due to women's lesser body heat, women's reproductive organs were located internally, whereas men's were external. Pre-modern science recognized only one physiological sex – the male – portraying female anatomy as an inferior, internal variety. The vagina was nothing other than an inverted penis, the ovaries, interior testicles, and menstruation and lactation, bodily fluids that with sufficient (i.e., male) "heat" would be semen (Laqueur 1990).

Sexual dimorphism, the anatomical division of the human species into male and female, emerged in the eighteenth century as an integral component of the politics of modernity. As natural science displaced theology in Enlightenment metaphysics, the "one sex" model of embodiment that had dominated European political thought and practice for nearly two millennia gave way to a "two sex" model that posited white men and women as incommensurate beings. Opposite sexes supplanted the embodied souls that had been ordered along a continuum on the basis of proximity to the divine. Reproductive organs became the sign of self-evident opposition. In the eighteenth century, the emerging "natural philosophy" conceived human biology in terms of sexual dimorphism, "a fixed oppositeness, that was somehow foundational and beyond culture," providing a "natural foundation" for differentiated social roles and responsibilities, legal status, as well as divisions of power and opportunity (Laqueur 2012, 1).

In the midst of Enlightenment proclamations of universal rights derived from the "self-evident truth" that all men are created equal, political theorists and republican revolutionaries in both the United States and France extrapolated from the new biological dimorphism grounds for excluding women from membership in the political community. Asserting that reproductive physiology determines individual character and political capacity, republican revolutionaries on both sides of the Atlantic adopted the notion that sexual difference dictates proper political status and behavior, insisting that any transgressions of the gendered political order threatened the very basis of society and civilization. To shore up women's supposed biological incapacity for politics, male law makers passed legislation barring women from participation in political clubs, political organizations, political parties and from political office (Landes 1988, 1998).

Although sexual difference was described in terms of Nature's laws that could be violated only with catastrophic consequences, the sexualization of women was closely linked to a gendered political critique of aristocratic life. Republican revolutionaries portrayed court politics as a system of patron–client relations that reduced the "nobility" to sycophants vying for royal favor through intrigue, manipulation, secret negotiations. The terms used to denounce the aristocracy were thoroughly gendered, courtiers were characterized as effeminate, passive, and dependent on the monarch's favor, soft, and mired in luxury (Clark 1998).

Montesquieu was the first to advance a proposal for the domestication of women in his treatise, *Spirit of Laws* (1748). His rationale was simply put: to avoid the "effeminacy of men" imposed by absolute monarchy and the corruptions of "unnatural women" in salons, the republic *must* domesticate women. As Joan Landes (1988, 38) has noted, "The forward march of civilization," according to Montesquieu, "requires the domestication of women; in a more advanced society women will be sure to occupy their proper place. The domestic woman is accommodated to her new surroundings, her narcissistic vanity and licentious use of freedom are curbed, and her nature, like that of a domesticated animal, is made to fit a depoliticized domestic environment … Private virtue within the male-defined, restricted family, Montesquieu hopes, will provide the foundation for a patriotic and virile political constitution." Montesquieu was not alone in linking critiques of feminized courtiers and dissipated aristocrats to "unnaturally powerful" women. On the contrary, this potent cluster of negative associations became embedded in republican discourses on both sides of the Atlantic.

Although men held the preponderance of power within feudal aristocracies, a peculiarly gendered discourse associating corruption with women's rule circulated widely among republican reformers in the British colonies in North America as well as in France, providing a rationale for the exclusion of women from rights of citizenship (Offen 2000). Republican political theorists and practitioners actively sought to create an exclusively male political assembly, "free from women's corrupting influence." Rousseau developed the theoretical argument, which was enacted first by American revolutionaries and subsequently by French revolutionaries.

Despite his claim in *The Social Contract* (1762) that the only legitimate political system is one that promotes liberty and equality, Rousseau afforded women no place among the citizenry in his proposed democratic polity. Instead, he characterized women as a threat to the political order. "Never has a people perished from an excess of wine; all perish from the disorder of women" (Rousseau 1758, 109). Rather than fostering women's liberty on equal terms with men, Rousseau cultivated the ideology of "republican motherhood," insisting that women's contribution to democratic politics lies in childbearing and childrearing. Only when restricted to the home could women develop the "natural morality" requisite to the nurturance of future male citizens. Indeed, Rousseau grounded the right of democratic participation on a principle of *resemblance*, an embodied likeness that he imagined his ideal male citizens would share by virtue of being farmers who owned land and were masters of their households – households in which men ruled over women and children.

Across the Atlantic, concerns with the "disorder of women" surfaced in surprising ways in the newly independent states. Despite women's critical contributions to the revolutionary struggle against Great Britain, at the moment of victory, women were excluded from participation in the design of political institutions and from equal participation within those institutions. Although they claimed to hold no truck with feudal hierarchies and titles of nobility, between 1776 and 1783 when designing their constitutions in the midst of the American Revolution, twelve of the original 13 states forming the United States excluded women from the rights of citizenship. Reflecting Quaker influence, New Jersey's first constitution awarded voting rights to single women who owned property. This right was rescinded in 1807.[2] The only reference to women in the *Federalist Papers*, the newspaper articles written to explain and justify the provisions of the U.S. Constitution, involves a discussion of the "dangers posed to the safety of the state by the intrigues of courtesans and mistresses."

The cryptic reference to political dangers posed by women reflects the transnational circulation of misogynous discourses among "revolutionary" men who characterized themselves as proponents of human liberty. Coupling abuses during the reign of Russia's Catherine the Great (1762–1796) with depraved sexual mores associated with life at the French court, some male reformers on both sides of the Atlantic began castigating women for the evils of monarchical rule. In the context of the French revolution, for example, the radical republican journalist Louis-Marie Prudhomme "invoked the bad effects of women's intrigues during the monarchies of Louis XV and Louis XVI as an argument against women's inclusion in the nation" (Offen 2000, 58). Alleging that "The reign of courtesans precipitated the nation's ruin; the empire of queens consummated it," Prudhomme (1791) argued against the extension of full rights of citizenship to women, a demand which was being pressed forcefully by Olympe de Gouges and Condorcet. Following the tradition set by the American revolutionaries, the French National Assembly voted not only to exclude women from rights of citizenship, but in 1793 voted to ban women's participation in political clubs and to prohibit the existence of popular women's associations, effectively foreclosing all avenues of women's political participation (Landes 1988, 144–46; Offen 2000, 61–63).

The gender inequalities enshrined in the laws of new "republics" exacerbated inequalities entrenched in custom and tradition (Smart 1992). Feudal and colonial hierarchies were grounded in class, family ties, nationality, gender, and race. Although the republican revolutionaries claimed to break with such feudal hierarchies, the constitutions created within the first "liberal republics" replicated and strengthened hierarchies tied to gender, race, and class, by denying equal citizenship and rights of political participation to women, Blacks, and those without property. Women who loudly protested the imposition of *de jure* gender inequality (i.e., inequality established by law) were dealt with harshly. Indeed, Olympe de Gouges, author of *Déclaration des droits de la femme* (*Declaration of the Rights of Woman*, 1791), was sent to the guillotine by republican revolutionaries. Even after the failure of the first French republic, exclusionary gender practices were carried forward. In 1804 the *Code Napoleon*, later imposed on much of Europe, classified women as "incapacitated" and excluded them, along with children, convicted criminals, and the insane, from political life. Indeed, the Napoleonic Code deprived women of the right to perform as civil witnesses, to plead in court in their own names, or to own property without their husband's or father's consent.

By excluding women from full citizenship, male law makers used the law as a means to produce not only sex-segregated political spaces, but to reshape gender identities within the confines of emerging conceptions of "separate spheres." Asserting that men and women have different "natures," proponents of the emerging gender ideology insisted that men and women be assigned to sex-segregated social and economic roles for their own happiness, as well as for the good of society. Indeed, French aristocrat, revolutionary and diplomat Talleyrand (1754–1838), who assisted in writing the *Declaration of the Rights of Man*, went on to persuade the French National Assembly that women's "share should be uniquely domestic happiness and the duties of the household." In his *Report on Public Instruction* (1791) presented to the Assembly on behalf of the Committee on the Constitution, Talleyrand argued that "in accordance with the will of nature," women should renounce political rights in order to ensure their happiness and their long-term protection (Offen 2000, 59).

Biologization offered a new conceptualization of "the sexes," which was quickly appropriated by philosophers, political revolutionaries, and men of science in the eighteenth century to subordinate women. This new form of biological determinism suggested that "sex" has a systemic influence not only upon one's role in reproduction, but upon the operations of the human mind (Laqueur

1990). The new "domestic model of womanhood," which assigned women to the home and reframed her political work as mothering, profoundly reshaped the terms of political discourse.

In the second volume of *Democracy in America*, Alexis de Tocqueville (1840, 223) analyzed the new sex segregation as akin to divisions of labor introduced by modern manufacturing:

> The Americans have applied to both sexes the great principle of political economy which governs the manufacturers of our age by carefully dividing the duties of man from those of women in order that the great work of society may be the better carried on. In no country has such constant care been taken as in America to trace two clearly distinct lines of action for the two sexes ... American women never manage the outward concerns of the family, or conduct a business, or take part in political life ... If, on the one hand, the American woman cannot escape from the quiet circle of domestic employment, she is never forced on the other hand to go beyond it ... Nor have the Americans ever supposed that one consequence of democratic principles is the subversion of the natural authorities in families. They hold that every association must have a head in order to accomplish its object, and that the natural head of the conjugal association is man. They do not therefore deny him the right of directing his partner, and they maintain that in the smaller association of husband and wife as well as in the great social community the object of democracy is to regulate and legalize the powers that are necessary, and not to subvert all power.

As de Tocqueville so keenly observes, rather than giving substance to the promise of equality, the new republics made sex socially relevant in a way that it had not been formerly. Under feudal monarchy, masculinity carried some privileges, but they were not vast. Under ordinary circumstances class status trumped sex in determining a person's life prospects. Within the emerging republics, however, "sexual difference" was written into law. At just the moment that bourgeois claims to universality raised hopes for the elimination of all social distinctions before the law, gender discrimination was encoded into the founding constitutions of "free nations." Thus Joan Landes has argued that the republic's most important legacy was the cultural inscription of gender in social life. As an emerging national form, "the Republic was constructed against women, not just without them" (Landes 1988, 171). Similarly, historian Claire Moses has pointed out that "Women had been reduced to the status of a legal caste at the same time that the ancient regime legal class system was abolished for men. Women's status had worsened, if not in absolute, then in relative terms. The code would serve as a rallying point for feminist protest not only because it discriminated against women but also because it intensified women's sense of sex identification" (Moses 1984, 18).

The ideal of republican motherhood was, of course, thoroughly racialized – an ideal constructed for white middle-class women that did not apply to enslaved women, whose children could be sold according to a slave-master's will and whose exploited labor transcended the boundaries of public and private spheres, as well as gendered divisions of labor embraced by the rising bourgeoisie. Yet, this racialized conception of sexual difference, which emerged in the eighteenth century, was deployed in the nineteenth century as an index of "civilization." Thus, Richard von Krafft Ebing (1886), the founder of "sexual science," could assert unequivocally: "The secondary sexual characteristics differentiate the two sexes; they represent specific male and female types. The higher the anthropological development of the race, the stronger these contrasts between man and woman" (cited in Markowitz 2001, 391). Similarly, Havelock Ellis claimed, "In more civilized races, where male taste and female beauty are fully realized, women have developed wide hips and large breasts … Broad hips, which involve a large pelvis, are necessarily a characteristic of the highest human races, because the races with the largest heads must be endowed also with the largest pelvis to enable their large heads to enter the world" (cited in Markowitz 2001, 402).

On this view, civilization was a racialized-gendering force that altered physical embodiment. Although purportedly driven by "Nature," this "civilizing process" benefited inordinately from legislation. Over the course of the nineteenth century, male law makers in nations across the globe adopted the norm of republican motherhood as a part of their modernizing projects, passing laws that barred women from politics and the professions, and restricted them to the private sphere.[3] As "civilized" nations embraced the exclusion of women from the public sphere as an indication of "more advanced civilization," those with colonial empires imposed sex-segregation on colonies in Africa and Asia as a "civilizing" measure (Towns 2009). These colonial impositions displaced earlier indigenous forms of women's political authority (Okonjo 1994, Oyewumi 1997).

Despite the overt political means by which these exclusions and restrictions were enacted, the growing authority of science afforded them a "natural" justification: disparate male and female anatomies carried "natural" mandates for social roles – mandates implicated in the very survival of the species. As biological determinist frames gained ascendency, the political work involved in the subordination of women was rendered invisible and replaced with fictive pasts accredited by evolutionary theories that posited male dominance as natural and universal.

Within the version of biological dimorphism cultivated over the twentieth century, male and female were construed as "natural kinds," although the basis for their differentiation changed over time from claims about gonads (reproductive organs such as testes and ovaries), internal morphology (seminal vesicles and prostate as opposed to vagina, uterus, and fallopian tubes), and external genitalia (penis and scrotum/clitoris and labia), as well as secondary sex characteristics (body hair, facial hair, breasts) to arguments about chromosomes (XY/XX) and hormones (androgens/estrogens). But the typical correlates of biological sex do not conform to the demands of "natural kinds" any better than do grounds adduced to support claims about race. Feminist science scholars have demonstrated that "there are no behavioral or physical characteristics that always and without exception are true only of one gender" (Kessler and McKenna 1978, 1). Chromosomes, hormones, sperm-production, and egg-production, all fail to differentiate all men from all women or to provide a common core within each sex. "No matter how detailed an investigation science has thus far made, it is still not possible to draw a clear dividing line even between male and female" (Devor 1989, 1). Indeed, both men and women have testosterone and estrogen in their systems and the human "X" chromosome, wantonly mischaracterized as the "female" chromosome, is not only common to both men and women, but carries a large collection of male sperm genes (Richardson 2012). Even the insistence that there are two and only two sexes is mistaken. As biologist Ann Fausto-Sterling (1993) has pointed out, using strictly biological criteria, there are not two but five sexes "in nature." In addition to males and females, there are multiple modes of intersexuals – "herms" (persons born with both a testis and an ovary), "merms" (persons born with testes and some aspect of female genitalia), and "ferms" (persons who have ovaries combined with some forms of male genitalia).

The social sciences have done no better than the natural sciences in their efforts to identify behavioral differences that conform to the definition of a natural kind. Attitudinal and behavioral "sex differences" reflect social attributions that have nothing to do with natural differences. Within social science research, indicators of "biologically based femininity" typically include interest in weddings and marriage, preference for marriage over career, interest in infants and children, and enjoyment of childhood play with dolls. While indicators of "biologically based masculinity" include high activity levels, self-assurance, and a preference for career over marriage (Devor 1989, 11–15). Psychological inventories of "masculinity" and "femininity" manifest the misogynist tendency to define socially-valued traits such as being logical, self-confident, ambitious, decisive, and knowing one's way around the world as "male." Less valued characteristics are ascribed to "the female" (e.g., being talkative, gentle, sensitive to others' feelings, interested in appearance, manifesting a strong need for security) (Devor 1989, 32). Even with all the cultural bias built into such indicators, empirical studies have not been able to clearly differentiate men and women in the cultures that produced them. "'Normal femininity' of the psychological test variety may actually be a rare commodity. In one study of college-aged females, only 15% of the heterosexual sample tested as feminine on a widely accepted sex role inventory. The remaining 85% scored as either masculine or as some combination of masculine and feminine" (Devor 1989, 15). Differences cast in terms of averages, tendencies, and percentages do not meet the criteria for a natural kind.

Rather than being given in nature, sexual dimorphism is imposed by human beings who are trying to make sense of the natural world. As Suzanne Kessler and

Wendy McKenna noted, this imposition is as characteristic of scientific inquiry as it is of everyday observation. "Scientists construct dimorphism where there is continuity. Hormones, behavior, physical characteristics, developmental processes, chromosomes, and psychological qualities have all been fitted into dichotomous categories. Scientific knowledge does not inform the answer to the question, 'What makes a person a man or a woman?' Rather it justifies (and appears to give grounds for) the already existing conviction that a person is either a man or a woman and that there is no problem differentiating between the two. Biological, psychological, and social differences do not lead to our seeing two genders. Our seeing two genders leads to the 'discovery' of biological, psychological, and social differences" (Kessler and McKenna 1978, 163).

Biologism Resurrected

As Dorothy Roberts (2011, 27) has noted, "Science is the most effective tool for giving claims about human difference the stamp of legitimacy … once scientists were committed to understanding human beings as divided into races [and sexes], they believed that human biology *could not* be studied without attention to race and sex." Despite ample evidence generated over the past century that biological determinism is fundamentally flawed and morally suspect, some quite eminent scientists continue to circulate reductionist arguments. Socio-biologists, evolutionary psychologists, and physical anthropologists, for example, continue to insist that sexual "difference" is dictated by the demands of species survival. Defining men as "sperm producers" and women as "egg producers," they suggest sexual dimorphism exists to foster diversity, providing richer opportunities for genetic variation than asexual modes of reproduction, and thereby affording survival advantages for particular gene pools. Socio-biologists characterize heterosexual intercourse as a form of "cooperation" to produce zygotes; yet they also suggest that species survival "mandates" different sexual practices for men and women. Because, they claim, sperm are "cheap" – males supposedly produce 100 million sperm per ejaculation – sexual promiscuity affords advantages for the promotion of male genes. Eggs, on the other hand, are "costly" – females produce only 20 to 30 viable eggs over the course of a lifetime – therefore, females are more inclined toward fidelity and monogamy as strategies to promote the survival of their gene pool. The putative adaptive advantages afforded by sex-specific sexual practices are claimed to generate distinctive traits associated with masculinity (aggressiveness) and femininity (coyness). Gendered divisions of labor – from fictive accounts of man-the-hunter, woman-the-gatherer to contemporary claims about men's overrepresentation and women's underrepresentation in positions of power, wealth, and prestige – are similarly explained in terms of the survival advantages (Wilson 1975, 1978). Rooting their claims in neuroscience, genetics, and evolutionary psychology, best-selling authors such as Simon Baron Cohen (2004) and Steven Pinker (2002) have reinvigorated old debates about innate sexual differences, "hard-wired" in the brain that purportedly affect cognitive abilities, communication skills, and the capacity to perform a host of social and political roles.

Critics have pointed out pervasive and systemic flaws in the sociobiological account of biological sex. At a methodological level, sociobiology falls prey to circular reasoning that violates the norms of scientific inquiry. Because they assume that existing traits are genetic adaptations, sociobiologists offer no empirical evidence to demonstrate that particular traits or behaviors are "heritable." They advance purportedly universal claims about sex differences drawn primarily from observations of baboons; but offer no justification for their selection bias. Research on some 200 other primate species provides no credible evidence to support sociobiological claims. In particular, claims about "costly eggs" and "cheap sperm" that undergird claims about sex-specific sexual practices have been found to be invalid and unwarranted. In addition, the notion advanced by socio-biologists that the rich and vast domains of culture are "genetically" based mistakenly assigns responsibility to nature for the design of human institutions (Gould 1980; Fausto-Sterling 1986; Fedigan 1992; Tang-Martinez 1997). Unable to provide scientific evidence to support their unwarranted claims, sociobiologists proffer a defense of a narrow range of male-privileging, heteronormative behaviors by attributing survival advantage to them.

Although scientific claims about sex differences in the brain are enormously popular, gaining widespread media attention, they too are seriously flawed. Rebecca Jordan-Young (2010) has provided systematic evidence that studies that treat the brain as an "accessory reproductive organ" suffer from a host of methodological flaws. Her detailed examination of the "quasi-experiments" and "proxy variables" deployed in "brain organization studies" demonstrate not only that it is impossible to identify any "hard-wired" male-typical or female-typical behavior, but particular studies are riddled with inconsistencies, ambiguities, and contradictions.

Despite their patent inadequacy as accounts of embodiment, sexuality, or gendered social practices, biological reductionist arguments surface regularly in popular culture and in academic discourses. Following noted anthropologist Claude Levi-Strauss (1969, 1971), many accept a conception of culture as an elaborate mechanism devised to create interdependence and cooperation in the reproduction of the species. Philosopher Stephen Smith (1992), for example, makes explicit a host of assumptions that are often taken for granted. Smith suggests that species reproduction requires sexual differentiation, therefore culture creates that differentiation through processes of gendering in order to insure the perpetuation of the species, but culture masks its role by attributing the original difference to sex itself. "Since men and women have significantly different reproductive risks and opportunities in evolutionary terms, their guiding sex-related emotions must be sex-differentiated, that is, there must be different female and male sexual natures" (124). Defining gender as a "conventional formation of a plastic humanity" (15), Smith suggests that culture shapes what is perceived as a body. Through "embodiment," "the community stipulates what counts as a male/female body, what life will be like in a male/female body in relation to other bodies, what norms (and latitudes) of character and conduct are associated with these bodies, and who is male and female" (91). When culture takes up the task of molding human nature, then, its aim is to enhance its own *construction* of what is *naturally given*, marking sex differentiations through language, character, and social roles. According to Smith, gender differentiation is culture's contribution to "heterosexuality's postulated union of male and female specializations" (80). Indeed, he suggests that "Confronting sex differences makes me realize that I need a partner to reproduce ... A gendered being teams with other gendered beings" (71, 55). Echoing sociobiological presumptions, Smith suggests that the cultural creation of gender complementarity serves the larger purpose of species survival.

Smith's account operates within the confines of a "base/superstructure" model of the sex/gender distinction (Connell 1987, 50; Laqueur 1990, 124). Within this model, the body is assumed to provide the raw material which culture can refine in various, but limited ways. Thus, gender is assumed to be "hard-wired," at least, in part. The presumed naturalness of gender, its purported emergence in the absence of force or coercion, turns on a presumption of hard-wiring. When nature is imagined as the ground of cultural constructions of gender, discussions of gender seldom move far beyond presuppositions concerning inherent sex differences. R. W. Connell explained this recurrent problem in accounts of sex and gender by suggesting that in our culture "the notion of natural sex difference forms a limit beyond which thought cannot go" (1987, 66). Although feminist historians such as Mary Poovey (1988), Ludmilla Jordanova (1989), and Thomas Laqueur (1990) have provided detailed accounts of the emergence of the base/superstructure model of sex/gender since the 17th century, its naturalizing tenets are hard to shake. In the words of Thomas Laqueur, "It is a sign of modernity to ask for a single, consistent biology as the source or foundation for masculinity and femininity" (1990, 61). Despite centuries of feminist mobilization and the emergence of a vibrant Trans movement[4] over the past few decades, myths of sexual dimorphism continue to circulate widely in the 21st century.

Resurrecting Biological Race

As the history of the past four centuries has made clear, biological accounts of race are not only wrong but pernicious, supporting dehumanizing practices that range from enslavement, and the abuses of eugenics to genocide. In the aftermath of World War II, the newly created United Nations Educational, Scientific, and Cultural Organisation (UNESCO) issued a "Statement on Race" (1950) crafted by an international committee of experts, which declared that race is not "a biological phenomenon but a social myth" (Roberts 2011, 43). Physical anthropologists and geneticists objected to the UNESCO report and issued their own "Statement on the Nature of Race and Race Differences" (1951) one year later. Although the physical anthropologists and geneticists rejected the "racialist position regarding purity of the races and the hierarchy of inferior and superior races to which this leads," they insisted that "it is possible, though not proved, that some types of innate capacity for intellectual and emotional response are commoner in one human group than another" (Roberts 2011, 44). Despite continuing lobbying by some scientists to vindicate a notion of biological race, the defects of biological accounts gained increasing recognition. "The 1963 Preamble of UN Declaration on the Elimination of all Forms of Racial Discrimination stipulated: that any doctrine of racial differentiation or superiority is scientifically false, morally condemnable, socially unjust, and dangerous, and that there is no justification for racial discrimination either in theory or practice" (Rabinow and Rose 2003, 17–18). An international declaration did not eradicate all racialist discourses, "but a biological understanding of racial categories no longer was 'in the truth' in political or policy discourse … The link between biological understandings of distinctions among population groups and their socio-political implications seemed broken or at least de-naturalized" (Rabinow and Rose 2003, 17–18).

The findings of the Human Genome Project were supposed to dispel any lingering suspicion that there might be innate biological, intellectual or emotional racial differences. "When it became clear that humans shared over 98% of their genome with chimpanzees, and that intra-group variations in DNA sequences were greater than inter-group variations, it appeared that genomics itself would mark the terminal point of biological racism" (Rabinow and Rose 2003, 18). Such optimism was short-lived, however. And in an ironic twist, a new molecular discourse on race emerged from genomic thinking. Like investments in sexual dimorphism, convictions concerning racial difference persist despite repeated falsification. As Dorothy Roberts (2011) has carefully documented in *Fatal Invention: How Science, Politics, and Big Business Re-create Race in the Twenty-First Century*, some geneticists, molecular biologists, medical researchers, and pharmaceutical corporations have resurrected notions of genetic difference for a host of purposes that range from genealogy and back-to-one's-roots tourist ventures to "race-based" medicine. "Commercial aspirations of pharmaceutical companies, as well as the biomedical industry's quest for new strategies in diagnosis, drug development, and marketing fuel multiple projects to map diversity at SNP (single nucleotide polymorphisms) level – the 0.1% of the three billion base pairs of the human genome seems to provide ample space for racial differentiations … The core racial typology of the nineteenth century – white (Caucasian), black (African), yellow (Asian), red (Native American) – provides the dominant mold for this new genetic knowledge" (Rabinow and Rose 2003, 18).

What is hailed in the media and widely circulated in popular culture as racialized "genetic difference," however, has nothing to do with "natural kinds." As the Human Genome Project proved there are no genetic boundaries that demarcate a handful of large discrete human groups. In their absence, twenty-first-century scientists have turned to continents to conceptualize race as did their eighteenth-century predecessors. Because there are no sets of genes that belong exclusively to one human group, molecular biologists have turned to counting "alternate alleles" associated with certain gene mutations, correlating them with selective samples from particular geographical regions (Roberts 2011, 52–54). As Dorothy Roberts has noted:

> This reconfiguration of race for the genomic age hinges on applying two key concepts to genetic information: statistical probability and geographic ancestry. With the advent of worldwide genomic population studies, many scientists are using statistical estimates of gene frequencies that differ among geographic populations as a more objective, scientific and politically palatable alternative to race ... Population biologists using a statistical approach do not actually trace the ancestry of particular individuals to place them in racial categories. Rather, they infer groupings from the statistical frequencies of particular DNA sequences sampled from distinct populations around the globe.
> *(Roberts 2011, 57–58)*

The circularity of this process may easily escape notice, especially as scientific terminology is offered to sustain these problematic inferences. Roberts scrupulously traces the multiple steps in this methodology to show how presuppositions about race structure research findings. For example, genetic scientists Neil Risch and Esteban Burchard "define race on the basis of the 'primary continent of origin.' Ancestry, on the other hand, 'refers to the race/ethnicity of an individual's ancestors, whatever the individual's current affiliation.' In other words, race is where one's ancestors come from and ancestry is the race of one's ancestors." (Roberts 2011, 64). Like 18th-century taxonomists, these scientists sample a handful of ethnic groups to represent an entire continent. Three sub-Saharan populations were represented by two pygmy groups and the Lisongo; a selection of Chinese, Japanese, and Cambodians represented East Asia; and a sample of North Europeans and northern Italians were used to represent Caucasians. Roberts points out that this flawed sampling method, which is now built into the infrastructure of genomics research, mimics a basic tenet of racial thinking. Assuming that races are composed of uniform individuals, any individual or small sample of individuals can represent the whole group. These problematic sampling techniques were also shored up by unsustainable assumptions about select groups as "pure" types, unsullied by global migration and centuries of miscegenation (65). When pressed, population biologists acknowledge that their continent-based models are far from perfect. As Roberts notes, people from India do not fit the "Asian genetic cluster" and Northern and Eastern Africans do not fit the "genetic profile of Africans." Moreover, when researchers "do not try to fit findings into pre-determined boxes, genomic population studies have discovered that (1) many of the individuals sampled fit in more than one cluster, and (2) the clusters leave out whole groups who do not fit anywhere" (Roberts 2011, 66).

In the various partitions of the human population orchestrated by population biologists, variation within group (93–95 percent) is far greater than variation between groups (5 percent). Nonetheless, on such shaky foundations, the new "biological reality of race" is being constructed. Thus, Roberts concludes that the geographic approach to the genome "misperceives continental populations as natural groupings ... as bounded, isolated, and static, amenable to scientific sampling, analysis, and classification" (75). Rather than providing scientific grounds for the existence of biological races, assumptions about race structure the design and execution of these population studies. As Roberts succinctly puts it:

> Race serves as an unquestioned organizing principle for the collection, analysis, and reporting of genetic data. Far from carefully scrutinizing the scientific validity of racial classifications, the researchers simply insert race into their studies ... Lab scientists not only assumed that African American and Caucasian DNA samples had significantly different allele frequencies, but they also perceived each as the other's *opposite* race. They predicted that black and white DNA would always produce dramatically disparate findings. When findings did not confirm expectations, results were rejected as due to contaminated samples ... yet, the findings produced by scientists' faulty use of race as a research variable are taken to confirm the very racial categories that are being employed in such a sloppy manner.
>
> *(Roberts 2011, 68–72)*

Assumptions about race as a biological category have also resurfaced in genetic explanations for health disparities in ways that mask the social and environmental causes. Like geographical approaches to the genome, genetic explanations of racial disparities in health and longevity suffer from a troubling circularity. "Scientists observe racial disparities in health and hypothesize they are caused by biological difference based on an ideological premise that race is a biological category. After collecting data on health disparities, they conclude that unexplained differences between racial groups must be genetic, which they claim proves that races are biologically different" (Roberts 2011, 119). Rather than considering the complex ways that social disadvantage affects people's experiences, environments, and access to resources, including health care, some medical researchers have attributed higher incidences of asthma, hypertension, maternal mortality, and premature death to "genetic distinctions between racial groups." Roberts points out that such race-based surmises suffer from what "statisticians call the problem of residual confounding: falsely concluding that there is a causal relationship between two variables (here, genetics and health outcomes) because other variables (racial discrimination, poverty in early life, wealth, income, neighborhood segregation, environmental racism) have not been measured" (117).

Conclusion

The history of biologization indicates that science and politics collaborate in making the raced-sexed body the ground for a social order purportedly ordained by Nature. As the racialized and gendered body is constructed as given, pre-political, and apolitical, the role of science and politics in fostering white supremacy and male dominance is naturalized and rendered close to invisible. Biological determinism masks dimensions of embodied power and places the political construction of racial and sexual hierarchies beyond the boundaries of the discipline of political science. Naturalized bodies also hide the intricate power relations through which racialized gendering operates in interpersonal, national and international relations.

Esther Lezra (2015, 2) has pointed out that the construction of race was a mechanism through which Europe came to know itself. "Portraying Blacks as savage enabled whites to imagine themselves as civilized. Establishing slavery as the master sign of 'not freedom' permitted exploited wage labor to masquerade as freedom. Portraying agrarian societies as remnants of the past helped legitimate urbanism, industrialization, and state-building as technical features of modernity rather than as the self-interested projects of elite groups and classes." Biologization, then, was not an aberration or a mistake; it was constitutive of European men's self-production as the most advanced "civilization," entitled by "Reason" and "Nature" to rule all lesser others, which is to say, the majority of the world's racialized and sexed population. The science and politics of bodies are thus integrally related to the creation and perpetuation of a known world that legitimates hierarchies of difference. And perhaps most importantly, biologism enables a form of "unknowing": the brutality of colonization, conquest, displacement, dispossession, enslavement, and dehumanization are omitted from official histories as discourses about white men's civilizing mission convey a very different story.

Notes

1 "Degraded and degenerate" are the terms that Louis Agassiz, Harvard professor and founder of the National Academy of Sciences, used to describe Black Americans. The conviction that Blacks must be a different order of humanity than Europeans inspired Agassiz to advance the theory of polygenesis, which suggested that different races descended from different ancestors. Agassiz claimed that it was the duty of science "to settle the relative rank among the races, the relative value of the characters peculiar to each, in a scientific point of view" (Roberts 2011, 32).
2 Judith Apter Klinghoffer and Lois Elkis. "The 'Petticoat Electors:' Women's Suffrage in New Jersey, 1776–1807." *Journal of the Early Republic* 12(2): 159–93 [1992].
3 For a list of these exclusionary laws, see Hawkesworth (2012, 33–35).
4 The term Trans has been developed to provide an umbrella term for the movement that includes transgender, gender variant, transsexual, Intersex, and gender-nonconforming people. For a sophisticated account of this complex category, see Bettcher (2013).

4

FROM RACIAL AND SE...

The project of w...
inspiration and ide...

...ynolds 2008, 4)

Biologization encourages t... ...ution that embodiment is easily captured within simple systems of classification: two sexes, three (four or five) races. By contrast, intersectionality theorists emphasize that embodied power involves multiple overlapping and interactive dynamics that structure relations ranging from sexual intimacy and family formation to national belonging, transnational migration, and organized conflict. These complex dynamics are masked not only by the naturalization of race and sex, but also by the demarcation of public and private spheres championed by liberal political theory since the seventeenth century. Claims concerning "negative liberty," a private sphere free from intrusion by the state, create the impression that liberal democratic states play no role in relation to sexuality, marriage, reproduction, family formation, employment, religion or voluntary associations. Presumptions concerning disembodied politics mask the role of the state in constituting the public and the private domains and the manifold inequalities that pervade them.

The United States characterizes itself as both the embodiment and the defender of liberal democratic ideals, yet from its earliest legislation, it has enacted laws that privilege propertied "white" men, according them rights and immunities denied to others.[1] This chapter draws upon historical and contemporary policies and practices to explore the complexities of gendered racialization and racialized gendering. By examining laws that structure national belonging, the chapter illuminates state practices of embodied power that sustain hierarchies of difference despite guarantees of formal equality. Drawing attention to racialization,

tes how embodied power
onal, the transnational, and the
mbodied power can be found in all
ge, adoption, education, environment,
ation, welfare, zoning), this chapter focuses
s of citizenship associated with nation-building,
curitization.
tribute to racialization, gendering, and sexualization as
e disciplines of anthropology, critical race studies, cultural
nd sexualities studies, literary criticism, media studies, post-
es, and sociology have scrupulously demonstrated. But the state's
e simultaneous production of advantage and disadvantage is seldom
in political science outside the "content specializations" of the politics of
ender, race, and ethnicity. Precisely because racing-gendering is so frequently naturalized, this chapter calls attention to state practices that create and maintain embodied difference.

Constructing the Boundaries of Belonging

To illuminate intersectional asymmetries as relations of power requires a vocabulary that challenges categorization schemes, which posit race and sex as discrete systems. In earlier work (Hawkesworth 2003, 2012), I used the term "racing-gendering" in an effort to capture the simultaneous production of relations of domination and subordination as women and men were positioned as members of particular races, classes, ethnicities, and nationalities. Through such racialized gendering, the state devises policies that differentiate affluent, working class, and impoverished heterosexual white men and white women from men and women of color, demarcated by pigment, ethnicity, ancestry, religion, as well as class and sexual orientation. Public policies are the means by which the state affirms, privileges, and secures the dominance of whites, while marginalizing and excluding other groups. Constitutional guarantees of equality before the law would make it appear impossible for the state to be involved with any such hierarchical organization of social groups, but contrary to liberal notions about negative liberty (a sphere free from state intervention) and legal neutrality (the idea that the law applies equally to all), U.S. history is rife with laws, policies, norms, and practices that categorize, classify, separate, and segregate in ways that create and sustain a social order with profound consequences for self-understandings, interpersonal relations, possibilities for belonging, and life prospects.

State practices of racialized gendering have produced observable and widespread inequalities in wealth, income, political representation in government, life expectancy, and other markers of human well-being. Although certain processes define racialized gendering (the production of hierarchies of difference and their justification through appeals to notions of superiority and inferiority), racial categories themselves have not been static. They have varied over time in accordance with the cultural and political imperatives of specific locales. Thus, systems of racial classification in the United States differ substantially from those in Brazil, the United Kingdom, the Middle East, South Asia, or East Asia. Racial classifications also shift over time in conjunction with processes of migration, state management of difference, litigation, and popular tolerance for "assimilation." Where some groups are allowed to "become white" (e.g., Irish, Italians, and Jews in the U.S. context), others are rendered "unassimilable" (e.g., Blacks, Asians, and Native Americans) (Haney-Lopez 1996; Haney-Lopez 2004). The last chapter traced the use of the law during the colonial period and the early years of the republic not only to exclude enslaved Blacks from citizenship, but to strip them of humanity by declaring them "property." This section expands the frame to consider state and federal policies in the U.S. that structure the boundaries of belonging in ways that maintain fairly rigid social, economic, and political hierarchies.

In the early twentieth century, W. E. B. Du Bois (1910) defined race as a form of power that aggregates disparate people into one group that is accorded rights and privileges, while simultaneously designating others as inferior, denying them these rights and privileges, while also subjecting them to multiple forms of degradation.[2] Following Du Bois, sociologists Michael Omi and Howard Winant (1986) conceptualized "racial formation" as an active process that differentiates certain groups by physically separating them, diminishing their status, and subjecting them to mechanisms of control that do not apply to other groups within the population. Although not exclusively due to state action, Omi and Winant emphasized that collective political action plays a crucial role in limiting the freedom, deploying the labor power, constraining upward mobility and economic advancement of those classified as racial "minorities." The white majority, acting through the official institutions of state, determines who will be deemed eligible for citizenship and accorded rights that protect their lives and properties, and who will be excluded from legal protections and subjected to coerced labor, dispossession, immiseration, or even annihilation (Omi and Winant 1986, 66–68).

In the United States, racialized gendering involved multiple groups and various policy instruments from the earliest days of the new republic. As noted in the last chapter, enslaved men and women – both those imported from Africa prior to 1808 and those born on American soil – were reduced to the status of property by legal mandate. Both Black men and Black women were stripped of legal personhood understood in common law in terms of self-possession, the ownership of one's own life, mind, body, and labor, as well as long established rights of privacy, speech, association and self-defense. Yet as Hortense Spillers (1987, 40) eloquently noted, enslavement entailed a "vortex of raced-gendered hierarchies" that played out differently for enslaved men and women. In one sense, slave women were systematically degendered, subjected to the same grueling labor regimes as their male counterparts even while pregnant. According to Jennifer

Morgan's (2004) meticulous research, 76 percent of enslaved women in the British colonies performed fieldwork, comprising the majority of the agricultural labor force. Yet, enslaved women were also specifically gendered in relation to sexual exploitation and coerced reproduction. Prior to 1800, African women constituted 80 percent of the women who crossed the Atlantic. Given the paucity of Anglo women in the colonies, African women suffered unparalleled levels of sexual assault. After the end of the slave trade, slave owners appropriated the reproductive labor of enslaved women to produce, enhance, and pass on their wealth through inheritance (Morgan 2004). Enslaved men could also be raped, as is made clear in the autobiography of Frederick Douglass (1845). This brutal mode of feminization, in combination with laws prohibiting enslaved men from marriage, legally recognized paternity, or the right to protect their loved ones from abuse by white owners, engendered the trope of slavery as "emasculation." Yet, that rhetoric masks the complex modes of gendered dehumanization within slavery, as well as gendered modes of resistance. As Angela Davis (1972, 87) noted, for enslaved women, even domestic drudgery could become a form of resistance:

> With the black slave woman, there is a strange twist of affairs: in the infinite anguish of ministering to the needs of the men and children around her (who were not necessarily members of her immediate family), she was performing the only labor of the slave community which could not be directly and immediately claimed by the oppressor. There was no compensation for work in the fields; it served no useful purpose for the slaves. Domestic labor was the only meaningful labor for the slave community as a whole (discounting as negligible the exceptional situations where slaves received some pay for their work). Precisely through performing the drudgery, which has long been a central expression of the socially conditioned inferiority of women, the black woman in chains could help to lay the foundation for autonomy.

Like Blacks (enslaved and free), Native Americans, the original inhabitants of the land, were denied citizenship. Their exclusion was justified on the grounds that they were "sovereign" peoples or independent nations, possessing the right to self-governance, including the right to enter into binding treaties with the government of the United States. Yet the provisions of these "international" treaties were seldom respected for any length of time by the white settlers. Eradication rather than coexistence with Native peoples characterized the views of many settlers. In his *Notes on Virginia*, for example, Thomas Jefferson (1782) envisioned the eradication of the Native Americans, placing graveyards on maps in territories that were home to thriving Indigenous communities (Holland 2001). While some white settlers endorsed intermarriage between white men and Native women as a means to assimilate the Indigenous and gain access to Native lands, others imagined much more brutal tactics.[3]

The violent removal of the Cherokee nation exemplifies these tactics. The Cherokee had signed peace agreements in 1785 and again in 1791 to secure their land holdings in Alabama, Georgia, North Carolina, and Tennessee. With the discovery of gold in Georgia in the 1820s, however, the Georgia legislature passed a series of laws to strip the Cherokee of their rights under these treaties and the U.S. Congress appropriated $30,000 to abrogate Cherokee land titles in Georgia. By 1828, the sovereign Cherokee people were being re-conceptualized as "ultimately inassimilable and doomed to extinction" to use the words of U.S. Supreme Court Justice Joseph Story (cited in Kitch 2009, 129). Testifying before Congress in support of the 1830 Indian Removal Act, President Andrew Jackson argued that the Cherokee ought to be grateful for U.S. government assistance in relocation because "removal" to the West was in their best interest. When the Cherokee failed to manifest appropriate gratitude for and compliance with this "assistance," President Jackson authorized use of the U.S. military to forcibly remove the Cherokee from their ancestral lands. Of the 15,000 who were forced to follow the "Trail of Tears," 4,000 died *en route* to the new "Indian Territories" in what later became the state of Oklahoma. Rather than recognizing the responsibility of the U.S. government for this extraordinary loss of life, proponents of westward expansion took these deaths as evidence that Indigenous peoples were bound for "extinction." In 1848, U.S. Senator Thomas Hart Benton, a Jacksonian Democrat who represented Missouri from 1821 to 1851, asserted that it was up to the "Indians" to choose civilization or "extinction ... the fate of all people who have found themselves in the track of the advancing Whites" (Kitch 2009, 129).

Through racialized gendering, the United States actively created itself as a white nation, which accorded full citizenship only to white men. The policy instruments deployed toward that end included property law, suspension of birthright citizenship for people of color, marriage law, immigration and naturalization policies, and war-making. As a settler society in the new world, the United States proclaimed itself a nation of immigrants, but only some immigrants were deemed eligible for citizenship. Through laws governing "naturalization," the U.S. Congress determined which immigrants could become citizens. The Nationality Act of 1790 unequivocally articulated the founding vision of a white race-nation, restricting the right of naturalized citizenship to "free white persons" of good moral character – evidenced by having lived in the country for five years without incurring any criminal record.[4] The rules governing "naturalized" citizenship consolidated the hierarchy of Anglo-Saxon over African American and Native American already embedded in the suspension of birthright and miscegenation laws and laid the foundation for intensive contestation over the legal meaning of "white person." For more than a century, changing immigration laws, court decisions, and census categories contributed to shifting definitions of who was "white" and who was "non-white," ascribing racialized meanings to physical features and ancestry in the process (Haney-Lopez 1996).

In 1855, in the midst of widespread mobilization for the abolition of slavery and the enfranchisement of women, Congress further codified exclusions from citizenship, stating that the "capacity for full citizenship was inherent in the self-governing man only and not in any person encumbered by bonds of dependence" (Cott 1998, 1457). Although slavery and women's dependency were created by laws and therefore subject to alteration, Congress treated dependency as if it were an unalterable condition. Women's rights advocates attempted to use the courts to secure the rights of "free white persons." In several cases, they argued that as "persons" born in the United States, women fit the definition of citizens established in the 14th Amendment to the Constitution and therefore qualified for full rights, including the right to practice professions such as law and medicine, the right to vote and the right to hold elective office. In *Bradwell v. Illinois* (1873), *Minor v. Happersett* (1874), and *In re Lockwood* (1884), however, the Supreme Court consistently held that women were not "persons" in the constitutional sense. In the eyes of the law, "persons" were male, a constitutional interpretation that was not officially overturned until 1971 in *Reed v. Reed*.[5]

As the United States pursued its policy of Manifest Destiny, expanding its territorial boundaries from the Atlantic to Pacific Oceans, it resorted to warfare not only to displace Native Americans, but also to acquire the northern half of Mexico. The 1848 Treaty of Guadalupe Hidalgo, which ended the Mexican-American War, gave residents of the conquered territory the option of leaving their land or becoming U.S. citizens. More than 70,000 Mexican nationals were coerced into citizenship (McWilliams 1968, 51–52), but the terms of their citizenship were far from equal. Although the treaty promised to respect the property, language, and religion of the new citizens, none of these promises was kept as white settlements expanded across these territories. In 1930, the census enumerated Mexican Americans as a separate "race." During the Depression in the 1930s, 240,000 Mexican American citizens by native birth, along with 160,000 Mexican nationals, were deported, nearly 20 percent of the Mexican population of the United States at that time. As Mae Ngai (2004, 75) has noted, "The repatriation of Mexicans was a racial expulsion program exceeded in scale only by the Native American removals of the nineteenth century."

The Nationality Act also introduced legal status distinctions between citizens and aliens, clearing new ground for the construction of racial hierarchies. Over the course of the nineteenth and twentieth centuries, increasingly restrictive immigration laws and naturalization policies produced new categories of racial difference by distinguishing between "assimilable" (European) aliens, deemed eligible for citizenship after fulfilling the residency requirement, and "unassimilable" aliens, deemed permanently ineligible for citizenship. As Mae Ngai (2004) has carefully documented, the legal designation "alien ineligible for citizenship" created a new subject population, resident within the borders of the nation but barred forever from the possibility of citizenship. Without rights, aliens deemed ineligible for citizenship were condemned to a "condition of racial otherness, a badge of foreignness that cannot be shed," an encompassing stigma that dramatically affected their children, born on U.S. soil and, as such, citizens by birth (Ngai, 2004, 8).

In the early 1850s, white citizens in California launched campaigns against Chinese immigrants, complaining that immigrants provided "cheap labor," that lowered the wages of white workers and therefore should be considered a form of unfair competition (Lake and Reynolds 2008, 18). Responding to citizens' demands, the California legislature passed a tax on "alien" miners and a "landing tax" on Chinese immigrants, shoring up the notion that the gold fields and the manufacturing sector should be the preserve of white men. When the U.S. Supreme Court struck down these laws, vigilante committees mobilized to use extra-judicial means to drive away the "alien race." When the Chinese tried to use the justice system to call these vigilantes to account, the California Supreme Court ruled that Chinese could not give evidence against a white man, extending legislation providing that "no Black, or Mulatto person, or Indian, shall be allowed to give evidence" to include Chinese (Lake and Reynolds 2008, 19). When California convened a constitutional convention in 1878 to revise the 1849 Constitution, some participants advocated adoption of the racial restrictions on citizenship that had been included in the federal Nationality Acts of 1790 and 1870. Their justification for such a stance was simply white supremacy: "This state should be a state for white men …the State has a right of self-preservation. It is the same right that a man of family has to protect his house and home … We want no other race here. The future of this republic demands that it shall be a white man's government, and that all other races be excluded" (Lake and Reynolds 2008, 31).

As California state law constructed Chinese men as workers who threatened the security of white employment, Chinese women were routinely depicted as prostitutes. Federal immigration law deployed the stereotype of the lascivious Chinese woman as a means to interfere with Chinese family reunification and family formation. Although the ratio of Chinese men to women in the U.S. in the mid-nineteenth century was 22 to 1, the Page Act of 1875 banned the immigration of Chinese women for "lewd and immoral purposes" (Siu 1987; Berger 2009). The humiliations devised by border control agents to enact this provision both prevented married Chinese women from entering the country and deterred the migration of married and single women. California had passed an anti-miscegenation statute in 1850, which "prohibited marriage between a white person and a Negro, a Mulatto, or a Mongolian" (Ngai 2004, 115). By banning marriage to white women and making migration of Chinese women difficult, state and federal law conspired to make it near impossible for Chinese men to marry and build families. By constraining both family formation and employment prospects, the state contributed to the feminization of Chinese men, pressuring them to work as domestics, providing cooking, cleaning, and laundry services – labor traditionally performed by women. Although state action was largely responsible for the low numbers of Chinese women admitted to California, the fraternal societies created by Chinese men in "Chinatowns" fueled allegations by white citizens concerning Chinese men's "deviant" sexuality (Ting 1995, Hsu 2003).

The Chinese Exclusion Act of 1882 barred all Chinese contract laborers from entry into the United States and prohibited Chinese nationals already resident in the country from acquiring naturalized citizenship. Although the title of the 1882 legislation named only the Chinese for purposes of exclusion and ineligibility for citizenship, a series of court cases and subsequent immigration acts expanded the category, "aliens ineligible for citizenship," to include all "Asians." Constructing the "Asian" as "a peculiarly American racial category," U.S. immigration law homogenized all the peoples of East Asia and South Asia, creating a fictive sameness among all nations "from Afghanistan to the Pacific, except the Philippines which was an American territory" (Ngai 2004, 37). Barring half the world's population from entering the United States, this provision also codified the principle of racial exclusion in the main body of American immigration and naturalization law.

Mae Ngai (2004, 202) points out that immigration laws that altered the status of Asian nationals already living and working in the United States created the "first illegal aliens as well as the first alien citizens. Although the Supreme Court ruled in 1898 that Chinese born in the US were citizens, the premises of exclusion – the alleged racial unassimilability of Chinese – powerfully influenced Americans' perceptions of Chinese Americans as permanent foreigners. Excluded from the polity and for the most part confined to Chinatown ghettos and an ethnic economy, Chinese Americans remained marginalized from the mainstream of society well into the twentieth century."

The Japanese nationals who migrated to California were typically better educated than Irish, Italian, or Polish immigrants, but that did not spare them the racial animosity of the white citizenry. Although the United States signed a treaty with Japan in 1894 that assured free immigration, Japanese workers in California encountered growing hostility as their numbers increased. In response to a request from the United States, the government of Japan agreed to deny passports to laborers seeking to enter the U.S. in 1900. But the number of Japanese migrants continued to rise as workers who had obtained passports to Canada, Mexico, or Hawaii subsequently moved to the United States. Fueled by inflammatory articles in the press, white residents' antagonism against the Japanese intensified, culminating in the creation of the "Japanese and Korean Exclusion League" in 1905. The following year, the San Francisco School Board mandated that all Asian children be placed in a segregated school (Foner and Garraty 1991).

School segregation, a thoroughly local matter according to the division of governmental jurisdictions within the U.S. federal system, had international ramifications. The government of Japan protested San Francisco's discriminatory law. Concerned with Russian expansion in the Far East, President Theodore Roosevelt sought to preserve harmonious ties with Japan by persuading the San Francisco School Board to rescind the segregation order. In 1907, Roosevelt concluded the "Gentlemen's Agreement," designed to allay Californians, concern about Japanese migration. Under the terms of the agreement, Japan once again agreed to deny passports to laborers intending to enter the United States and recognized the "right" of the U.S. to exclude Japanese immigrants holding passports originally issued for other countries.

The skilled Japanese farmers who had migrated to California initially worked as farmhands until they amassed sufficient resources to lease farm land or purchase small farms. By 1913, they owned 26,000 acres of land and leased an additional 235,000 acres, dominating the production of berries, beets, and cut flowers (Lake and Reynolds 2008). Although their success conformed to the American mythos of "self-making" and the promise held out to immigrants that the United States was indeed a land of opportunity, Japanese farmers were denounced rather than celebrated for their farming expertise. Members of the California legislature began agitating against "foreign" land ownership. In the words of California State Senator J. D. Phelan (1913), Japanese farmers had "exterminated the white settler in many districts. In the place of a sturdy white population – assimilable and homogeneous – we have an alien, incapable of assimilation, loyal to his home government, and hence composing a permanent foreign element in our midst. In other words, we have created a race question, against which all history has warned us: where two races are endeavoring to live side by side, one must take the inferior place or an irrepressible conflict is precipitated" (cited in Lake and Reynolds 2008, 265–66). Later in 1913, California passed an Alien Land Act that prohibited aliens ineligible to citizenship (i.e., Chinese, Japanese, and Koreans) from owning land, while also imposing limits on the right to lease land, a law that was subsequently replicated in Arizona, Idaho, Kansas, Louisiana, Montana, New Mexico, Oregon, and Washington.

The Transnational Politics of Racialization

The epigraph for this chapter calls attention to the paradoxical politics of racialization. Although state laws to consolidate the privileges accorded to white male citizens primarily affected domestic populations living within state borders, they also envisioned transnational ties. Men who could trace their ancestry to diverse and antagonistic national communities within Europe were presumed to share the property of whiteness, and accorded rights within the United States on that basis. But exclusionary laws pioneered in the United States also had transnational reach and international implications. The discriminatory laws against Asians enacted in California (and the terms of debate that surrounded them) were reproduced in Australia and South Africa and reverberated internationally in the first two decades of the twentieth century (Lake and Reynolds 2008).

Just as it had reacted against school segregation in San Francisco, the government of Japan lodged a formal complaint against California's 1913 Alien Land Act. The terms of Japan's complaint were designed to persuade North Americans that it too was a "civilized nation." Japan noted that it shared the conviction that advanced civilizations should use law to institutionalize gender segregation, thereby heightening "sex difference." Thus in 1890, Japan's Imperial Diet issued the Law on Assembly and Political Association (*Shukai Oyabi Seishaho*) banning women from political participation and from joining political parties (Molony 2010). Moreover, Japan followed the United States in adopting the principles of Manifest Destiny, expanding its territory and imperial rule over the Korean peninsula. With the outbreak of World War I, Japan declared war against Germany, joining the British, French, and Russian forces. Despite its alliance with the Triple Entente, the Japanese continued to experience multiple forms of racial discrimination by these "civilized" powers.

In response to their continuing maltreatment, the government of Japan crafted a nondiscrimination clause for inclusion in the Covenant of the League of Nations. To support its proposal, Japan emphasized that the principle of equality of nations was the foundational concept of international law. Moreover, "the colored races" comprised "62 percent of the whole of mankind" and as the majority of the global population, they deserved equal respect and equal treatment (Lake and Reynolds 2008, 285). The language Japan drafted for inclusion in the Covenant was supported by a majority of the participants in the 1919 Peace Commission: "The equality of nations being a basic principle of the League of Nations, the High Contracting Parties agree that concerning the treatment and rights to be accorded to aliens in their territories, they will not discriminate, either in law or in fact, against any person or persons on account of his or their race or nationality" (Lake and Reynolds 2008, 289). Canada, Australia, New Zealand, South Africa and the United States, however, opposed the nondiscrimination clause. Although Woodrow Wilson had led the Japanese to believe that he supported the nondiscrimination principle, he used his role in chairing the session to defeat the proposal by requiring a unanimous vote rather than a majority vote as had been required for other articles (Lake and Reynolds 2008, 301).

Far from being a wholly domestic matter, racialization shaped the decisions of the Paris Peace Conference and the creation of the League of Nations with long-term consequences. Marilyn Lake and Henry Reynolds suggest that Japan's sense of betrayal by its wartime allies fueled its militarism over the following decades. In an essay, "Illusions of the White Race," published in the *Asian Review* in January 1921, the former Japanese Prime Minister Marquis Shigenobu Okuma denounced white racism:

> Whites are obsessed with the mistaken theory that they are superior to all other races. Asian nations are fully peers of European nations, yet they are discriminated against because of the color of their skin. The root lies in the perverted feeling of racial superiority entertained by the whites. If things are allowed to proceed in the present way, there is every likelihood that the peace of the world will be endangered.
>
> (Okuma 1921, 170)

Thus racialization created a disjuncture between the principle of the equality of nations, which underlies international law, and the principle of self-determination embraced within white settler societies that fueled decisions to exclude certain people of color from the boundaries of belonging.⁶

Racialization under the Guise of Race Neutrality

Within the United States, local, state, and federal laws worked collaboratively to impose subordinate status on those racialized as "Asian." The United States Supreme Court upheld the California and Washington laws prohibiting land ownership by aliens ineligible to citizenship in 1921. The Court ruled that "alien land laws did not discriminate against the Japanese because the laws applied to *all* aliens ineligible to citizenship, masking the racial foundation of the concept" (Ngai 2004, 46–47). Laws in many western states also barred aliens deemed ineligible for citizenship from professional occupations, including law, medicine, teaching, and real estate. In addition to condoning the denigration, exclusion, and total deprivation of rights to those deemed permanently foreign and unassimilable in the American race-nation, U.S. immigration law contributed to the "invention and codification of new racial categories ... that put Europeans and non-Europeans on different trajectories of racial formation" (Ngai, 2004, 13). The Johnson-Reed Immigration Act passed in 1924 once again shored up white supremacy, but without using the language that citizenship was restricted to "free white persons."

In *Impossible Subjects: Illegal Aliens and the Making of Modern America*, Mae Ngai illuminates the complex racialization involved in the concept of "national origin" deployed in the Johnson-Reed Immigration Act, a concept invented to engineer the racial composition of the population. Assuming that "the American nation was, and should remain, a white nation descended from Europe," the Johnson-Reed Act established a national-origins quota system based on a "whitened" past that was sure to promote a whitened future. Put simply, "eliminating nonwhite peoples from the formula" enabled larger numbers of white Europeans to migrate to the United States (Ngai 2004, 25). The state's definition of national origins also erased any sense that African Americans, who comprised 9 percent of the U.S. population in 1920, or Asian Americans "really belonged" to the American race-nation.

The Johnson-Reed Act restricted immigration by imposing a quota system purportedly linked to the demographics of the U.S. population in 1920. To implement the quota system, the 1924 law required information about the "nation of origin" of the resident population. The difficulty, however, was that the nation's first census in 1790 did not include information about national origin or ancestry. Indeed, Ngai points out that the census did not differentiate foreign born from native born until 1850 and did not record the parental nativity of native born until 1890. Further complicating the task of quota apportionment, immigration was unrecorded before 1820 and not classified according to national origin until 1899, when the Immigration Service began designating immigrants by "race or people." Making the project of calculating national origin even murkier, many boundaries in Europe changed after the World War I, necessitating a "translation of political geography to reattribute origins and allocate quotas according to the world in 1920" (Ngai 2004, 25–26).

As Ngai (2004, 25) notes, the calculus of numerical restriction devised by the Quota Board to count ancestry was far from innocent:

> The Quota Board defined immigrant stock as all persons who entered the United States after 1790 and their progeny. The law defined "nationality," the central concept of the quota system, according to country of birth. Although the statute made no reference to race, race entered the calculus and subverted the concept of nationality in myriad ways. Ironically, nationality did not mean "country of birth" as far as defining the American nationality was concerned. *The law excluded nonwhite people residing in the United States in 1920 from the population universe governing quotas.* The law stipulated that "inhabitants in the continental United States in 1920 do *not* include (1) immigrants from the Western Hemisphere or their descendants, (2) aliens ineligible for citizenship or their descendants, (3) descendants of slave immigrants, or (4) the descendants of the American aborigines." The Quota Board ... discounted from the population all blacks and mulattoes, eliding the difference between the descendants of slave immigrants and the descendants of free Negroes and voluntary immigrants from Africa. It discounted all Chinese, Japanese, and South Asian persons as "ineligible to citizenship," including those with American citizenship by native birth. The provision also excluded the Territories of Hawaii, Puerto Rico, and Alaska, which American immigration law governed and whose natives were U.S. citizens. In other words, to the extent that "the inhabitants of the continental United States in 1920" constituted the legal representation of the American nation, the law excised all nonwhite, non-European peoples from that vision, erasing them from American nationality.
>
> *(Ngai 2004, 26, emphasis added)*

The shift in the Johnson-Reed Act to "race-neutral" criteria in order to exclude people of color set a pattern for subsequent legislation in the twentieth century. Racial exclusions pervaded New Deal policies, although the language of race appeared nowhere in the actual legislation. The National Labor Relations Act of 1935, which protected workers by granting them the right to organize and bargain collectively, the Social Security Act of 1935, which created unemployment insurance and a contributory scheme to fund pensions for the elderly, and the Fair Labor Standards Act, which established minimum wage and maximum hours, excluded agricultural and domestic workers – the occupations in which the majority of workers of color were concentrated. Overt racism did sometimes manifest itself in government policies, as was the case in segregation of schools and the armed services (prior to the end of World War II), the deportation of hundreds of thousands of Mexican American citizens and Filipinos, who were U.S. nationals, during the 1930s. And the construction of Japanese-Americans as inherently alien, unassimilable, disloyal, and a potential threat to national security was central to the government decision to deny Japanese American citizens their constitutionally-guaranteed right of *habeus corpus*, strip them of their possessions, and place 120,000 in internment camps for the duration of World War II, a decision subsequently upheld by the U.S. Supreme Court in *Korematsu v. United States* (323 U.S. 214, 1944). But whether the terminology adopted was explicitly race-specific or race-neutral, citizens of color were repeatedly excluded from the legal protections afforded by citizenship. Despite the 14th Amendment's guarantee of equal citizenship and equal protection of the laws, racialized U.S. citizens often had "no rights that white men had to respect" to paraphrase the infamous *Dred Scott* decision (*Dred Scott v. Sandford* 60 U.S. 393, 1857).

Constructing Racialized-Gendered Tiers of Citizenship

Many like to think that racialized gendering is an artefact of the past. Whatever racialized policy instruments may have been deployed over the course of U.S. history, they no longer have any role in "post-racial" America, where public policy is scrupulously colorblind (Haney-Lopez 2014). Yet, embodied power continues to structure government interventions whether the domain involves poverty, social services, environmental degradation, economic incentives for businesses, education, immigration, or securitization. Neoliberal political discourse, however, renders the racialized-gendered policy mechanisms invisible.

Consider, for example, Loïc Wacquant's (2002) assessment of "Americans' imagined community" in the 21st century: "On the one hand, stand praiseworthy 'working families,' implicitly white, suburban, and deserving; on the other hand, a despicable 'underclass' of criminals, loafers, and leeches – by definition dark-skinned, undeserving, and personified by the dissolute teenage 'welfare mother' and the dangerous street 'gang banger.' The former are exalted as the living incarnation of genuine American values: self-control, deferred gratification, subservience of life to labor. The latter is condemned as the loathsome embodiment of their abject desecration, the 'dark side' of the 'American dream' of affluence and opportunity for all, believed to flow from morality anchored in conjugality and work."[7] Neoliberal rhetoric celebrates personal responsibility, suggesting that these dramatically different conditions can be accounted for by individual choice. Yet, as Michael Lewis (1978) pointed out four decades ago, explanations that individualize success and failure mask both structural forces and state policies that produce racialized-gendered-classed outcomes.

For the better part of the twentieth century, residential segregation was not a matter of personal choice. Local ordinances that mandated racial segregation were operative well into the 1960s, when they were replaced by mortgage lending practices that "redlined" certain neighborhoods as white only, reserving others for people of color. Local and federal policies collaborated in highway construction plans, urban renewal projects, and the siting of public housing units to ensure the perpetuation of "ethnic enclaves" – more accurately characterized as ghettos. Residential segregation had profound effects on the quality of public schools, which were funded by local property taxes. Indeed, direct and indirect state action has enabled what Robert Reich (1991) called a "secession of the successful" from civic life. "In many cities and towns, the wealthy have in effect withdrawn their dollars from the support of public services and institutions shared by all and dedicated the savings to their own private services."

When school desegregation "with all deliberate speed" was mandated by the U.S. Supreme Court in *Brown v. Board of Education* (347 U.S. 483, 1954), local school authorities worked with white parents to create and support white-only "private" schools (often under the rubric of "Christian Academies"), while seriously underfunding the remaining public schools in which African-American students were clustered.[8] In the context of U.S. federalism, it is the responsibility of state governments to draw the boundaries of school districts. Yet, when "white flight" generated all-white suburban schools, leaving city schools 80 to 90 percent African American and Latino/a, states refused to redraw school districts to foster integration, a move sustained by the U.S. Supreme Court in *Milliken v. Bradley* (418 U.S. 717, 1974). In a 5–4 decision, the court ruled that school districts were not obligated to desegregate unless it could be proven that the lines were drawn with racist intent.[9] Thus, 60 years after the school desegregation order, more than 80 percent of Black children remain in "minority-majority" schools; while the vast preponderance of white students remain in white-majority schools. Like their predecessors in the pre-Brown days, racially-segregated schools are far from equal. The severely underfunded urban schools, which serve students of color whose family incomes fall below the poverty line, have been likened to "institutions of confinement whose primary mission is not to educate but to ensure 'custody and control' ... children are herded into decaying and overcrowded facilities that resemble fortresses, complete with razor wire on outside fences, bricked up windows, heavy locks on iron doors, metal detectors at the gates, and hallways patrolled by armed guards" (Wacquant 2002).

Tricia Rose (2013, 454) has noted that "Black urban poor communities are the product of a century's worth of systematic discrimination, spatial containment, and targeted disaccumulation of community resources." Schools may be the most visible evidence of that discrimination, but they are far from the only evidence. De-industrialization of cities in the "rust belt" is often discussed solely in terms of the profit-maximizing decisions of private corporations that relocate plants where they can find cheaper labor. But that is far from the whole story. States and municipalities in the "sun-belt" have offered large financial incentives and long-term tax abatement to lure industry to their jurisdictions. The federal government has negotiated treaties such as the North American Free Trade Agreement (NAFTA) that facilitate the free flow of capital across national borders and encourage the establishment of free trade zones offshore. As stable blue-collar employment disappeared from northern cities, state and municipal governments offered considerable financial incentives for gentrification programs, which were a boon to white urban "homesteaders," while driving up the cost of real estate and rents in ways that further pushed low-income residents into dilapidated sectors of cities. Spatial containment contributes to over-crowding in poorly constructed and poorly maintained public housing and in increasingly deteriorating private rental units. In 1968, the National Advisory Commission on Civil Disorders (NACCD), which had been appointed by President Lyndon Johnson to investigate the riots that had rocked the nation, devastating 23 cities including Watts in Los Angeles (1965), Chicago (1966), Detroit (1967), and Newark (1967), linked the fundamental causes of racial unrest to white actions and behaviors that produced segregation and poverty in "the racial ghetto." "Segregation and poverty have created in the racial ghetto a destructive environment totally unknown to most white Americans. What white Americans have never fully understood – but what the Negro can never forget – is that white society is deeply implicated in the ghetto. White institutions created it, white institutions maintain it, and white society condones it" (National Advisory Commission on Civil Disorders 1968, 1).

Competition for the jobs that are available in urban centers is intense. Multiple studies have documented continuing patterns of racial discrimination in hiring that significantly disadvantage African Americans in the competition for jobs. Carefully-crafted studies by the Urban Institute have demonstrated that having a "black name" on a résumé halves an applicant's chances of securing a job interview (Sehgal 2015, 13). Black unemployment is typically twice the rate of white unemployment. In the aftermath of the 2008 economic crisis, the increase in Black unemployment was seven times greater than that experienced by whites (Roberts 2011, 297). Neoliberal privatization has also had disproportionate negative effects on Black workers. As Patricia Cohen (2015, A1, B5) has noted, "One in five black adults works for the government, teaching school, delivering mail, fighting fires, driving busses, processing criminal justice and managing large staffs. They are about 30 percent more likely to have a public sector job than whites, and twice as likely as Hispanics. Since 2007, half a million public sector jobs have been cut. When normal growth of population is factored in, there are 1.8 million fewer jobs in the public sector for people to fill. Cuts in government employment disproportionately hurt Black professionals, who lost their jobs at a higher rate than whites, concentrated in a shrinking sector of the economy. As schools shift to part-time positions without benefits, Blacks are particularly hard hit."

People of color had been targeted for predatory loans in the mortgage scandal that contributed to the 2008 economic crisis. As a consequence, foreclosures in their neighborhoods outpaced foreclosures in white neighborhoods. A study by

Cornell University indicated that "mostly Black and mostly Latino neighborhoods lost homes at rates approximately three times higher than white areas. Today Blacks are far less likely to own homes or have sizable retirement savings, two primary ways most families accumulate wealth" (Cohen 2015, B5). Thus, a recent report issued by Demos and the Institute for Assets and Social Policy at Brandeis concluded that "the U.S. racial wealth gap is substantial and is driven by public policy decisions … In 2011 the median white household had $111,146 in wealth holdings, compared to just $7,113 for the median Black household and $8,348 for the median Latino household. From the continuing impact of redlining on American homeownership to the retreat from desegregation in public education, public policy has shaped these disparities, leaving them impossible to overcome without racially-aware policy change" (Sullivan et al. 2015). Racial disparities are equally pronounced with respect to "zero or negative wealth, which is the condition of 35 percent of Black households and 31 percent of Latino households, compared with 15 percent of white households" (King and Smith 2011).

Quite apart from any choices made by individuals, a compendium of forces contributes to personal insecurity in high-density impoverished communities of color. As Shatema Threadcraft (2014, 738) has noted, "African Americans did not possess equal formal political power relative to members of the wider society. They did not have equal access to employment-oriented skill acquisition or equal access to employment itself. They did not experience equal treatment within the criminal justice system. On the contrary, they suffered political and economic marginalization despite Constitutional guarantees of equality under the law. And they were subjected to racially-motivated heightened scrutiny and disproportionate police harassment, intimidation and violence."

Racialized-gendering pervades public discourses concerning low-income communities of color and the public policies devised to address them. Black and Latino youth are constructed as threats, subjected to hyper-surveillance, and disproportionately arrested and incarcerated (Cacho 2012; Alexander 2010). As legal scholar Ian Haney-Lopez (2014, 50–51) has pointed out, "Blacks are less likely than whites to commit crime, but are far more likely to be arrested and convicted." The racial composition of police forces, changes in policing practices, new DNA technologies, and the "war on drugs" have all contributed to the "criminalization" of Black and Latino youth (Cacho 2012; Roberts 2011).

Elijah Anderson (1999) has pointed out that "ghetto" residents have frequent encounters with police, yet they have far less personal security than members of the wider society. The police who patrol inner city neighborhoods are disproportionately white. In 2015, people of color comprise 25 percent of the police officers across the United States, but in major cities, the percentage of whites on the force is 30 percent greater on average than their presence in the population. According to a survey conducted by the Bureau of Justice Statistics in 2007, the disproportion of white police officers was greatest in densely-populated communities of color. For example, in the St. Louis suburb, Ferguson, Missouri, the police force is 55 percent more white than community residents; in the Maple Heights section of Cleveland, the force is 70 percent more white than the local population. The police are 76 percent more white in Chicago, 69 percent more white in Los Angeles, 62 percent more white in Houston, 59 percent more white in Washington, DC, 57 percent more white in Atlanta, and 53 percent more white in Boston than the communities of color they are patrolling. Rather than enhancing the physical safety of urban residents in contexts where intraracial violence poses serious challenges, certain policing practices jeopardize the rights, well-being, and lives of Black and Latino men.

Since the terrorist attacks on the World Trade Towers and the Pentagon in 2001, racial profiling has gained new legitimacy in U.S. "securitization" measures.[10] Police frequently use race or ethnicity as the grounds for "reasonable suspicion" to stop and frisk motorists and pedestrians. Dorothy Roberts (2011, 279) has catalogued the stark disparities in policing motorists: Blacks and Latinos constitute 5 percent of the drivers in Florida, but 70 percent of those pulled over by the Florida State Police; in New Jersey, Blacks and Latinos are 15 percent of the drivers but 42 percent of those stopped (and 73 percent of those arrested); in Maryland, Blacks and Latinos are 21 percent of the drivers on the roads, but 80 percent of those stopped and searched. In New York City, walking can be as hazardous as driving. In the words of a class action suit filed by the Center for Constitutional Rights, the New York Police Department has been relentless in pursuing "race-based and suspicionless stops and frisks":

> From 2004 through 2009, city police officers stopped people on the street and checked them out nearly three million times. Many were patted down, frisked, made to sprawl face down on the ground, or spread-eagle themselves against a wall or over the hood of a car. Nearly 90 percent of the people stopped were completely innocent of any wrongdoing. An overwhelming majority of the people stopped were Black or Hispanic. Blacks were nine times more likely than whites to be stopped by the police, but no more likely than whites to be arrested as a result of the stops. While crime has been going down, the number of people getting stopped has been going up. More than 575,000 stops were made in 2009 – a record. But 504,594 of those stops were of people who had committed no crime, were issued no summonses and were carrying no weapons or illegal substances … nearly 150,000 stops over this six-year period lacked any legal justification at all. An additional 544,252 stops lacked sufficiently detailed information from the officers involved to determine their legality.
>
> (Herbert 2010, A23)

African Americans comprise approximately 25 percent and Latinos, 28 percent of the population of New York City, yet they were 80 to 87 percent of those stopped and frisked in the five-year period tracked by the Center for Constitutional Rights. The racial disparity is heightened when gender and age are taken into account as these stops primarily target Black and Latino men under the age of 35. Stripped of the presumption of innocence and subjected to routine police harassment, Black and Latino youth have devised strategies for self-protection. In the words of Elijah Anderson:

> The code of the streets is actually a cultural adaptation to a profound lack of faith in the police and judicial system – and in others who would champion one's personal security. The police, for instance, are most often viewed as representing the dominant white society and as not caring to protect inner-city residents. When called, they may not respond, which is one reason many residents feel they must be prepared to take extraordinary measures to defend themselves and their loved ones against those who are inclined to aggression.
> *(Anderson 1999, 34)*

Thus, certain police practices may exacerbate violence, rather than heightening security.

The "War on Drugs" has been the principal policy fueling the criminalization of Black and Latino youth. Yet the racialized gendering integral to this policy has thoroughly distorted public perceptions of crime. As Michelle Alexander (2011, 7) has pointed out, "drug crime was declining, not rising, at the moment that the war on drugs was declared." Indeed, the "incidence of crime remained constant from 1973 to 1993, then fell sharply," as policing practices dramatically increased the prison population from 200,000 in 1970 to 2.3 million in 2010 (Wacquant 2008, 111; Haney-Lopez 2014, 50–51). Although people of color and whites use illegal drugs at roughly the same rate (6.4 percent among whites compared to 6.4 percent among Blacks and 5.3 percent among Latinos), in some states Black men are admitted to prison at rates 20–50 times greater than white men (Alexander 2010, 7). In 2010, a national survey on drug use indicated that young African Americans aged 18 to 25 were less likely to use illegal drugs than the national average; yet young Black men were 12 times more likely than white men to be sent to prison on drug charges (Roberts 2011, 279). Pronounced racial disparities in incarceration rates are a recent phenomenon. African Americans became a majority of those entering prison only in 1989. And although ethnic patterns of criminal activity have not fundamentally changed in the past six decades, the ethnic composition of the U.S. inmate population has reversed – from 70 percent white in 1950 to nearly 70 percent Black and Latino in 2002 (Wacquant 2002). By 2014, 1 of every 106 white men over the age of 18 had been in prison, compared to 1 in 36 Latinos, and 1 in 15 Black men (1 in 9 Black men aged 20 to 34) (Haney-Lopez 2014, 53).

The consequences of incarceration are stark: African Americans who have been incarcerated face 42 percent reduction in expected lifetime earnings, which constitutes a $300 billion loss of earnings for all offenders (Haney-Lopez 2014, 53). State and federal laws deny welfare payments, veterans' benefits, and food stamps to anyone held in detention for more than sixty days. The Work Opportunity and Personal Responsibility Act of 1996 excludes most ex-convicts from Medicaid, public housing, Section 8 housing vouchers, and related forms of assistance (Wacquant 2002). In addition, "thirty-nine states forbid convicts placed on probation from exercising the right to vote; and thirty-two states also disenfranchise parolees. In fourteen states, ex-felons are barred from voting even when they are no longer under criminal justice supervision – for life in ten of these states. The result is that nearly 4 million Americans have temporarily or permanently lost the ability to cast a ballot, including 1.47 million who are not behind bars and another 1.39 million who served their sentences in full. A mere quarter century after acceding to full voting rights, one black man in seven nationwide is banned from the electoral booth through penal disenfranchisement and seven states permanently deny the vote to more than one-fourth of their black male residents" (Wacquant 2002).

The U.S. shift to mass incarceration occurred just as the National Advisory Commission on Criminal Justice Standards and Goals (1973) issued a report recommending that "no new carceral institutions for adults should be built and existing institutions for juveniles should be closed." Far from inhibiting crime, the Commission asserted that "the prison, the reformatory, and the jail have achieved only a shocking record of failure. There is overwhelming evidence that these institutions create crime rather than prevent it" (Alexander 2010, 8). The disproportionate number of Black and Latino men in the prison population also has an unintended consequence. It contributes to the perception of African American and Latino men as dangerous "criminals" – a racialized-gendered depiction that haunts police as well as public perception. Indeed, investigation of the spate of deaths of young Black men in police custody in 2014 indicated that "fear" of Black and Latino youth is precisely what caused police officers to use their firearms or extreme force to "subdue" unruly suspects (Isoke 2016). The circularity is vicious, indeed: policing practices subject Black and Latino young men to excessive surveillance, increasingly negative encounters with police officers, and disproportionate arrest and incarceration for minor offenses, causing the prison population to soar. The soaring prison population contributes to the "criminalization" of Black and Latino youth, who devise strategies for self-defense, including refusal to cooperate politely with stop and frisk policies, which the police perceive as unruly behavior that requires force to subdue, culminating in increasing numbers of suspicious deaths of "suspects" of color in police custody. Thus it is no coincidence that Blacks and Latinos are overrepresented among those who die from police violence. Although African Americans comprise 12.6 percent of the U.S. population, they were 32 percent of the victims of police homicides between 2003 and 2009.[11] Latinos constitute 15 percent of the U.S. population, but they were 20 percent of those killed by the police while in custody between 2002 and 2009.¹² In these tragic instances, the exercise of embodied power becomes deadly.

Scholars have offered a range of explanations to account for the contradiction between falling crime rates and the exponential increase in the U.S. prison population. Some suggest that changes in the technology used in policing have had a major impact. Matt Taibbi (2014, 94–95), for example, notes that the introduction of CompStat, a quantitative data base, in New York, Los Angeles, Philadelphia, Washington, DC, and other cities changed the incentive system for police work. Beginning in the 1990s, precincts were required to submit weekly reports on police activity from the number of tickets issued to the number of arrests. Although initially introduced to track crime, quantitative data seemed to provide a ready measure of police performance and was quickly adopted to serve as criteria for promotion. With this shift in personnel policy, the number of marijuana arrests increased by a factor of ten in New York City between 1996 and 2000. "By the mid-to-late 2000s, police stops had multiplied all across the board for a range of seemingly minor offenses. The numbers by 2012 would be 600,000 summonses a year, more than three times the levels from the late 1990s" (Taibbi 2014, 95). In contrast to arrests for major crimes, 150,000 of these summonses each year were for marijuana possession; 140,000 were for violations of open container laws; 80,000 were for disorderly conduct; 20,000 were for riding bicycles on the sidewalk (Taibbi, 2014, 95).

Dorothy Roberts (2011, 264–65) notes that the DNA Fingerprint Act of 2005, which was included as a provision in the reauthorization of the Violence Against Women Act (VAWA), authorized U.S. law enforcement agents to take and store DNA from anyone arrested or detained and it allows CODIS (the FBI's Combined DNA Index System) to retain permanently DNA profiles submitted by states. Under the provisions of this act, 47 of the 50 U.S. states have begun to collect DNA from all those arrested for a felony, allowing no right to refuse. The DNA profile is then entered into CODIS. Mandatory extraction and permanent storage of DNA profiles taken at the time of arrest wreak havoc on the presumption of innocence. In California, for example, 30 percent of those arrested are not convicted of any crime. Yet, once their DNA has been entered into a permanent data base used to screen for "criminal involvement," the innocent are positioned as perpetual suspects who are far more likely to be questioned and arrested again. According to Roberts (2011, 264), "The U.S. now has 8 million offender samples … because of rampant racial bias in arrests and convictions, government-amassed DNA databases constitute another race-based technology emerging from genetic science. DNA repositories are gathered without consent and are maintained for purpose of implicating people in crimes."

The precariousness of being placed under permanent "genetic surveillance" is intricately related to the fallibility of "DNA prints." In contrast to the authority accorded to DNA profiles on popular crime shows, "DNA evidence is not infallible: genetic material has to be retrieved, transferred, transported, identified, labeled, analyzed and stored, creating opportunities for error at every stage ... [through] poor calibration and improper maintenance of equipment, inadequate record keeping, contamination of samples" (Roberts 2011, 270).[13] Moreover, genetic fingerprints created by crime labs are not absolutely unique. Because they match only 13 loci, multiple people can match a DNA profile (Roberts 2011, 272). Despite the fallibility of DNA evidence, police and prosecutors often use DNA profiles to extract confessions from those arrested and to negotiate plea bargains. The success of the "Innocence Project" in exonerating the wrongful convictions of 330 persons, who had served an average of 14 years in the penitentiary (18 of whom had been on death row), indicates how fraught being placed under permanent suspicion can be (www.innocenceproject.org). Roberts also emphasizes that some police departments are turning to DNA prints in criminal investigations "to predict the race of an unknown suspect," a prediction that rests upon multiple scientific flaws, such as confusing probabilistic population estimates with definitive individual identification, relying on inadequate reference data bases, errors in computer-generated statistical models, and the fundamental flaw of equating genetic ancestry with race (Roberts 2011, 262).

Where Taibbi and Roberts suggest that quantitative approaches to policing and technological innovations such as DNA profiling may explain the vast increases in the prison population, other scholars argue that an adequate explanation must move "beyond a crime and punishment schema [to] rethink the prison as a political institution, a central component of the state" (Wacquant 2008, 111). Michelle Alexander (2011, 13), for example, conceptualizes "mass incarceration as a tightly networked system of laws, policies, customs and institutions that operate collectively to ensure the subordinate status of a group defined largely by race."[14] Lynne Haney (2010) characterizes mass incarceration as a way to warehouse and neutralize those rejected by the deregulated service economy. Indeed, she suggests that prison not only "contains" but extracts labor from African Americans and Latinos displaced by mass unemployment and welfare retrenchment:

> With the 1979 Justice Systems Improvement Act's repeal of many restrictions against prison labor, there was a resurgence of prison work programs. Since then 36 states have enacted policies allowing companies to set up shop in prisons, textiles, data entry, and light industry. Companies ranging from IBM to Starbucks to Revlon, Boeing, and Microsoft now use prison labor. Their profits can be enormous: minimum wage requirements do not apply; large portions of inmates' wages can be deducted to cover room and board, leaving pennies in take-home pay. California's Joint Venture Program promises to give businesses a "competitive edge" while "instilling a work ethic in idle prisoners"
> *(Haney 2010, 77)*[15]

Mass incarceration has also affected women of color, although they comprise a much smaller proportion of the prison population in the United States. Over the past 35 years, however, women's incarceration rates have increased more rapidly than men's. Women constitute roughly 7 percent of state and federal prisoners, but their numbers have increased by 650 percent since 1980, as compared to a 300 percent increase for men. Most women are serving time for drug-related offenses and property crimes; slightly less than 10 percent have been convicted of violent offenses (Haney 2013, 105). The huge gender disparity in incarceration rates suggests that jails and prisons have become the dominant state institutions for controlling men of color, but women of color are subjected to other modes of social regulation and control as well, such as state and federal welfare policies and child protective services.

Since its inception, U.S. welfare policy has been a mechanism for racialized gendering (Fraser 1989; G. Mink 1995). Restricted primarily to women recipients deemed morally worthy by state bureaucrats, welfare has been "dispensed in a disparate and racially unequal manner not just in the Jim Crow era, but since the Voting Rights Act" (Darling 1998, 161). Racial bias in determinations of eligibility insured that "African American and Latinos remained underrepresented on the welfare rolls, despite high levels of need" (Mettler 2000, 12). Although racial disparities in the allocation of benefits have typified welfare policy, and the majority of welfare recipients are white, cultural stereotypes of the typical welfare recipient are highly racialized. The typical welfare recipient is imagined to be an inner-city Black woman, who irresponsibly has large numbers of children, is promiscuous, uneducated, and refuses to work. Several studies have demonstrated that the racist attitudes fueling the misperception that welfare recipients are overwhelmingly black influence white opposition to welfare (Gilens 1995, 1996). There is also evidence that entrenched racism has shaped decades of policymakers' efforts to "reform" welfare by curtailing benefits (Lieberman 1995; Quadagno 1994; Hancock 2004; Hawkesworth 2003).

As welfare "dependency" has been racialized, the facts pertaining to welfare use have been grossly distorted. Both Black and white women resort to welfare when beset by crises such as illness, unemployment, domestic violence, or divorce and remain on welfare for less than a year; indeed 80 percent of recipients rely on welfare for less than two years. But in the 1990s, proposals for "welfare reform" framed poverty as a matter of personal responsibility, particularly in relation to marriage and "responsible fatherhood and motherhood." Asserting that the nation confronted a "crisis of out-of-wedlock births," the Republicans proposed legislation designed to "ensure that the responsibility of having a child belongs to the mother and father, rather than to the mother and the U.S. taxpayer" (Meyers 1993).[16] Several of the key provisions of the Republican welfare reform targeted teen pregnancy in particular, and out-of-wedlock births more generally, on the assumption that "the increase in the number of children receiving public assistance is closely related to the increase in births to unmarried women" (Personal Responsibility and Work Opportunity Reconciliation Act of 1996 [PRWORA], Public Law 104–193, 42 USC 601, Sec. 101 (5) C). Although the empirical inspections, head tax, literacy tests, border-crossing cards, visa requirements ... produce 'illegal' entrants – those who lack proper documentation." In the aftermath of the 2001 attacks on the World Trade Towers and the Pentagon, however, "securitization" measures have proliferated, deploying levels of racialized gendering that blur the boundaries between national and international "threats" to national security and between public and private domains within domestic and international spheres. Embodied power assumes more extreme forms as the nation is conceived as a "homeland" in need of protection from terrorism. Private militias have declared themselves public servants as thousands of white vigilantes ("Minutemen") have converged on ranches spanning the Mexican border, pledging their guns and their lives to protect the United States from what they see as security threats lurking south of the border. On a smaller scale, armed white vigilantes ("Oath Keepers") have taken to patrolling city streets in communities of color to ward off what they perceive as internal threats to "law and order." Yet, in its efforts to protect national borders, the state has withdrawn constitutional protections of the private sphere. The USA PATRIOT Act (2001) authorizes securitization measures that suspend the right of *habeas corpus*, as well as Fourth Amendment guarantees against unwarranted searches and seizures.[22] According to securitization logic, public protection necessitates the erosion of civil liberties, the legitimation of racial and ethnic profiling; heightened surveillance; and detention without due process of law. On U.S. soil, those who appear "suspicious" have been arrested and detained without being charged with criminal offense and without access to counsel. In U.S. airports and in territories outside the United States, foreign nationals have been arrested and rendered to "black sites" in Djibouti, Egypt, Poland, Romania, and Syria for interrogation and confinement. Hundreds of men captured by U.S. forces in Afghanistan were shipped to a military base in Guantanamo Bay, Cuba for indefinite detention and interrogation. In 2003, a federal appellate court unanimously upheld a 2002 federal court ruling, which held that the 650 detainees had no legal rights in the United States and could not petition the courts to review their detentions.

Resurrecting "clash of civilization" discourses (Huntington 1996), the "war against terrorism" declared by President George W. Bush's executive order (October 7, 2001), pitted a "coalition of the willing against the Taliban regime in Afghanistan and the Al Qaida network, a non-state actor operating clandestinely within and across the national borders of some sixty states. In November 2001, the Bush Administration issued a Military Order on the Detention, Treatment and Trial of Certain Non-Citizens in the War against Terrorism (66 Fed. Reg. 57,833, November 13, 2001), which suspended basic constitutional protections, authorizing the establishment of military tribunals, indefinite detention of enemy combatants, as well as noncitizens associated with newly designated terrorist networks, denial of detainees' *habeas corpus* and basic constitutional rights, including a presumption of innocence, the right to be informed of charges against them, and the right to legal representation. The Bush Administration also declared that the

Geneva Conventions protecting prisoners of war did not apply to terrorists. Within this amorphous struggle, the figure of the "Muslim" assumed a particular racialized and gendered form. As Liz Philipose has noted:

> The concept of the "Muslim" has long circulated as a homogenizing fabrication, having little to do with the diverse beliefs, practices, geographies, histories or ethnicities of people who identify as Muslim. Yet the new raced-gendered grammar that collapses "Muslim" into "terrorist" has certain unique features, peremptorily designating any act, speech or movement made by a Muslim, or people perceived to be Muslim, as the act, speech or movement of a terrorist. Resting on gendered assumptions of men as hyper-patriarchal and misogynistic, and women as victimized and ubiquitously burqa-clad, the "Muslim terrorist" becomes the container for gendered attributes that signify the anti-modern, religiously fanatical and sexually deviant terrorist. Like older modes of racialization, this new racial grammar relies on visual cues to signal the deeper, hidden nature of the terrorist. It incorporates faulty biologism, suggesting that physical traits are keys to the interior moral turpitude of the individual terrorist. And it recklessly universalizes terrorist propensities to those marked by the visual cues. Invested in rigid distinctions between masculinity and femininity and clearly defined parameters of acceptable (hetero)sexuality, this new racial grammar links gender, sexuality and desire to lineage, heredity and kinship.
>
> *(Philipose 2007b, 1048)*

Securitization measures since September 2001 have been explicit acts of embodied power. Although the laws enabling these actions adopt race-neutral language, the decisions concerning whom to arrest are raced and gendered, specifically targeting men whose appearance conforms to the stereotype of a "Muslim terrorist." In the initial sweep of "suspicious" individuals, Arab, Muslim, and South Asian men fit the racialized profile. In November 2001, the Department of Justice (DOJ) announced that it had placed 1,182 people into secret custody since September 11th (Constitution Project 2004). The grounds offered for these detentions varied, ranging from expired immigration visas and material witness orders to suspicion of being an enemy combatant. Following this initial disclosure, the DOJ released no further information on the number of detainees and refused to disclose their identities.

The treatment of detainees swept up because they fit this profile involved a particular mode of racialized gendering – "feminization," which Timothy Kaufman-Osborn (2005) has aptly defined as scripted practices of subordination. While in detention, the detainees were "subject to harsh conditions, inconsistent with basic human rights standards" (Constitution Project 2004). Those arrested for overstaying their immigration visas, for example, were held in solitary confinement, subjected to physical and verbal abuse, including strip searches each time they were removed from or returned to their cells, exposed to extreme cold without adequate clothing, housed with convicted criminals, and denied reasonable medical attention. Most of the detainees, who had been arrested on U.S. soil, were released within three to five months; none were charged with terrorist acts. Despite the suspension of due process rights of innocent Arab, Muslim, and South Asian men, the U.S. Supreme Court upheld the validity of these racialized dragnets in *Ashcroft v. Iqbal* in 2009 (Haney-Lopez 2014, 118).[23]

Although the Justice Department characterizes the PATRIOT Act as a means to "preserve life and liberty,"[24] that account remains at great remove from the treatment of 136 individuals who were arbitrarily deprived of their freedom, kidnapped, transferred to black sites under the jurisdiction of 54 foreign governments and subjected to "extraordinary rendition" – extreme interrogation techniques that violate international conventions against torture (Open Society Foundation 2013).[25] During the George W. Bush Administration, the DOJ authorized "enhanced interrogation techniques, which included "walling" (quickly pulling the detainee forward and then thrusting him against a flexible false wall), "water dousing," "waterboarding," "stress positions" (forcing the detainee to remain in body positions designed to induce physical discomfort), "wall standing" (forcing the detainee to remain standing with his arms outstretched in front of him so that his fingers touch a wall four to five feet away and support his entire body weight), "cramped confinement" in a box, "insult slaps," (slapping the detainee on the face with fingers spread), "facial hold" (holding a detainee's head temporarily immobile during interrogation with palms on either side of the face), "attention grasp" (grasping the detainee with both hands, one hand on each side of the collar opening, and quickly drawing him toward the interrogator), forced nudity, sleep deprivation while being vertically shackled, and dietary manipulation (Open Society Foundation 2013).

Three official reports make it clear that sexual humiliation was part of the treatment of prisoners in Bagram Air Base and other camps in Afghanistan, Abu Ghraib Prison and other sites in Iraq, Guantánamo, and other secret black sites (Briggs 2015). Claiming that their goal was to extract "actionable intelligence," to borrow a phrase from Donald Rumsfeld, interrogators sought to elicit information or force confessions through sexualized interventions designed to violate the detainee's sense of self and human dignity. Combining moral debasement with physical and sexual battery, interrogators intimidated detainees through a panoply of tactics that ranged from strip searches mixed with physical groping designed to produce outrage twinned with shame, physical pain and despair; sadistic objectification (torturers entertaining themselves by issuing a barrage of orders for hours, requiring their often naked prisoners to stand, sit, kneel, grovel in quick succession), and forcing detainees to simulate homosexual intercourse, to rape by soldiers, and rape involving animate and inanimate objects. As Tim Kaufman-Osborn (2005, 609) has pointed out, interrogation practices at Abu Ghraib and Guantánamo manifested a "logic of emasculation, where the aim of disciplinary techniques is to strip prisoners of their masculine identity and turn them into caricatures of terrified and often infantilized femininity." In his detailed analysis of detention practices authorized by the CIA, the DOJ, and U.S. *Military Interrogation Manuals*, Kaufman-Osborn notes that gender was constitutive of the technologies designed to break prisoners down:

> Stripping male prisoners ... emasculates prisoners by exposing them in a way that is familiar from representations of women, including but by no means limited to those conventionally labeled pornographic ... Much the same logic is apparent in the practice of smearing prisoners with red ink said to be menstrual blood; here emasculation is a function of staining the male body with that which is taken to mark women's bodies as distinctively female, and as such, a source of degradation.
>
> *(Kaufman-Osborn 2005, 609)*

Kaufman-Osborn points out that these tactics can be effective only because of the implicit power hierarchy structured by gender. "Scripted practices of subordination achieve their ends through the manipulation of gendered stereotypes, all of which work precisely because degradation, weakness, and humiliation remain very much identified with matters feminine" (2005, 616).

The dynamics of feminization shape the language used to refer to detainees, as well as their treatment. To capture the ambiguity of their status, detainees in Afghanistan and Iraq are known by the acronym PUC (pronounced puck), referring to a "person under control." As Danchev (2008, 95) has noted, the use of the acronym facilitates depersonalization. In daily banter, PUC designates a nonperson, about whom soldiers have few moral compunctions, and so they joke that it is time to "fuck a PUC," that is, administer a beating. The purpose of these "aggressive interrogation techniques" is to render the detainees compliant. "Softening up," "sexing-up," and "smoking" (forced physical exertion, sometimes to the point of unconsciousness, accompanied by deprivation of food, water, sleep) are tactics endorsed by Military Intelligence to so demoralize PUCs that they will want to cooperate.[26] Detainees are feminized in front of their peers to produce generalized effects. Through interrogation strategies designed to establish and maintain control, the hyper-masculine interrogators (whether men or women) facilitate the descent from subject to abject by intensifying shame, helplessness, and fear, thereby sapping the will to resist. In the process of being humiliated, degraded, and subjected to processes of "voluntary" or involuntary self-abasement, detainees are often "reminded they are less than human, that animals have more freedom and love than they do" (Danchev 2008, 93).

As instances of racialized gendering, Laura Briggs (2015, 26–27) has suggested that these interrogation techniques should not be construed as merely opportunistic exploitation – something that "happens when young soldiers get out of hand." On the contrary, these routinized bureaucratic techniques result from years of psychological, biomedical, and anthropological research funded by the CIA. Anthropologist Raphael Parai's *The Arab Mind*, for example, which was used to train interrogators, "circulates the notion that Arabs are particularly vulnerable to sexual humiliation ... Arabs only understand force; their biggest weakness is shame and humiliation" (Briggs 2015, 29). Having been taught that Arab men embody "a racialized masculinity that is ... too stiff, too proud, too archaically patriarchal," interrogators are trained to sexually humiliate detainees. Their goal is not pain *per se* but an assault on the will and spirit in order to "break" the prisoner and lead him to cooperate. Informed by Orientalist assumptions about Arab men, sexually abusive interrogation tactics "produc[e] difference at the level of the body ... sexually humiliating Arab men produces them as a race apart ... Torture produces Arab men as different; a masculinity so unrecognizable that it does not share a common humanity" (Briggs 2015, 27, 34).[27] It is a painful irony that the brutal feminization of Middle-Eastern and South Asian men in detention has been publicly justified as a means to "rescue" Muslim women.

In another painfully ironic twist, Anna Sampaio (2015) has demonstrated that post-9/11 securitization measures have racially profiled Latino/a immigrants and citizens, as well as Arab, Muslim, and South Asian men. Through processes of racialization and gendering that mark some citizens as worthy of protection and others as dangerous threats to national security, recent immigration and securitization policies have blurred the boundaries between citizens and immigrants, and between immigrants and terrorist threats with devastating effects on the U.S. Latino/a community. Consistent with long-established practices that position ethnic minorities as unassimilable aliens, contemporary securitization measures construct Latina/o citizens as "alien" and Latina/o immigrants as "threats," which makes it appear "reasonable" to constrict and encumber their rights. Indeed, again adopting the rhetoric of a clash of civilizations, Samuel Huntington (2004, 31–32) suggested that "The persistent inflow of Hispanic immigrants threatens to divide the United States into two peoples, two cultures, and two languages. Unlike past immigrant groups, Mexicans and other Latinos have not assimilated into mainstream U.S. culture, forming instead their own political and linguistic enclaves – from Los Angeles to Miami – and rejecting the Anglo-Protestant values that built the American dream."

The 2001 PATRIOT Act and the 2002 Homeland Security Act authorized an expansion of law enforcement powers and systematic collaboration among law enforcement officials at local, state, and federal levels, resulting in the surveillance of thousands of U.S. citizens engaged in constitutionally protected activities and the deportation of hundreds of thousands of undocumented immigrants as potential threats to U.S. national security (Kretsedemas 2008, Sampaio 2015).[28] To demonstrate the scope and consequences of racial targeting by law enforcement agencies, Sampaio investigates a series of domestic operations initiated by the newly created Department of Homeland Security (DHS) that combined the forces of federal and state law enforcement agencies to root out "terrorist threats" to the country. Afforded names akin to foreign military operations, these initiatives included "Operation Tarmac," "Operation Community Shield," and "Operation Wagon Train."[29] Operation Tarmac, for example, drew resources from DHS, DOJ, the Departments of Transportation and Customs along with the Social Security Administration, U.S. Attorney's Office, Federal Aviation Administration and other agencies to investigate "persons of unknown origin" working at airports and other federally secured facilities around the country (Sampaio 2015). Characterized as "a highly effective weapon in the domestic war against terrorism," Operation Tarmac investigated more than 750,000 employees working for hotels, restaurants, cleaning services, and airlines at more than 1900 airports across the United States, culminating in the arrest and deportation of several thousand Latino/as who had been working as janitors, food service workers, gardeners, construction workers, mechanics and baggage handlers. According to the Department of Homeland Security and the U.S. Attorney's Office, the grounds for the arrests and deportations were "possession of false identification." Not one of the immigrants detained or deported as part of Operation Tarmac had any relationship to terrorist activity.

Like Operation Tarmac, subsequent national security directives used race neutral language to characterize initiatives to "protect critical infrastructure," yet these operations had disproportionate effects on Latino/as living in the United States. Although the September 11 terrorists had entered the United States through Canada, these operations focused on the U.S. border with Mexico. And Administration spokespersons frequently conflated undocumented workers from Mexico and Central America with terrorists and criminals. In 2002, Attorney General John Ashcroft, for example, warned that "In this new war on terrorism our enemy's platoons infiltrate our borders … their tactics rely on evading recognition at the border and escaping detection within the United States." Similarly, Homeland Security Secretary Michael Chertoff tied false social security numbers to terrorism: "illegal documents are used not only by illegal immigrants, but they are used by terrorists who want to get on airplanes and criminals who want to prey on our citizens" (cited in Sampaio 2015). By emphasizing illegality and portraying a false driver's license or a fake social security card as a criminal rather than a civil offense, proponents of securitization policies elevated what had been minor infractions into deportable offenses. The 2005 Operation Wagon Train focused specifically on fraudulent IDs used to secure employment. Targeting manufacturing plants, food processing plants, and fisheries, the coordinated action of federal and state agencies resulted in the arrests of thousands of undocumented workers – nearly all of whom were migrant workers from Mexico or Central America. Those detained were charged with presenting false information regarding their immigration status, use of false documentation to obtain employment, or overstaying a visa. If convicted of these charges, the immigrants would face penalties ranging from two to ten years in prison plus fines up to $250,000 in addition to deportation. Most of those rounded up, simply opted for deportation. As with Operation Tarmac, Wagon Train yielded no evidence of terrorist activity; the deported workers had no links to terrorist organizations (Sampaio 2015, Chapter 5).

The association of Latino/a immigrants with criminality and threats to national security seriously distorts the nature of economic migration and the contributions that undocumented workers make to the U.S. economy. Labor economists have demonstrated that undocumented workers do not compete with skilled laborers for jobs, they complement them.[30] In the construction trades, for example, undocumented workers perform routine tasks on worksites, thereby freeing up skilled workers like carpenters, electricians, and plumbers to focus on their specializations. From 1990 to 2007, this division of labor increased documented workers' pay by 10 percent (Davidson 2013, 18). Although immigrants send remittances home, shoring up the local economies of their nations of origin, they spend most of the wages they earn on rent, utilities, transportation, and food, thereby contributing to local businesses in the communities in which they reside. Using their "fraudulent" social security cards, undocumented workers pay state and federal taxes and contribute to social security – for benefits they will never claim. According to Stephen Goss, the chief actuary for the Social Security Administration, "undocumented workers contribute about $15 billion a year to social security through payroll taxes. They only take out $1 billion (very few undocumented workers are eligible to receive benefits). Over the years, undocumented workers have contributed up to $300 billion, or nearly 10 percent, of the $2.7 trillion Social Security Trust Fund" (Davidson 2013, 18). Although they are working without documentation, immigrants benefit the overall economy, a fact rendered invisible by discourses that racialize and criminalize them.

To further "secure the nation," Immigration and Customs Enforcement (ICE, formerly the Immigration and Naturalization Service) launched programs in conjunction with local law enforcement agencies to identify and apprehend immigrants classified as "fugitives." Operation Return to Sender, which began in 2006, and the Secured Communities program, launched in March 2008, enlisted local police to run federal immigration checks on and share electronic data for immigrants arrested for any infraction, no matter how small (most arrests involved traffic violations, disorderly conduct, or simply unlawful entry), and to orchestrate raids in search of immigrants for whom deportation orders had been issued but not yet executed. Non-citizens with outstanding removal orders were classified as "alien absconders," a category that made undocumented migrants sound particularly menacing. Operation Community Shield, which united ICE agents with the DOJ and local police departments in cracking down on street gangs, also heightened the impression that Latino youth – citizen and noncitizen – were thugs who posed a serious threat to local communities. Initially focusing on *Mara Salvatrucha* (MS-13), a broad association of Salvadoran, Guatemalan, Honduran, Ecuadorian, and Mexican youth, Operation Community Shield expanded to target all street and prison gangs with foreign-born members, rounding up and deporting more than 5,000 gang members by 2007 (Sampaio 2015).

Although the "war on terror" was a key initiative of the G. W. Bush Administration, measures to secure national borders continued during President Obama's two terms in office. According to the Department of Homeland Security, the Obama Administration "returned" (i.e., turned back at the border) 1,609,055 undocumented migrants and "removed" 1,974,688 undocumented workers living within the U.S. from 2009 through 2013, a rate that surpassed any previous president and was nine times the rate during the early Clinton Administration. According to ICE data, 97 percent of the removals were from Mexico, Central and South America and the Caribbean.[31] More than twice as many of the removals had no criminal record, yet the Obama Administration emphasized that it was targeting "criminal aliens." Indeed, in a speech in November 2014, President Obama noted that "over the past six years, deportations of criminals are up 80 percent" (Bump 2014).

Sampaio (2015) notes that policy discourses that depict Latino/a immigrants as criminals, aliens, security risks, or indeed, terrorists have a chilling effect on Latino/a citizens as well. Not only are the highly militarized raids of worksites and neighborhoods a form of public spectacle designed to intimidate entire communities, but Latino/a citizens too are subject to mass surveillance, and are at risk of arrest in raids conducted by law enforcement officials who expect identity documents to be fraudulent. Prior to the twenty-first century U.S., citizens were not required to carry identity papers as they moved across the country. Yet, in 2010, Arizona passed a securitization measure which requires citizens to prove their national identity, lest they be mistaken for an undocumented worker and arrested. The "Support Our Law Enforcement and Safe Neighborhoods Act" (S.B. 1070) made it a misdemeanor for an alien to be in Arizona without carrying proof of lawful entry, and authorized state law enforcement officers to determine an individual's immigration status during a "lawful stop, detention or arrest," when there is reasonable suspicion that an individual is an "illegal immigrant." The Arizona law, thus, mandates racial profiling, leaving it to the local police to decide who "looks" undocumented. Although the American Civil Liberties Union challenged the constitutionality of the act, the U.S. Supreme Court has upheld the provision that requires police to determine the immigration status of someone arrested or detained when there is "reasonable suspicion" they are not in the U.S. legally. Since its passage in 2010, two dozen states introduced similar legislation, and five states have passed comparable bills (Alabama, Georgia, Indiana, South Carolina and Utah). Under these provisions, "driving while Latino/a" or "walking while Latino/a" is becoming as perilous as driving or walking while Black.

The voting rights of citizens have also been under attack since 2010. Twenty-two states (18 of which have Republican-controlled legislatures and executives) have passed laws that make it more difficult to register to vote, requiring proof of citizenship to register, cutting back on early voting, eliminating election day registration, and imposing new restrictions on voter registration drives. Although proponents of these restrictions claim that they are simply trying to prevent voter fraud, the laws target African American and Latino/a communities for "voter suppression." A study by the Brennan Center for Justice at the New York University Law School found that "of the 11 states with the highest African American turnout in 2008, 7 passed laws making it harder to vote. Of the 12 states with the largest Hispanic population growth in the 2010 Census, 9 have new restrictions in place. And of the 15 states that used to be monitored closely under the Voting Rights Act because of a history of racial discrimination in elections, nine passed new restrictions" (Weiser and Opsal 2014). These laws also raise financial obstacles to voting as it can cost anywhere from $100 to $175 to obtain proof of citizenship when fees, transportation, and wages lost while waiting are taken into consideration.

Although the 14th Amendment to the U.S. Constitution guarantees citizenship to anyone born on U.S. soil, in 2013 the state of Texas prohibited registrars from issuing birth certificates to babies whose parents provided *matriculas*, identification cards issued by Mexican consulates in the United States, rather than a U.S. driver's license or visa as a valid form of identification. Hundreds of immigrant parents along the southern Texas border have been denied birth certificates for U.S.-born children, creating a critical disadvantage for Latino/a children who have a right to access medical care, travel, school enrollment and other benefits available to U.S. citizens (Hennessy-Fiske 2015).[32]

Conclusion

Embodied power operates in complex ways in the contemporary United States, affecting domestic and foreign policy. Despite formal guarantees of equal citizenship, racialized gendering is used by local, state, and federal governments to produce and maintain asymmetries with respect to individual liberties and immunities, educational and employment opportunities, income and wealth disparities, prospects for upward mobility, as well as civil and political rights. Far from marking natural attributes, racialization and gendering are productive processes with palpable effects. Racialized-gendering involves the production of difference, political asymmetries, and social hierarchies that simultaneously create the dominant and the subordinate. Whether manifested in explicit racial profiling or cast in "race-neutral" language, racialized gendering can subject people of color to heightened scrutiny, police surveillance, arrest, detention, deportation, or expatriation. Whether innocent or guilty, those racialized as "Black," "Brown," "Latino/a" or "Muslim" are positioned as objects of reasonable suspicion and subjected to unwarranted intrusions by the state. Whether constructed as suspicious or as threats, people of color are situated in public discourse as matters of collective concern – rather than as equal members of the collective – and they are subjected to regulation in ways that lack the beneficial aspects of privacy associated with negative liberty and the constitutional guarantees of citizenship. Embodied power affirms the privileges of some, while placing others beyond the boundaries of belonging, a placement that can jeopardize livelihoods, custody of one's children, the capacity to exercise the rights of citizenship, physical integrity, and even life itself.

In the international sphere, recent deployment of embodied power entails abrogation of the Geneva Convention, indefinite detention of those classified as "enemy combatants" and noncitizens believed to be associated with newly designated terrorist networks, the establishment of military tribunals, and denial of detainees' fundamental rights to *habeas corpus*, the presumption of innocence, the right to be informed of the charges against them, and the right to legal counsel. Racialized gendering has legitimated sustained military interventions to produce regime change in Afghanistan and Iraq; and it has structured daily interactions between the military forces of the "coalition of the willing" and local residents.

Whether exercised in the domestic sphere or in the context of international relations, embodied power is far too pervasive to be neglected by those committed to the study of contemporary politics.

Notes

1 Although many associate claims about white privilege with critical race studies of the late twentieth century, numerous pieces of legislation passed by the U.S. Congress and by state legislatures made special provisions for "white" persons, dating from the 1790s. Public debates over a host of issues also made explicit reference to color as a criterion for demarcating privilege and disadvantage as this chapter documents. For a fascinating discussion of litigation over who counts as "white" and the extraordinary equivocation of the courts on that question, see Ian Haney-Lopez (1996).

2 In "The Souls of White Folks" (1910), Du Bois noted that the invention of "race" was very recent, the product of a certain way of thinking advanced by Europeans and Americans of European descent. "This assumption that of all the hues of God whiteness alone is inherently and obviously better than brownness or tan leads to curious acts ... The European world is using black and brown men for all the uses which men know. Slowly but surely white culture is evolving the theory that 'darkies' are born beasts of burden for white folk. It were silly to think otherwise, cries the cultured world, with stronger and shriller accord. The supporting arguments grow and twist themselves in the mouths of merchant, scientist, soldier, traveler, writer, and missionary: Darker peoples are dark in mind as well as in body; of dark, uncertain, and imperfect descent; of frailer, cheaper stuff; they are cowards in the face of mausers and maxims; they have no feelings, aspirations, and loves; they are fools, illogical idiots, – 'half-devil and half-child' ... But what on earth is whiteness? ... Whiteness is the ownership of the earth forever and ever, Amen!"

3 By contrast, marriage between Native men and white women was actively discouraged as a threat to the purity of "white blood." For a discussion of concerns about blood mixtures and white "hypodescent," see Kitch (2009).

4 The restriction of citizenship to "free white persons" was replicated in the Nationality Acts of 1870 and 1906. In *Reproducing the State*, Jacquelyn Stevens (1999) introduces the concept of "race-nation" to emphasize that state control over the form of intimate

relationships has been the key means through which to determine the membership in a political society. In marked contrast to liberal origin myths about the social contract, links between citizens and states have been forged by laws pertaining to birth, kinship, and territory.

5 In the same era that it held that women were not "persons" in the constitutional sense, the U.S. Supreme Court ruled that corporations were "persons" in this sense and, as such, entitled to certain rights and immunities. See, for example, Chief Justice Morrison Waite's dicta in *Santa Clara County v. Southern Pacific Railroad* (118 U.S. 394, 1886), and the Court's opinion in *Pembina Consolidated Silver Mining Co. v. Pennsylvania* (125 U.S. 181, 1888): "Under the designation of 'person', there is no doubt that a private corporation is included."

6 Lake and Reynolds (2008, 322) also note that in 1946 when asked to reflect upon the causes of World War II, the emperor of Japan tied war to rejection of the proposed equality clause: "If we ask the reason for this war, it lies in the contents of the peace treaty signed at the end of the First World War. The racial equality proposal demanded by Japan was not accepted by the powers. The discriminatory sentiment between the white and yellow races remains, as always, and the rejections of immigrants in California. These were enough to anger the Japanese people."

7 Wacquant's reference to an "imagined community" is a covert reference to Benedict Anderson's (1991) definition of a nation.

8 The all-white school board in Prince Edward County, Virginia, for example, decided to close the public schools for four years rather than integrate, removing books and school furniture to the new Christian Academy. For detailed accounts, see Titus (2014) and Green (2015).

9 As George Lipsitz (2011, 35) points out, however, it is precisely the maintenance of residential segregation that allows "the advocates of expressly racist policies to disavow any racial intent."

10 In one of his final official acts, Attorney General Eric Holder issued guidelines to prevent racial profiling in December 2014. Seven U.S. states have laws prohibiting racial profiling, but these laws are seldom enforced.

11 U.S. Department of Justice, *Arrest Related Deaths, 2003–2009*, p. 1.

12 Ibid., p6.

13 Forensic genetic analysis examines the arrangement of alleles located at a selected number of loci on the DNA molecule, where the sequence varies greatly among individuals. The sequence at each position is converted into a series of numbers, which becomes the DNA profile. The FBI standard uses 13 loci to create a profile. If two samples match at all 13 loci, the odds are extremely high that they come from the same individual. If fewer than 13 match, it suggests a relative of the person arrested may be involved (Roberts 2011, 268).

14 Alexander argues that the use of incarceration as a mechanism of subordination and social control becomes clear when systems of punishment are viewed in comparative perspective. "Between 1960 and 1990, official crime rates in Finland, Germany and the U.S. were close to identical. Yet the U.S. incarceration rate quadrupled, while the Finnish rate fell by 60 percent and the German rate remained stable" (2011, 7).

15 Ian Haney-Lopez (2014) has noted that contemporary prison labor systems replicate the "Convict Leasing" program that was launched post-Reconstruction and remained operative until the mid-1940s. "The 13th Amendment allows involuntary servitude as punishment for crime whereof the party shall have been duly convicted. To meet its economic needs, the South built a criminal justice system around imprisoning Blacks. Fines for minor infractions morphed into jail time. Selective prosecution of Blacks surged. New crimes made their way onto the books … then jails leased convicts out as laborers … At one point, Alabama earned nearly 12 percent of its total annual revenue from leasing convicts to private enterprise (plantations, corporations, mines, steel

manufacturing) (39) ... Those men swallowed alive by the prison-leasing system were almost always 'convicts' only as a thin, cruel subterfuge, arrested by self-serving sheriffs and tried before venal judges for trivial offenses (40) ... The system's ubiquity and caprice assured that virtually no Black man was safe unless under the protection and control of a white landowner or employer ... Blacks went into sharecropping, a relationship itself akin to slavery, partly because they needed white bosses to protect them" (41).

16 U.S. Representative Jan Meyers [R-KS] was one of the first to frame welfare reform in terms of personal responsibility. This quote was taken from a floor speech accompanying her introduction of welfare reform legislation in early 1993. Although this bill died in committee during the 103rd Congress, many of its provisions were incorporated in the Personal Responsibility and Work Opportunity Reconciliation Act of 1996.

17 As the Center on Hunger, Poverty and Nutritional Policy at Tufts University documented, these assumptions conflict with the facts. The growth of single-parent families has been primarily among the non-poor. From 1970 to 1990, the number of female-headed households increased from 6 million to 11 million, mostly among the non-poor. Sixty-five percent of single-parent families were not living in poverty (Brown 1995). Moreover, the Census Bureau demonstrated that economic factors such as low-wage jobs accounted for approximately 85 percent of the child poverty rate. A 1993 Census Bureau study showed that the poverty rate was due mainly to changes in the labor market and the structure of the economy.

18 The 1996 Act required 30 hours/week of unwaged work in order to receive benefits under Temporary Assistance to Needy Families (TANF); the number of workfare hours was increased to 40 during the George W. Bush Administration.

19 Between 1919 and 1964 at least 30 states passed legislation to allow involuntary sterilization for "eugenic" purposes. In 1972 alone, the federal government funded 100,000 sterilizations of Black women. In Puerto Rico, eugenic legislation was passed in the late 1930s; by the 1970s, more than 35 percent of women of childbearing age had been sterilized (Davis 2003, 152).

20 As White and Rog (2004, 393) have documented, 1 in 10 children in predominantly Black Central Harlem is taken into foster care, compared with 1 in 19 children in Latino-dominated Hunts Point and 1 in 200 white children in predominantly white Ridgewood and Glendale in Queens.

21 According to the Children's Bureau (2012), American Indian/Alaska Native children have the highest rates of placement in foster care.

22 The full title of the legislation is Uniting and Strengthening America by Providing Appropriate Tools Required to Intercept and Obstruct Terrorism Act; USA PATRIOT Act is the acronym.

23 In 2015, the Second Circuit Court of Appeals reinstated complaints in a lawsuit against former Justice Department officials, charged with violating the rights of Arab or Muslim immigrants in the immediate months after the September 11th terrorist attacks. The lawsuit, which had been filed on behalf of eight former detainees in 2002 by the Center for Constitutional Rights, seeks to hold former Attorney General John Ashcroft, former FBI Director Robert Mueller, and former Commissioner of the Immigration and Naturalization Service James W. Ziglar accountable for subjecting immigrants to harsh confinement on the basis of their race, national origin, and religion. (Metropolitan Detention Center (MDC) and Passaic County Jail officials were also named as defendants in the lawsuit.) In January 2013, a federal court had dismissed the complaints after concluding there was no evidence the officials had any "intent to punish" the plaintiffs, who allege their rights were violated. In reversing this decision, the Second Circuit Court of Appeals held that the conditions of confinement were

established and executed with punitive intent and hence, the Justice Department officials were not entitled to "qualified immunity."
24 The website created by the Department of Justice to explain the USA PATRIOT Act is subtitled "Preserving Life and Liberty" (www.justice.gov/archive/ll/highlights.htm).
25 According to the Open Society Foundation's report *Globalizing Torture*, the following nations assisted the CIA with extraordinary rendition: Afghanistan, Albania, Algeria, Australia, Austria, Azerbaijan, Belgium, Bosnia-Herzegovina, Canada, Croatia, Cyprus, the Czech Republic, Denmark, Djibouti, Egypt, Ethiopia, Finland, Gambia, Georgia, Germany, Greece, Hong Kong, Iceland, Indonesia, Iran, Ireland, Italy, Jordan, Kenya, Libya, Lithuania, Macedonia, Malawi, Malaysia, Mauritania, Morocco, Pakistan, Poland, Portugal, Romania, Saudi Arabia, Somalia, South Africa, Spain, Sri Lanka, Sweden, Syria, Thailand, Turkey, United Arab Emirates, United Kingdom, Uzbekistan, Yemen, and Zimbabwe.
26 These "softening up" tactics were declared to be legally permissible by the U.S. Attorney General and officially authorized by the G.W. Bush Administration, and in October 2006, by the U.S. Congress.
27 Briggs notes that abusive treatment of detainees is a normal part of the U.S. conduct of war, dating at least to the 1899–1902 Philippine-American war. The most recent techniques emerged in the context of CIA funded research between 1953 and 1964 (2015, 27–28).
28 Philip Kretsedemas (2008) notes that Immigration and Customs Enforcement (ICE) uses memoranda of understanding to recruit states as partners in immigration enforcement, but state legislatures have also passed more than 300 laws since 2001 requiring police and state workers to verify immigration status and apprehend unauthorized immigrants.
29 Sampaio (2015) traces the proliferation of these militarized operations over the first decade of the twenty-first century. Like Operation Tarmac, Operation Safe Travels, Operation Joint Venture, Operation Access Denied, Operation Fly Trap, Operation Safe Sky, and Operation Plane View involved multiple federal agencies including major departments (Defense, Justice, Homeland Security, Transportation, Labor, Agriculture), as well as a myriad of agencies and bureaus within them (i.e., INS, FBI, Social Security Administration/Office of the Inspector General, Transportation Security Administration, U.S. Marshals Office, U.S. Attorney's Office, Federal Aviation Administration, Civil Aviation Security Field Office, U.S. Customs).
30 The picture is not quite as straightforward with respect to competition for jobs typically held by U.S. adults who do not have high school diplomas. Several studies have suggested that undocumented workers have lowered the wages of unskilled service workers from 0.4 to 7.4 percent (Davidson 2013, 17).
31 U.S. Immigration and Customs Enforcement. FY 2013 ICE Immigration Removals, *ERO Annual Report*, www.ice.gov/doclib/about/offices/ero/pdf/2013-ice-immigration-removals.pdf.
32 Attorneys representing 19 parents of 23 children denied birth certificates filed a law suit in U.S. District in Austin in May 2015, arguing that the decisions are unconstitutional and an unlawful form of racial discrimination.

5
WAYS OF SEEING, MODES OF BEING

> Racialization does not just produce an "other" – it also produces the same.
> *(Laura Briggs 2015, 33)*

> The Eurocentric perspective of knowledge operates as a mirror that distorts what it reflects ... the image perceived is not just composite, but partial and distorted.
> *(Anibal Quijano 2000, 556)*

In *Ways of Seeing*, a BBC series aired in 1972 and subsequently published as a book, art historian John Berger advanced a simple claim: "The way we see things is affected by what we know or what we believe" (Berger 1972, 8). Crystallizing insights from the philosophy of science, Berger's claim challenged key tenets of modern empiricism,[1] most notably, the view of the mind as a mirror that faithfully reflects the external world. Using examples from visual culture, Berger drew attention to several features of perception at odds with notions of "neutral observation." Perception is partial, both in the sense that it is incomplete and in the sense that it attends to things of interest to the viewer: "we only see what we look at. To look is an act of choice" (Berger 1972, 8). Perception is context dependent: "We never look at just one thing; we are always looking at the relation between things and ourselves" (Berger 1972, 9). In addition, perception is structured by social values. Rather than capturing "things as they are" – altogether independent of the mind of the knower, Berger emphasized that "every image is humanly created and embodies a way of seeing" (Berger 1972, 10). Berger sought to alter common-sense assumptions about perception in order to foster critical reflection about sexist and consumption-oriented ways of seeing circulating in the second-half of the twentieth century. His insights also have important ramifications for the study of politics.

Empiricist assumptions have been central to the development of the discipline of political science and to the scientific study of politics in the twentieth and twenty-first century (Tanenhaus and Somit 1967; Greenstein and Polsby 1975; Finifter 1983; Seidelman and Harpham 1985).[2] Positing a simple and direct relation between knower and known, mainstream approaches within the discipline suggest that the senses can be trained to accurately report the external world, minimizing subjectivity, bias, and cultural or linguistic distortions. Precisely because controlled observation is understood to purge bias, empiricist strategies for the acquisition of knowledge are said to be "neutral" and "value-free." From the empiricist view, scientific investigations can grasp objective reality, because the subjectivity of individual observers can be controlled through careful adherence to quantitative analytical techniques, hypothesis testing, and theory generation.

As Berger pointed out, however, confidence about an unmediated apprehension of the "given" by a receptive observer misconstrues both the nature of perception and the nature of the world. Controlled observation does not "clear" the mind to receive an image of the given, it imposes a particular order upon the external world through a process of selection, interpretation and directed attention. Observation is always linguistically and culturally mediated. Scientific observation adds additional filters devised in accordance with discipline-specific norms. As Karl Popper (1959, 1972a, 1972b) pointed out, scientific observation is necessarily theory-laden. It begins not from "nothing," nor from the "neutral" perception of given relations, but rather from immersion in a scientific tradition which provides frames of reference or conceptual schemes that organize reality and shape the problems for further investigation. Within political science, observations of the political world are "theory-laden." They depend on a constellation of theoretical presuppositions that accredit certain data as significant. Theoretical presuppositions shape perception and determine what will be taken as a "fact"; they confer meaning on experience and control the demarcation of significant from trivial events; they afford criteria of relevance according to which facts can be organized, tests envisioned and the acceptability or unacceptability of scientific conclusions assessed; they accredit particular models of explanation and strategies of understanding; and they sustain specific methodological techniques for gathering, classifying, and analyzing data. Theoretical presuppositions set the terms of disciplinary debate and organize the elements of political research. Moreover, they typically do so at a tacit or preconscious level and for this reason, they appear to hold unquestionable authority.

As critics of mainstream political science have long noted, "facts" can be collected only after they have been designated as worthy of attention by theoretical presuppositions. A "fact" is a theoretically constituted entity. Indeed, "the noun, 'experience', the verb, 'to experience' and the adjective 'empirical' are not univocal terms that can be transferred from one system to another without change of meaning ... Experience does not come labeled as 'empirical', nor does it come self-certified as such. What we call experience depends upon assumptions hidden beyond scrutiny which define it and which in turn it supports" (Vivas 1960, 76). Any attempt to identify an "unmediated fact" must mistake the conventional for the "natural," as in cases which define "brute facts" as "social facts which are largely the product of well-understood, reliable tools, facts that are not likely to be vitiated by pitfalls ... in part [because of] the ease and certainty with which [they] can be determined and in part [because of] the incontestability of [their] conceptual base" (Murray 1983, 321). Alternatively, the attempt to conceive a "fact" that exists prior to any description of it, prior to any theoretical or conceptual mediation, must generate an empty notion of something completely unspecified and unspecifiable, a notion that will be of little use to science (Williams 1985, 138). "Ideally, scientists would like to examine the structure of the world which exists independent of our knowledge – but the nature of perception and the role of presuppositions preclude direct access to it: the only access available is through theory-directed research" (Brown 1977, 108).

This chapter explores some of the theoretical presuppositions that organize and structure political research and popular understandings in ways that render embodied power invisible. Presumptions about individualism, colorblind perception, methodological individualism and methodological nationalism singly and in combination make it exceptionally difficult to perceive racialization, gendering, and sexualization. By determining the meanings of observed events, identifying relevant data and significant problems for investigation, indicating strategies for solving problems and methods by which to test the validity of proposed solutions, these ways of seeing push embodied power below the threshold of visibility.

Distinctive ways of seeing configure the visible and the intelligible, ordering the world in ways that make certain courses of action reasonable and certain forms of explanation plausible. By drawing attention to some things and not others, they shape evidence, which in turn plays a formative role in public opinion, policy debates, litigation, and social relations. As interpretive frameworks, individualism, colorblindness, methodological individualism and methodological nationalism structure belief – and relations of doubt, skepticism, uncertainty, and trust that follow from belief. By providing constellations of concepts that structure perception, these ways of seeing influence understandings of the past, present, and future. The following sections explore how four distinctive ways of seeing – individualism, colorblindness, methodological individualism, and methodological nationalism – structure a conceptual order that carries important implications not only for interpersonal relations and social policies, but also for transnational activism, and international affairs.

Individualism

Integral to the overthrow of ascriptive hierarchies associated with feudalism, liberal individualism postulates a fundamental equality of persons and insists that each person has a right to freedom and self-determination. What it means to be an individual, the processes by which individual identity is constituted, the nature of the individual's relation to other people and to social institutions, and the scope and depth of the possibilities for self-realization, however, have been topics of intense debate among those committed to the protection of individualism.[3]

As a regime of rights, individualism posits abstract individuals unencumbered by race, sex, gender, ethnicity or sexuality. As suggested by the doctrine of legal neutrality, constitutions recognize "citizens" and "persons," who appear to be altogether disembodied. In positing formal equality, individualism asserts that all that differentiates people within the private sphere is, in principle, irrelevant in the eyes of the law. The system of public law concretizes this equal status by guaranteeing equal rights and immunities to all regardless of the differences in group membership, wealth, power, and prestige that characterize their existence in the private sphere. The status of the citizen purportedly enshrines the essential equality of all persons despite whatever differences may exist in private life. It affords markedly different individuals a formal public persona as a basis for meaningful equality in the political realm.

In a system of representative government serving a society known for its heterogeneity and multiplicity of interests, liberal individualism becomes synonymous with the right to participate for purposes of self-protection and to form groups to promote private interests. Each individual is equally entitled to compete in the public forum to press claims, to advance interests, and to air perceived grievances. The guarantee of equal political rights offers the assurance to individuals and to groups that their views will receive due consideration in the policy-making process. Equal citizenship affords' different persons an equal weapon for self-defense through the simple act of political participation. Moreover, because representative governments define fair laws in procedural rather than substantive terms, the right to participate is depicted as the most meaningful equality that the state can accord its citizens. Whether wealthy or poor, Black, Latino, Asian American or white, man or woman, straight or gay, the individual as citizen can, in principle, influence the legislative process. The inequalities characteristic of the private sphere are supposedly overridden by equal political rights in the political sphere. Indeed, claims about the "equality of all citizens" immunize liberal individualism from the systemic effects of racial, gender, and sexual hierarchies.

The liberal creed assumes that the formal equality of citizens will not be contaminated by the inequality characteristic of the private realm. In donning the public persona of the citizen, the individual is expected to transcend the experiences of private life. Constraints imposed by the realities of socioeconomic status, class differentials, or collective identities based on race, sex, sexuality, ethnicity or religion are expected to be obliterated by the uplifting balm of equality before the law. Indeed, in the latest theoretical reformulation of the liberal creed, John Rawls (1971) claimed that the experience of equal citizenship is sufficiently powerful to generate a sense of "being equal" in the self-image of each citizen. The political equality guaranteed by a just constitution culminates in the dissemination of equality of self-respect.[4]

As a normative precept endorsing equality before the law, individualism has many virtues, but as a way of seeing the world, it also has a number of drawbacks. It renders the processes and effects of racialization and gendering unintelligible. The scripted practices of domination and subordination that situate individuals as members of particular races, sexes, and ethnicities are privatized. The role of the state in producing and sustaining inequalities is made inconceivable by the very notion of formal equality and legal neutrality. Systematic oppression is reduced to private troubles, which the self-determining individual is expected to rise above. By minimizing persistent structural constraints, individualism masks the contradictions that arise when formal equality coexists with systemic mechanisms of exclusion.

Feminist scholars have pointed out that the abstract individual is far from disembodied. In fields as diverse as law, philosophy, and science, the unmarked individual is defined in terms of norms grounded in the experiences of white, privileged men (Brown 1995, Scott 1996, Squires 1999). Struggles for equality, then, can require those subordinated by racialized gendering to assimilate to norms premised on their exclusion. Thus, individualism sustains a kind of tokenism, promoting women who "act like men" and people of color who "act white," which insulates exclusionary norms from critical interrogation and transformation. To paraphrase Wendy Brown (1995, 153), "equality as sameness is a [raced-] gendered formulation of equality because it secures [race and] gender privilege through naming women [and people of color] as difference and [white] men as the neutral standard of the same."

Proponents of individualism, who conflate neutrality with white male-defined norms, often demand forms of equal (i.e., identical) treatment that mask the double-binds, which result from the exercise of embodied power. When women, for example, are expected to manifest self-sacrifice and subservience – to subordinate their interests to those of family, partner, spouse, boss – they cannot conform to the expectations for an unencumbered individual. Recent studies of domestic labor, for example, indicate that women who work outside the home continue to work fifteen hours more per week than their male partners despite the fact that surveys indicate that 80 percent of women and 70 percent of men report that they want an egalitarian relationship in which they share breadwinning and family care responsibilities (Gerson 2010). Yet, the desire for equality is elusive: "women are still paid less at every educational level and in every job category. They are less likely than men to hold jobs that offer flexibility or family-friendly benefits. When they become mothers, they face more scrutiny and prejudice on the job than fathers do" (Coontz 2013, SR 7). When the demands of child-care provision and employment conflict, women working in professional positions are "twice as likely to quit work as other married mothers when their husbands work 50 hours or more a week and more than three times as likely to quit when their husbands work 60 hours or more" each week

(Coontz 2013, SR7). Although they frame their decisions to give priority to mothering as an individual choice, the choice to stay home comes with a significant price tag. "Thirty percent of opt-out moms who wanted to rejoin the labor force were unable to do so, and of those who did return, only 40 percent landed full-time professional jobs ... the typical college-educated woman lost more than one million dollars in life-time earnings and foregone retirement benefits" as the penalty for opting out (Coontz 2013, SR 6).

Many women workers in the United States do not have the luxury of opting out. Class and race profoundly affect decisions about mothering in ways that defy norms concerning equal individuals. In 40 percent of the households with children under the age of 18, women are the primary or sole breadwinners. Women hold a disproportionate share of poorly paid jobs (i.e., earning less than $10/hour): women are 76 percent of the lowest-waged workers; women of color constitute 37 percent of the lowest-paid workers; 24 percent of the lowest-waged workers are mothers with children under the age of 18. Low-income women who are sole breadwinners cannot choose to stay home to care for their children. Their incomes are essential to family survival. Those who lose their jobs and apply for Temporary Assistance to Needy Families (TANF) are required by law to devote 40 hours/week to unwaged labor as a condition for the receipt of benefits. To "choose" welfare is to choose mandatory work for benefits whose dollar equivalent is far below minimum wage rates – regardless of the age of children living at home. Individualism as a way of seeing nullifies the factors that constrain such choices, as well as their long-term effects. Within an individualist frame, a choice is a choice, regardless of the constraints that order individual preferences.

The individualist emphasis on choice frames group membership along the lines of voluntary association: individuals choose the groups to which they wish to belong, the duration of their membership, and their conditions of participation. Yet, this frame makes it difficult to perceive the operations of embodied power either in the production of racialized-gendered groups associated with a host of negative attributes, or in the placement of individuals within those groups – regardless of their wishes. As legal scholar Ian Haney-Lopez (2014, 87–88) has noted, "from the outset race was believed to involve both physical differences and distinctions in culture, behavior, and ability. Supreme Court Justice Harlan referred to 'lazy nigger, dirty Mexican, sneaky Chink' ... these vile terms inseparably conjoined biology and behavior: physical distinctions supposedly corresponded to innate behavior and cultural deficiencies. Indeed, as a way to justify inequality, race did its most destructive work by emphasizing temperament and ability, rather than mere differences in integument. More than skin pigment, it was nonwhite laziness, filthiness, and mendacity – and correspondingly, white industry, hygiene, and honesty – that supposedly explained inferior and superior positions in society."

Contrary to liberal individualist presumptions, there is nothing volitional about being racialized. Consider, for example, the 2009 arrest of Harvard Professor

Henry Louis Gates at his home in Cambridge, Massachusetts. Despite providing proof of residence in the form of both Harvard ID card and Massachusetts driver's license, Professor Gates was arrested and charged with disorderly conduct. The police, who had been summoned to the house by a neighbor on suspicion of a possible break-in, had convincing evidence that Professor Gates was not a burglar. But the combustible mix of racial profiling, presumptions about Black men in affluent white neighborhoods, and a perception of disrespect for police authority when Professor Gates refused to step out of his house as the white police officer demanded created the disorder with which Professor Gates was charged. Neither his eminence as a scholar nor his affluence as a Harvard professor could rescue Gates from the indignity of arrest, fingerprinting, and being processed at the local jail. The microphysics of embodied power in this instance involved the instant criminalization of a Black man, the suspension of any presumption of innocence, and the expectation of deference when a Black civilian interacts with white police. Individualism finds these dimensions of gendered racialization incomprehensible, preferring modes of accountability that individualize praise and blame. A report on the incident commissioned by the Cambridge Police Department, for example, attributed responsibility for the immediate misunderstanding and failed communications to both men. Entitled *Missed Opportunities, Shared Responsibilities*, the report did not acknowledge any power differentials between Black arrestee and white police officer; it simply concluded that "both of the individuals contributed to the outcome unintentionally" (Thompson 2010).

In failing to recognize how racialized-gendered subordination creates webs of relation that profoundly affect self-understanding, possibilities for belonging, prospects for freedom, and perceptions of linked fate with specific others, individualism misses political dimensions of individual aspiration and resistance. Ensnared by structures of domination while simultaneously exposed to the liberal notions of unfettered selves, the subordinated may internalize sexist, racist, and heteronormative stereotypes that circumscribe their desires and aspirations and burden them with potent doses of self-doubt and self-loathing. Liberation groups seek to transform internalized self-hatred into active modes of resistance, forging collective identities, and mobilizing groups to press for social transformation. Whether in the form of national independence struggles, or racial and sexual empowerment movements, embodied power engenders manifold modes of resistance – forms of oppositional politics to overcome marginalization by creating political institutions that can foster equal recognition, equal respect, and more equitable distribution of resources. Mired in assumptions about formal equality and individual opportunity, individualism is often hard pressed to make sense of such transformative politics. On the contrary, individualism endorses the status quo as an approximation of a just society, in which benefits and burdens are distributed on the basis of individual talent, effort, hard work, and desert. Starting from the premise of individual equality, and holding individuals responsible for the conditions under which they live, individualism remains impervious to the systemic racialized-gendered inequalities that structure contemporary life. Thus, Ian Haney-Lopez (2014, 36–37) notes:

> Most whites accept the connection between minorities and crime and by extension widespread racial inequality in society as part of the natural order of things ... Society is stratified by race, but this is not a social problem so much as an unpleasant fact of life ... Because many whites believe that major social institutions are racially fair *and* include vast racial disparities, simply informing them about dramatic race-correlated differences will not change their beliefs. Instead, and perversely, among those who accept dramatic racial inequalities as a normal and legitimate feature of society, hearing about discrepancies alone tends to solidify their beliefs regarding minority failings and society's basic fairness.

As a way of seeing, individualism accredits the existing order, assuming that each person's position within that order has been earned by personal effort, quite independent of race, gender, or sexual orientation.

Colorblind Perception

The idea that law and policy ought to be colorblind has a noble pedigree. It can be traced to an historic dissent by Justice John Marshall Harlan in *Plessy v. Ferguson* (163 U.S. 537, 1896) – the case in which the U.S. Supreme Court majority ruled that "separate but equal" was compatible with the 14th Amendment Equal Protection Clause. Quoting from the brief prepared by Homer Plessy's attorney Albion Tourgée, Justice Harlan articulated a norm that *ought* to be binding on U.S. law: "Our Constitution is colorblind, and neither knows nor tolerates classes among citizens" (559). Faced with the consolidation of a system of racial apartheid in the post-Reconstruction era, African American intellectuals including Tourgée used the metaphor of colorblind perception to envision an ideal of equality (Condit and Lucaites 1993). That ideal has echoed through countless anti-racism mobilizations, perhaps most famously in Martin Luther King's 1963 Dream Speech: "I have a dream that my four little children will one day live in a nation where they will not be judged by the color of their skin but by the content of their character." In 1963, as in 1896, colorblindness was invoked as an aspiration – not as a description of the world as it is.

Colorblindness as a way of seeing has quite a different valence than colorblindness as an aspiration. Indeed, colorblindness as a mode of perception makes growing racial inequalities invisible and unintelligible. Public opinion polls over four decades indicate that white Americans are strong believers in racial equality and actively disavow holding racist views or harboring racist animosities. "Colorblind" is how they characterize their stance, claiming they "do not see color, [do] not use color in evaluating people or situations, and thus believe themselves not to be contributing to whatever racial differences exist" (Rose 2013, 448). Indeed, taking the civil rights movement to have been a success, many white citizens consider it a testament to the quality of U.S. democracy that *de jure* segregation has ended, discrimination on the basis of race, sex, religion, or disability has been outlawed, an African American has twice been elected president of the United States, and the nation is well into a "post-racial" era. Convinced that blatant racism has long been left behind, many whites assume that African Americans are flourishing in the 21st-century United States.

According to a 2014 Gallop Poll, most whites believe that Blacks living in the U.S. have the same opportunities as whites: 74 percent reported that Blacks have equal employment opportunities; 80 percent believe educational opportunities to be equal; 85 percent claimed that Blacks and whites enjoyed equal housing. In 2009, 61 percent of whites said that "Blacks had achieved racial equality," up from 43 percent in 2000. A 2011 poll by the Pew Research Center indicated that more than half of whites thought Blacks, on average, were doing as well or better than whites financially. According to Michael Norton and Samuel Sommers (2011), not only do whites tend to think that anti-Black racism has been eliminated, many whites believe that racism against whites has increased significantly as racism against Blacks has decreased. In a series of polls, whites rated anti-white bias as more prevalent in the twenty-first-century U.S. than anti-Black bias (Norton and Sommers 2011). Although the perception of white victimization is not supported by any empirical evidence, it seems to be an artefact of colorblind perception. Recurrent polls sponsored by the *Washington Post*, the Kaiser Family Foundation and Harvard University have found that a majority of whites believe that Blacks are as well off or better off than whites: 46 percent of whites report that Blacks on average held jobs of equal quality to those of whites, 6 percent said that Blacks had jobs that were "a little better" than those held by whites, and another 6 percent said Blacks had jobs that were "a lot better" than those held by whites. Because an overwhelming majority of whites believe that Blacks have an equal chance to succeed, they also report that whites bear no responsibility for the problems Blacks face today, and that it is not the responsibility of government to ensure that all races have equal jobs, pay, or housing (Fletcher 2014).

Thus, colorblindness insulates whites from the glaring evidence of racial inequality in contemporary society. Census Bureau statistics and social science reports that document growing racial inequality are deemed to lack credibility. Certain facts that illuminate the effects of racialization and gendering become imperceptible, such as the fact that the median net worth of white households is 14.2 times greater than the wealth of Black households and 10.3 times greater than the wealth of Latina/o households. In 2012, 28 percent of African Americans, and 27 percent of Latino/as were poor compared to 10 percent of whites. One third of Black and Latino children grow up in poverty, compared with 13 percent of white children. Between 2000 and 2010, whites experienced a 7 percent drop in household income, while African Americans suffered a 17 percent decrease and Latinos, an 11 percent decrease (Harris 2012). The wealth gap between Blacks and whites increased fourfold between 1984 and 2007 (Roberts 2011, 297). According to the Centers for Disease Control (2013), the rates of premature death (before age 75) from strokes and coronary heart disease remain significantly higher for African Americans; the infant mortality rate for African American women was more than double that of white women; in 2010, Black women were four times more likely to die of pregnancy-related complications than white women – a death gap that has not improved in 20 years (Roberts 2011). Despite such glaring statistical disparities, only 16 percent of whites believe that racial discrimination is a continuing problem in the United States.

Colorblindness in conjunction with assumptions about equal opportunity suggests an alternative way to make sense of systemic racialized and gendered disparities. Differences in health, wealth, income, and mortality are attributed to biological difference, cultural depravity, or individual irresponsibility (Roberts 2011). Insulated from the everyday violence experienced by the racialized poor, many whites hold the poor responsible for their own plight (Quijano 2000). Convictions about colorblind perception rule out discrimination as an explanation for inequality, leaving racialized and gendered stereotypes to account for disparate outcomes (Haney-Lopez 2014, 78). As a way of seeing, colorblindness provides a potent immunity from "the punishing reality facing Blacks: extreme material hardships, overt discrimination, segregated and inferior schools, inadequate housing, lack of access to health care, labor market exclusion, and systematic police violence" (Haney-Lopez 2014, 85).

As a way of seeing, colorblind perception has also had dramatic effects on Supreme Court decisions over the past six decades. When the court struck down *Plessy v. Ferguson* in 1954, ruling that "separate but equal" was inherently incompatible with the Equality Clause of the 14th Amendment, it recognized that segregation imposed a "badge of inferiority" on Black citizens that had lifelong consequences. The court noted that the state's racialization of citizens involved an invidious distinction that required redress. Ending *de jure* segregation and integrating the public school system "with all deliberate speed" constituted the appropriate remedy for decades of state-sponsored racism. To undo systemic discrimination against African Americans, color-conscious remedies were essential. Rather than pretending to be colorblind, the state must take race into account to craft policies to counteract centuries of racialized gendering. With the passage of the Civil Rights Act of 1964 and the Voting Rights Act of 1965, the U.S. Congress introduced measures to ban discrimination in employment, accommodations, public programs and voting booths. With Executive Orders 11246 and 11375, the federal government launched "Affirmative Action," a policy that asked employers "to make good faith efforts to recruit qualified women and minority candidates" for open positions.[5] With these small steps, the government initiated programs to enable members of "disadvantaged groups" to surmount obstacles imposed by racial discrimination. To prevent the perpetuation of discrimination and to undo the iniquitous effects of social injustice, the government introduced policies that allowed race to be considered under narrow circumstances.[6]

The possibility of using race to craft remedies for ongoing discrimination has been enormously controversial. Claims about colorblind perception have figured prominently in those debates. As Ian Haney-Lopez (2014) has noted, a federal district court in South Carolina articulated a colorblind argument against integration as early as 1955: "The Constitution ... does not require integration. It merely forbids discrimination. It does not forbid such segregation as occurs as the result of voluntary action. It merely forbids the use of governmental power to enforce segregation" (*Briggs v. Elliott*, 132 F. Supp. 776, 777 [E.D.S.C. 1955], cited in Haney-Lopez 2014, 83). The argument that the colorblind constitution "should no more be violated to attempt integration than to preserve segregation" became a hallmark of William Rehnquist from his days as a speechwriter for Barry Goldwater through his appointment to the Supreme Court in 1972 and his elevation to Chief Justice in 1986.[7] Conservative justices appropriated rhetoric devised to promote civil rights in order to thwart government action in support of racial equality. In the *Regents of the University of California vs. Bakke* (438 U.S. 265, 1978), for example, the court curtailed the consideration of race in admissions decisions and lent credence to white claims concerning "reverse discrimination."[8] Speaking for the conservative majority, Justice Powell asserted: "There is nothing in the Constitution [which] supports the notion that [white] individuals may be asked to suffer otherwise impermissible burdens in order to enhance the societal standing of ethnic groups ... it cannot be said that the government has any greater interest in helping one individual than in refraining from harming another" (4904, 4906–4907). Skillfully avoiding the language of race, Justice Powell subsumed African Americans, Asian Americans, Latino/as and Native Americans under the rubric of "ethnicity." And in keeping with the precepts of colorblindness, he asserted that there was no warrant for treating one ethnicity different from any other. In a "nation of minorities where the white majority itself is composed of various minority groups, most of which can lay claim to a history of prior discrimination at the hands of the state and private individuals," it is the individual not the group who should be given careful consideration (4903).

The majority's opinion in the Bakke decision demonstrates how assumptions about colorblind perception in the context of individualist premises shift the discursive field from ongoing racial discrimination to legacies of past problems, transforming people of color from members of seriously disadvantaged groups to individuals indistinguishable from their white counterparts. This privileging of colorblindness took place in the context of an intense debate on the court about how to "see" race in the late twentieth century. In their dissent, Justices Brennan, Marshall, Blackmun and White insisted that racial discrimination remained an ongoing problem in the United States: "a glance at our dockets and those of the lower courts will show that even today officially sanctioned discrimination is not a thing of the past" (4912). Indeed, they argued that "the generation of minority students applying to the Davis Medical School since it opened in 1968 – most of whom were born before or about the time *Brown I* was decided – clearly have been the victims of discrimination" (4923). Justice Thurgood Marshall added: "It is unnecessary in twentieth century America to have individual Negroes demonstrate that they have been victims of racial discrimination, the racism of our society has been so pervasive that none, regardless of wealth or position has managed to escape its impact" (4931). In concluding their dissent, the justices urged that a commitment to neutral principles and to the concept of a colorblind constitution not be allowed to "become myopia which masks the reality that many 'created equal' have been treated within our lifetimes as inferior both by the law and by their fellow citizens" (4912).

Despite the direct confrontation over the distortions produced by a colorblind approach, the conservative majority consolidated by President Richard Nixon's appointment of Lewis Powell and William Rehnquist to the court has consistently held that the government cannot take race into account – whether it is being used for benign or invidious purposes. The court's current doctrine of colorblindness condemns all attempts to use racial considerations as means to redress injustice, while simultaneously rendering ongoing racial discrimination against minorities near impossible to perceive (Haney-Lopez 2014, 87). In a concurring opinion in *Adarand Constructors, Inc. v. Pena* (515 US 200, 241 [1995]), for example, Justice Clarence Thomas denounced affirmative action policies as "racial aesthetics," noting that "government sponsored racial discrimination based on benign prejudice is just as noxious as discrimination inspired by malicious prejudice." As Ian Haney-Lopez (2014, 92) has pointed out when entrenched as legal doctrine, "colorblindness shifts the harm of racism from degradation, exclusion, and exploitation to being treated differently on the basis of a socially irrelevant characteristic, which is never acceptable no matter how benign the motive. Colorblindness seems to appeal to lofty principle, while communicating sympathy for supposedly imperiled whites." Despite the appearance of racial neutrality, then, colorblindness operates as a racial code that works to white advantage: it contains racial content but is not consciously recognized as racial (Haney-Lopez 2014, 178).

Over the past six decades, colorblindness has been transformed from an aspiration for equal treatment to a code that renders systemic racial disadvantage invisible. Operating subtly to advantage whites, colorblindness places the issue of racial inequality in the past and shores up troubling notions of reverse discrimination. Within policy circles, colorblindness supports "race neutral" approaches, a political strategy of "de-racialization" to advance the interests of minority citizens (Hamilton 1977). Rather than press for race-based policies that "alienate" whites, colorblindness endorses legislation geared to help low-income people generally, such as full employment, improved income-maintenance programs, and universal health care (Aberbach and Walker 1973; Wilson 1980). Any attempt to address unique needs of people of color is condemned as racially polarizing and doomed (Swain 1993). Suggesting that race-conscious policies are tantamount to racism, "post-racialism considers efforts at racial repair politically unwise and counter-productive" (Haney-Lopez 2014, 202). The problem with such advice, however, is that it fails to come to grips with colorblindness as a means of rendering embodied power invisible. Race-neutral policies place racial justice beyond the realm of the possible, while allowing white privilege to operate unassailed.[9]

In addition to acting as a filter that screens out pervasive racial inequalities, colorblindness' demand for race-neutral policies masks racialized gendering in contemporary legislation that is neutral on its face, but has pronounced disparate racial impact. In the presidential election of 2008 – for the first time in U.S. history – African Americans turned out to vote at nearly identical rates to their white counterparts. Barack Obama's historic candidacy for the presidency accounted for this important achievement, as did a series of changes in electoral laws initiated under the auspices of the Voting Rights Act (VRA) of 1965 and its subsequent reauthorizations. To encourage Blacks to exercise their suffrage, states had introduced a number of innovations to encourage voting, such as authorizing voter registration at state department of motor vehicle offices and public assistance offices, allowing registration on election day, counting ballots mistakenly cast in the wrong precinct, and introducing early voting. Since 2010, 22 states controlled by Republican legislators have passed new laws to rescind those initiatives and to require photo identification at polling places. The grounds offered for such laws were race-neutral: to avoid voter fraud.[10] Yet the laws had a disproportionate impact on low-income people of color, particularly the elderly. The U.S. Department of Justice challenged these statutes as incompatible with the Voting Rights Act. But in 2013, the Supreme Court handed down a decision in *Shelby County v. Holder* (570 U.S. ____2013), striking down section 4b of the Voter Rights Act that established preclearance provisions, which gave the Department of Justice legal authority to challenge proposed changes in election laws in states that had engaged in voter suppression in the past.[11] Writing for the majority, Chief Justice John Roberts claimed that the preclearance provision was "based on 40 year-old facts having no logical relationship to the present day."[12] Denying the existence of racial discrimination in the 21st century, the court insisted that in the absence of proof of discriminatory intent, the federal government ought not interfere in the autonomy of states as they enacted legislation within their legitimate jurisdiction.

Although this colorblind doctrine is now the law of the land, Justice Ruth Bader Ginsberg pointed out in her dissent in *Shelby County v. Holder* that the court's ruling seriously distorted the facts pertaining to racial discrimination in relation to voting rights. Justice Ginsberg noted that the materials collected by the U.S. Congress in the context of debates over VRA reauthorization in 2006 indicated that there "were more DOJ objections between 1982 and 2004 (626) than there were between 1965 and the 1982 reauthorization" (490); indeed, in a majority of those objections, the Department of Justice found "calculated decisions to keep minority voters from fully participating in the political process" (cited in Rutenberg 2015, 47).

In 2014, a study by the Government Accounting Office found that voter ID laws in Kansas and Tennessee had reduced turnout by 2 to 3 percent in the 2012 election — a sufficient margin to swing an election in a close contest (Berman 2015). And materials submitted in litigation challenging a Texas statute that requires presentation of a photo ID at the polling place indicated that the law disproportionately affected low-income people of color, who tend to vote for Democratic candidates. As Judge Catharina Haynes noted in her opinion on behalf of the Fifth Circuit, Latino registered voters were 195 percent less likely to have a photo ID and Black registered voters were 305 percent less likely to have a photo ID than their Anglo peers. Although challenging the magnitude of the disparity, Texas officials acknowledged that the voter ID law disproportionately disenfranchised racial minorities. Their data indicated that 5.3 percent of eligible Black voters and 6.9 percent of eligible Latino voters lacked a photo ID, compared to 4 percent of eligible white voters. The Texas statute allows driver's license, U.S. passport, military ID, and concealed weapons permit to serve as valid identification at the polls, forms of ID that low-income voters are much less likely than affluent voters to have. The district court in this case credited expert testimony that 21.4 percent of eligible voters earning less than $20,000 per year lack identification mandated by the Texas law ID, compared to only 2.6 percent of voters earning between $100,000 and $150,000 per year (Millhiser 2015). In August 2015, the United States Court of Appeals for the Fifth Circuit ruled unanimously that the Texas law violated the Voting Rights Act. The State of Texas may appeal that decision.

Methodological Individualism

Beyond the influence of liberal individualist assumptions and presumptions about colorblind perception that circulate widely in the United States, Tim Luke (1987) has suggested that several dominant approaches within American political science are structured in accordance with methodological individualism. Both rational choice theory and political behavior studies take the individual as the basic unit of analysis. They define "individuals who make choices among certain values under certain constraints" as the domain of the politically observable; "then model the behavior of these observables in predictive or explanatory frames" (Luke 1987, 342).

Luke points out that methodological individualism has multiple dimensions, including *ontological individualism*, the assumption that individuals are the ultimate constituents of the social world (349); *epistemological individualism*, the assumption that all that can be known derives from observations about individuals (350);

psychological individualism, the presumption that mental objects are furnished solely by individual sense perception and experience (351); and *axiological individualism*: the notion that individuals are self-interested agents, who are motivated by subjectively-defined preferences and values (353). This combination of presuppositions constructs a way of seeing that construes politics as very much like economic markets – activities in which self-interested individuals engage in voluntary transactions to maximize their preferred outcomes. Within this frame, votes and decisions are the principle political currency; a group is nothing more than an aggregation of individuals; and political activity is simply a function of the aggregate of individual choices (342). Proponents of rational choice and political behavior approaches note that these presuppositions may fail to encompass all modes of human relationship, but insist that they are sufficient to enable accurate prediction of political outcomes ranging from electoral results to the outbreak of war. Within this research framework, correct predictions constitute the authoritative ground of science.

Quite apart from the question of accurate prediction,[13] the premises of methodological individualism offer a denuded conception of politics that fails to acknowledge that collectives such as states, institutions, and race-gendered formations have properties quite independent of and different from the individuals who comprise them, whether considered in terms of history, culture, values or power. Individual political action does not begin to exhaust the dimensions of political life or what can be known about the operations of states, nations, militaries, civil society organizations or international institutions. Although preference maximization may be one way to characterize the behavior of states, it may not be the most illuminating way to capture the complex mechanisms that shape determinations of "national interest," partisan politics, legislative behavior, or social conflict. Voluntary association and contractual agreement do not begin to capture the coercive powers of existing states, whether deployed in domestic or foreign policy. And the interplay of norms, laws, conventions, and customs in politics are not adequately depicted as subjective preferences. Perhaps most importantly for those concerned with embodied power, the reduction of the state to an aggregation of individuals completely misses the intricate ways that states produce raced-gendered-sexualized hierarchies that structure individual self-understandings, social relations, and life prospects.

To consider the manifold dimensions of politics occluded by methodological individualism, consider the Victims of Trafficking and Violence Protection Act of 2000 (P.L. 106–386, hereafter TVPA).[14] Treating trafficking as a problem of law and order within and beyond the borders of the United States, TVPA situates trafficking within an individualist frame. It defines sex trafficking as "the recruitment, harboring, transportation, provision, or obtaining of a person for the purposes of a commercial sex act"; and it defines a commercial sex act as "any sex act on account of which anything of value is given to or received by any person" (TVPA Sec. 103.8 (B)). Obliterating the distinction between coerced and

voluntary sex work and blurring the boundary
actional sex," TVPA seeks to severely punish t..
while funding interventions to "prevent" traffickin_
ficking.¹⁵ Designed to address trafficking within the
nations, TVPA requires the U.S. State Department t.
taskforce to combat trafficking and to establish a state
monitor and combat trafficking. In accordance with its monitc
Department is required to issue an annual report that evaluates .
of governments across the world in addressing trafficking. States th..
insufficient progress in anti-trafficking efforts may be subject to sanctions,
being deemed ineligible for loans from U.S.-led international ..
institutions.

Although TVPA positions the United States as a defender of individual rights, particularly the rights of women and children – who are characterized as the "chief victims" of this "contemporary manifestation of slavery" (TVPA section 102 (A)), implementation efforts have included the heightened criminalization of prostitution and intensified policing of street prostitution. U.S. citizens who are convicted of sex work can be sentenced to "rehabilitation" at facilities run by fundamentalist Christians, which include mandatory prayer sessions as part of the "rescue" process (Bernstein 2007b, 2010). In contrast to court-ordered rehabilitation, the majority of undocumented sex workers arrested in the United States have been deported. A small number of the undocumented who have been arrested for prostitution have been granted asylum on the condition that they assist law enforcement officials in the prosecution of their "traffickers" – a form of assistance that can place their family members in home nations in danger of retaliation by trafficking syndicates. In East Asia and Africa, funds to "prevent" trafficking and "protect" victims have been used to support brothel raids that liberate "traffic victims" and place them in worksites run by Christian evangelical organizations.¹⁶ In addition to employment as jewelry makers or textile workers, rehabilitative placement involves mandatory prayer sessions even for workers who do not identify as Christian (Shih 2013).

Beyond the gulf that divides the protection of individual rights from the politics of evangelical rescue, TVPA's individualist focus obscures the reality that trafficking is symptomatic of complex economic, political, and social dynamics associated with neoliberalism and marketization (Suchland 2015). In *Economies of Violence*, Jennifer Suchland (2015) draws attention to the political and economic context in post-socialist states that have fueled the growth of sex work – a context that individualized accounts of trafficking miss. Suchland documents the role of international financial institutions and advisors in the orchestration of "shock therapy" in the transition from state socialism to capitalism, and the role of the powerful centralized state in undermining the *de facto* property rights of workers in cooperative enterprises, transferring wealth to the new owners of the privatized companies. Contrary to notions of economic emancipation, newly-elected contributed to a "return of the serving classes" (Sassen 2002, 259). In the words of Barbara Ehrenreich and Arlie Hochschild (2002, 4), "In an earlier phase of imperialism, northern countries extracted natural resources and agricultural products – rubber, metals, and sugar, for example – from lands they conquered and colonized. Today, while still relying on third world countries for agricultural and industrial labor, the wealthy countries also seek to extract something harder to measure and quantify, something that can look very much like love." Sex work is one manifestation of the commodification of "love."

High rates of poverty and unemployment have long served as triggers for increasing numbers involved in sex work. In the era of structural adjustment, the growth in transnational sex work has been exponential. Yet, this increase has occurred at the same time that many states have adopted securitization measures and tightened border controls, which makes it increasingly difficult for undocumented women to cross borders. Women in desperate need of alternative circuits for survival have turned to networks of traffickers to facilitate their movement across borders (Sassen 2001). As Valerie Sperling (2009, 198–205) has documented, some trafficking operations are aided and abetted by international peacekeeping forces. In Bosnia, for example, key staff members of the International Police Training Force and the NATO-led stabilization Force organized a sex-trafficking ring that operated with impunity. When the ring was discovered, none of the traffickers were prosecuted for illegal activity. Instead, they were repatriated so that they could not serve as witnesses at trials of locals involved in the trafficking operation. Sperling points out that although a particularly blatant instance, the Bosnia operation replicates a long-established pattern of military command structures working with local administrators to ensure an ample supply of sex workers to accommodate the "needs" of soldiers on deployment. The U.S. military, like their counterparts in many other nations, liaise with local officials to guarantee a constant supply of "disease-free" sex workers (Enloe 2000, 2007; Enloe 2001). Precisely because sex-work is criminalized in most nations, trafficking typically involves a public-private partnership linking some government officials to trafficking syndicates – another fact obscured by individualized accounts.

The criminalization of sex work and the shaming of sex workers force prostitution into the underground economy – which makes it exceedingly difficult to estimate the number of sex workers in any country, much less the number of people trafficked for sex work. TVPA's elimination of the distinction between voluntary sex worker and trafficking victim further complicates the problem of accurate estimates of women and children coerced into sex work. Denise Brennan (2008) has pointed out that the federal government radically decreased its estimate of trans-border trafficking victims from 50,000 per year in 2000 to 14,500/year in 2006. Even the TVPA legislation itself manifested some ambivalence about estimates of trafficking victims in the U.S., capping the number of visas to assist victims at 5000 per year (Doonan 2014, 83). The politics surrounding such diverse estimates of trafficking are masked by individualized approaches. So too are the racialized gendering practices that structure the policing of trafficking in the United States. "According to U.S. Attorney Paula Chen, a full half of federal trafficking cases currently concern underage women in inner-city street prostitution. Enforcement-wise, this has resulted in an unprecedented police crackdown on people of color who are involved in the street-based economy – including pimps, clients, and sex workers alike" (Bernstein 2010, 57; 2007a). Whether the goal is prevention of trafficking or protection of those coerced into forced labor and forced sex work, the individualist assumptions that inform the policy and the implementation of TVPA provide an inadequate ground. In the words of Janie Chuang (1998, 66): "The narrow portrayal of trafficking as necessarily involving forced recruitment for the purposes of forced prostitution thus belies the complexity of the current trafficking problem, and overlooks numerous victims whose experiences diverge from more traditionally recognized forms of trafficking. Moreover, because international anti-trafficking law reflects this narrow conception of trafficking, the exigencies of modern manifestations of trafficking in women have rendered these laws inadequate to prevent and redress the trafficking problem." As the TVPA makes clear, individualist frames are simply incapable of accounting for the complexity of embodied power operating through interpersonal dynamics, institutional practices, national regimes, transnational circuits, and international economic forces associated with voluntary and involuntary sex work.

Methodological Nationalism

Although individualism has a powerful hold on the mental landscape in this neoliberal era, it coexists with a host of entrenched assumptions about the nation. Within American political science, and the social sciences more generally, in policy circuits, in the media, and in popular culture, a conception of the nation anchors a formidable way of seeing. In taking the nation-state as a fundamental unit of analysis, social scientists cast themselves as "realists," who simply describe the current world order. But assumptions about "the nation" move well beyond descriptions of territorial boundaries, populations, forms of governance, and types of political authority in the contemporary period. As Andreas Wimmer and Nina Glick Schiller (2003) have pointed out, contemporary conceptions of the nation presuppose a mode of belonging grounded in the notion of a "people." As a domain of identity, the nation suggests membership in an ethnicity that pre-exists the power politics of state formation. Thus, the nation is conceived as a people who share common "blood," origins, ancestry, language, culture, and history. As the metaphors of blood and lines of descent suggest, national belonging implies organic ties, something akin to an extended family that requires solidarity, shared sacrifice, and mutual support. Emphasis on common language, culture, and history also suggest linked fate, a common destiny as well as a shared geography. In certain formulations, the nation is taken to manifest certain inherent characteristics, a national character, which forges ties across generations. In the words of Edmund Burke (1790, §165), the nation involves a "partnership not only between those who are living, but between those who are living, those who are dead, and those who are to be born."

As a territorially bounded unit, the nation is also imagined to contain an economy, shaped by the natural resources available within territorial boundaries and fueled by the ingenuity of the people. As Suzanne Bergeron (2006) notes, in the aftermath of the Great Depression, economists framed the economy in terms of production, circulation, and consumption within the space of the nation. With the advent of econometrics, economists devised a new statistical indicator of national well-being, the gross national product (GNP), which not only provided an index of collective well-being but enabled economists for the first time in history to measure whole nations against each other (Bergeron 2006, 6).[17] By comparing GNP, nations could be rank-ordered according to levels of development, from the poorest to the most affluent, thereby lending a scientific imprimatur to notions of national superiority. In positing the national economy as its object of investigation, modernization theory organized national comparisons according to an assumed natural progression from subsistence agriculture to industrialization to a post-industrial, hi-tech, services-based system. Drawing lessons from their own success, "advanced" nations offer "development assistance" to the "underdeveloped" or "developing" economies of the Global South to enhance their growth and maturation. By attributing underdevelopment to the internal logic of national economies in the global South, this container notion of the national economy masks longer histories of colonial and patriarchal domination that structured inequities across systems of governance, education, and economic organization (plantation and slave systems), facilitated particular modes of resource extraction, and contributed to the construction of trade routes and markets within a "center-periphery" frame (Bergeron 2006).

Binding the "scientific eye" to the body of the nation, methodological nationalism accredits the nation as the only conceivable unit of analysis – whether the discipline is art, folklore, literature, music, history, politics, or sociology (Wimmer and Glick Schiller 2003). Historians mute the foreign origins of national projects by transforming them into "prehistories of the nation, referring for example to the colonial U.S., as opposed to British North American colonies" (Briggs et al. 2008, 627). In this way, academic work has helped to produce the nation as an imagined community. Through memorials and the management of memory, national governments shape an invented past, which structures the terms of national belonging. National governments also generate the statistics pertaining to health, wealth, population, employment, and growth that social scientists use to compare nations, and often, provide funding to support comparative studies. Within the frame of methodological nationalism, national borders demarcate the scope of investigation, contrasting domestic studies, with comparative approaches, or the examination of the relations among states (international relations). Civic education is conflated with cultivation of patriotism and fellow feeling, performance of civic duty, and heightening political participation. Cultural literacy is defined in terms of mastering the national iconography, and assimilation is taken as the appropriate norm for all who are allowed to join the national community.

When the nation anchors the way of seeing, however, a great deal about the origins and operations of contemporary nation-states is obscured. A romanticized notion of a people bound by blood masks the historical origins of nations in war, conquest, and colonization. And in the case of colonial settler societies, it masks the brutal construction of the racialized and gendered boundaries of belonging that reserved property ownership and citizenship to an elite white cohort. It hides the diversity within the population and the political force expended to suture the nation together, from quelling riots, subduing dissent, and breaking strikes to civil war. The myth of a stable, homogeneous population also masks the waves of immigration and migration that shaped the current population. As Philip Kretsedemas (2008, 559) has pointed out, in the 21st-century United States, for example, "the annual immigration levels for persons granted legal permanent residence peaked at 1.2 million in recent years; the annual flow of noncitizens has exceeded 33 million (conservatively estimated), and has exceeded 230 million per annum if counting all temporary arrivals." In contrast to solidarity grounded in shared rights, "nonimmigrants are admitted to US under temporary legal status with limited social and legal rights, virtually no political rights, and no guaranteed option for naturalization ... unauthorized migrants are in an even more precarious legal situation than nonmigrants. Some legal and human rights for unauthorized migrants have been recognized by federal courts ... but unauthorized migrants seldom assert their rights due to fears of deportation" (Kretsedemas 2008, 559–60). In contrast to the myth of a stable, homogeneous people, "the national population is ... an assemblage of different legal categories that are not on the same pathway to citizenship ... citizenry is just one population among many that reside in the national territory alongside populations of noncitizens" (Kretsedemas 2008, 560).

National territory has never been a uniform political space. While the state afforded some privileged persons rights, free land, and the possibilities of self-determination, it shackled, enslaved, and exploited others, and annihilated still more. In *Seeing Like a State*, James Scott (1998) points out that states have devoted great effort to producing a national population – efforts that have involved massive transformations of the physical landscape, the built environment, economic policies, educational practices, systems of regulation, and the appearance and demeanor of the people themselves:

> To make a society legible, states develop social simplifications that make a society seem to be administratively manageable. In this process, they marginalize

local knowledges that challenge managerial orderings. Social statistics, models, physical representations of space and place involve sweeping projects of social change informed by ideology of high modernism: a vision of rational engineering all aspects of social life to improve the human condition. The goal is transformation. Toward that end, the state creates a population with the characteristics easier to monitor and manage. Those who do not fit the model are left out of the frame, characterized as anomalies or pathologies which need to be transformed.

(Bergeron 2006, 30)

States have devised complex technologies to cultivate national identity, sufficiently strong to overcome differences associated with class, ethnicity, religion and gender – while designating certain "races" unassimilable. The state has funded all kinds of programs to build connections between the aspirations of authorities and the activities of individuals and groups:

… deploying humble and mundane mechanisms … inculcation of habits, standardization of systems of training, professional specialisms and vocabularies, invention of devices, surveys, health regimens … [through which] actors come to understand their situation according to similar language and logic, to construe their goals and their fate as in some way inextricable, they are assembled into mobile and loosely affiliated networks. Shared interests are constructed in and through political discourses, persuasions, negotiations, and bargains. Common modes of perception are formed, in which certain events and entities come to be visualized according to particular rhetorics of image or speech. Relations are established between the nature, character, and causes of problems facing various individuals and groups … intrinsic links form the basis for solutions. Regulatory techniques installed within citizens align their personal choices with the ends of government.

(Rose and Miller 1992, 19–20)

The intricate modes of embodied power exercised by governments in collaboration with academic experts who help design such interventions are all rendered invisible by methodological nationalism. The arduous work of nation building is masked by the presumption of naturalized national ties. "Americanization" courses devised to facilitate and accelerate assimilation disappear from the national memory. Educational programs that channeled affluent white public school children to pre-college courses, while consigning working class children to trade schools, and sequestering children of color in massively underfunded segregated facilities are relegated to a deep past, so far removed from the present that it is expected to have no contemporary effects. State mandates to preserve white citizenship, white police forces and fire departments, as well as official tolerance of white supremacist vigilante activities are muted by presumptions of national solidarity. As the national memory is salved by a fictive past, new grounds are laid for resentment against those who refuse to accredit the fiction of national unity. As the mythos of an inclusive nation displaces the history of racialized-gendering in the United States, many white citizens have come to believe that African Americans are "better off" than whites and that Black success is a threat to white middle-class status: "Blacks constitute the explanation for whites' vulnerability and for almost everything that has gone wrong in their lives ... whites came to understand themselves as victims of reverse discrimination or racial mistreatment: discrimination against whites has become a well-assimilated and ready explanation for whites' vulnerability, declining status, failures" (Haney-Lopez 2014, 71).

As a way of seeing domestic politics, methodological nationalism has unfortunate consequences. It occludes manifold dimensions of U.S. history associated with the quest to build and sustain a white race-nation, and it contributes to distorted perceptions of contemporary race and gender relations. But this way of seeing also has powerful consequences beyond the borders of the nation state. Methodological nationalism offers a political taxonomy of a world that is taken to be "naturally" divided up into homogeneous "peoples" – each bearing a particular nationality. Solidarity among a people within the territorial boundaries of the nation fosters suspicion of those without, who are readily positioned as threats – whether those threats are tied to disease and contamination, religious practices and culture, ideological beliefs and economic systems, a "flood" of immigrants, or military might. Methodological nationalism acknowledges national defense as the primary obligation of the state. Defending "the people" is always deemed to be legitimate even as the doctrine of national defense is expanded to encompass preemptive attacks to prevent possible future aggression.

Thus methodological nationalism shores up military operations in the "national interest" – exercises of lethal force that produce, reproduce, naturalize, and maintain racial, gendered, ethnic, and national hierarchies. For this reason, Briggs et al. (2008) characterize "the nation [a]s an ideology that changes over time with profound effects on wars, economy, movement of peoples, and relations of domination." A brief examination of claims to defend the nation advanced by multiple participants in the second Iraq War (2003–2011) illuminates how methodological nationalism gives rise to lethal forms of racialization, gendering, and sexualization.

When the U.S. invaded Iraq in March 2003 with the assistance of Britain and a few other members of the "coalition of the willing," President G. W. Bush offered two justifications linked to national interest. He sought to rid Iraq of weapons of mass destruction and to end its support for terrorist groups, including al-Qaida.[18] Although the U.S. acted without the authorization of the United Nations, it sought to legitimate its action with reference to the 1993 UN General Assembly Resolution on "Human Rights and Terrorism" (GA Res 48/122, 1993), which defines terrorism in terms supplied by methodological nationalism. According to the United Nations resolution, terrorism always and only involves non-state actors. Thus terrorism is defined as "activities wherever and by whomever committed, aimed at the destruction of human rights, fundamental freedoms and democracy, threatening the territorial integrity and security of states, destabilizing legitimate constituted governments, undermining pluralistic civil society and having adverse consequences on the economic and social development of states." By aligning U.S. national interest with the protection of freedom, democracy, and pluralist civil society, the G. W. Bush Administration drew a careful distinction between certain kinds of liberal and social democratic states and the regime of Saddam Hussein, who was depicted as a destabilizing force, vaguely associated with transnational terrorism, posing an imminent threat to order and security. Portrayed within an Orientalist frame, the nation of Iraq was characterized as a conglomeration of warring tribal societies with Sunni and Shiite factions vying for ascendancy in the southern and central regions and the Kurds fighting for autonomy in the north. The goal of "Operation Iraqi Freedom," then, was to rescue the Iraqi people from the oppressive rule of Saddam Hussein and from warring Muslim factions. In direct contravention of the principle of non-intervention in the internal affairs of other states, the U.S. overthrew the government of Iraq, disbanded the Iraqi military, and launched an eight-year military occupation. Although the exact number of deaths during this conflict is a matter of on-going debate, it is estimated that 4491 U.S. service members lost their lives, compared to 16,623 Iraqi military and police, and 27,000 Iraqi insurgents, and 161,000 civilians (Iraq Body Count 2015).

In attempting to document the scope of civilian deaths during the Iraq conflict, an additional dimension of racialized sexualization becomes apparent. As the movement for lesbian, gay, bisexual, and transgender (LGBT) rights has gained momentum, some activist organizations have hailed the achievement of gay rights as a marker of Western "progress."[19] Within this frame, the guarantee of the full rights of citizenship for LGBT persons is portrayed as an indication of heightened civilization, which is contrasted with barbaric practices of gay persecution. The creation of civil society spaces for LGBT mobilization, constitutional equality clauses, and marriage equality are juxtaposed against "political homophobia," the explicit use of homophobic and transphobic discourses by political officials to construct queer lives as a threat to the sanctity of the nation (Currier 2012). Denouncing same-sex desire and homosexual practices as a legacy of colonialism or an artefact of Western imperialism are standard tropes in political homophobia, typically accompanied by criminalization of those practices. These complex dynamics play out in the pages of a 2009 Human Rights Watch report, providing a powerful example of how terms of debate set by methodological nationalism infiltrate the work of nongovernmental organizations.

Entitled *"They Want Us Exterminated": Murder, Torture, Sexual Orientation and Gender in Iraq* (Long and Moumneh 2009), the Human Rights Watch report documents the murder of 743 gay men in Iraq between 2003 and 2009. Featuring testimony by survivors and witnesses, the report depicts brutal physical attacks prior to death, as well as mutilation of corpses postmortem. The murders are attributed to Moqtada al-Sadr's Mahdi Army, which fights under the banners of religion and morality, claiming to defend the honor of Iraq against multiple transgressions – including the "feminization" of Iraqi men. Articulating a virulent brand of political homophobia, the Mahdi Army is depicted as railing against the importation of homosexuality from the West. According to the Report, the Mahdi militia takes a particular style of Western dress (tight T-shirts and expensive jeans) as evidence that Iraqi men are being Westernized, feminized and in the process stripped of their authentic Iraqi manhood. Depicting the Muslim militants as caretakers of tradition, culture, and national authenticity, the report suggests that the Mahdi militia uses violent and lethal practices to police gender and sexuality in conflict-ridden Iraq. In the defense of a pure Iraqi culture, the Mahdi Army insists that same-sex desires, erotic practices, and emotional relationships have never existed in Iraq (an insistence which the report claims is at odds with Iraqi vernacular language, literature, and art). Wielding an invented past, the Mahdi Army kills for the sake of the nation's future. The Human Rights Watch report frames the brutal practices of the Mahdi militia as exercises of embodied power, which involve racialized gendering: Iraqi citizens are racialized as "Western" and sexualized as gay. Within this frame, political homophobia on the part of a savage version of fundamentalist Islam provides a compelling account of the "extermination" of hundreds of gay men. Yet, in making this case, the report manifests what Jasbir Puar (2007) has called "homonationalism," a linking of LGBT freedom and security to U.S. patriotic projects. By focusing primarily on the Mahdi Army and other fundamentalist militias, the report isolates these deaths from the U.S. military incursion.

In a subsequent work, Rasha Mounmeh (2015) – co-author of *"They Want Us Exterminated": Murder, Torture, Sexual Orientation and Gender in Iraq* – suggests that the Human Rights Watch report misses much of the complexity surrounding the deaths of these civilians. By focusing exclusively on "a campaign to exterminate gay men," the report elides the fact that the Mahdi Army and other sectarian militias targeted women "corrupted by the West" for assassination as well as gay men. Thousands of Iraqi women were murdered for working outside the home, wearing make-up or trousers, or walking the streets unveiled. They too were violently tortured and raped prior to death; their bodies were desecrated and placed on display postmortem to serve as a lesson to others. By masking the assassination of women, and figuring the gay men who were assaulted and murdered as "innocents," who were sacrificed solely because of their sexuality, the Human Rights Watch report positions the West as morally superior, a guarantor of gay rights, ready to intervene to save other oppressed queer subjects by granting visas and providing exit strategies to Europe and the U.S.[20] In this way, Human Rights Watch shores up the myth of the "civilized" West, while rendering invisible the role of U.S. forces in the deaths of more than 100,000 civilians during the second Iraq war. By constructing gay victims solely in terms of homophobic violence, the Human Rights Watch report also masks U.S. complicity in their deaths. Many of the men and women murdered by the sectarian militias had been employees of U.S. and coalition forces, serving as translators, facilitators, and organizers of logistical support. To militia members, these employees were "collaborators" with the enemy, aiding and abetting an imperial invasion. The U.S. military incursion in Iraq may not have been directly responsible for these deaths, but it clearly bears some responsibility for these assassinations. Any such responsibility is rendered invisible by methodological nationalism, which constructs a narrative of dueling visions of the nation, pitting the civilized liberal democracy against the barbaric Muslim *ummah*.

Establishing clear lines of causality for civilian deaths in war is a fraught undertaking under the best of circumstances, but it is near impossible in the context of competing nationalist frames. Both the U.S. alignment of its national interests with "freedom, democracy, and pluralism," and the Mahdi militia's embrace of a particular version of the Muslim nation (*ummah*) appeal to the prerogatives of a sovereign nation to defend its people against constructions of external threats. Methodological nationalism can be seductive, allowing sustained practices of racialization, gendering, and sexualization to masquerade as national defense even as the numbers of the dead proliferate. By naturalizing the nation, methodological nationalism renders invisible the exercise of state power in founding, building, and defending nation-states. It occludes the deployment of embodied power in forging national identity, structuring processes of belonging, and indulging in systemic practices of exclusion. It masks modes of racialization, gendering, and sexualization by appealing to invented pasts and deploying force to create imagined futures.

Conclusion

As the ways of seeing discussed in this chapter demonstrate, embodied power is rendered invisible by multiple assumptions that inform everyday perception as well as research paradigms. Individualist presuppositions push racialized and gendered divisions of labor in the home and in the labor force below the threshold of visibility. Assumptions about "colorblind" perception distort understandings of the economic condition of whites and people of color in ways that mask systemic disadvantage and sustain claims concerning "reverse discrimination." Methodological nationalism naturalizes and depoliticizes notions of national interest in ways that sustain political violence – whether that violence appeals to a defense of the freedom of women and LGBT rights or justifies assaults on "Westernized" women and gays who are constructed as a "threat" to authentic national traditions. In combination, assumptions about individualism, colorblindness, methodological individualism, and methodological nationalism sustain explanatory accounts that decontextualize and divert attention to contorted causal claims that neglect structural forces and blame those disadvantaged by systemic inequalities for the harms that befall them.

Operating singly and in concert, these powerful ways of seeing naturalize a host of social relations and mask the operations of power. In contrast to the apparent self-evidence of a world constituted by self-determining individuals and ordered by determinate peoples dwelling within the boundaries of their national homelands, racialization, gendering, and sexualization glimmer vaguely as ephemera, "their presence captured as negation, (written over, erased); as objects marked by their inability to count as proper proof ... a kind of evidence invisible to trained political scientists" and to the popular imagination (Muñoz 1996). Precisely because ways of seeing structure perception at a preconscious level, they sustain notions of neutral observation. But these notions can be contested. As John Berger emphasized, calling attention to specific ways of seeing and demonstrating how they shape perception and understanding, how they accredit certain kinds of evidence and explanation, while ruling out others, creates the possibility for critical engagement with formidable assumptions. When questionable presuppositions are moved from the tacit realm to the explicit, they can be subject to rigorous scrutiny, contested, and transformed.

Racialized gendering and sexualization operate in complex ways that precede and exceed the intentions and actions of individuals; they are embedded in constructions of national interest that play out both in domestic and international contexts with profoundly destructive consequences. If the scope of contemporary injustice is to be recognized and engaged in the study of politics, then units of analysis other than the individual and the nation-state are required to plumb the raced-gendered dynamics of interpersonal relations, institutional practices, and visual regimes, as well as national and international orders. Considering a range of analytical tools that make embodied power visible and intelligible is the topic of the final chapter.

Notes

1 Empiricism is a rich and varied intellectual tradition that has had a profound effect on theories of knowledge since Aristotle. Although they differ in many respects, ancient and modern empiricism suggest that human sensory perception is the source of knowledge and induction – the systematic observation of particular cases – enables reliable generalaization. Proponents of empirical inquiry have catalogued diverse challenges that must be overcome to attain an objective account of reality. Various accounts of scientific methods synthesize strategies to avoid error. For an overview of versions of empiricism and scientific method, see Hawkesworth (2006, Chapter 1, "Sources of Error and Strategies of Redress"). For a pragmatist critique of unmediated perception, see Richard Rorty (1979).
2 Hundreds of works could be cited to support this claim. For the sake of brevity, I have chosen a few well-known examples. With the exception of direct quotations, parenthetical references should be taken as representative rather than exhaustive.
3 In *Mind and Politics*, Ellen Wood (1972) argues that commitment to individualism as a social doctrine is compatible with two divergent interpretations of individuality, which she labels "dialectical individualism" and "metaphysical individualism." For a comprehensive analysis of individualism, see Lukes (1973).

4 In *A Theory of Justice*, John Rawls (1971, 544–45) argues that "The basis for self-esteem in a just society is not one's income share but the publicly affirmed distribution of fundamental rights and liberties. And this distribution being equal, everyone has a similar and secure status when they meet to conduct the common affairs of the wider society. No one is inclined to look beyond the constitutional affirmation of equality for further political ways of securing his status … In a well ordered society, then, self-respect is secured by the public affirmation of the status of equal citizenship for all." For demonstrations of the complex ways that Rawls misunderstands racism and sexism, see Mills (2015), Shelby (2007) and Threadcraft (2014).
5 In the mid-1960s, most open positions were filled by word of mouth using personal networks. Those positions that were publicly advertised were posted in newspapers by race and sex (i.e., "Help Wanted White Male, Help Wanted White Female, Help Wanted Black Male, Help Wanted Black Female"), reserving prestigious professional positions and skilled-craft jobs for white men, and requiring increasing levels of servility for jobs with much lower pay from workers in the residual categories. Title VII of the 1964 Civil Rights Act prohibited the restriction of jobs by race and sex unless these could be demonstrated to be "bona fide job requirements." Title VII also *prohibited* the use of quotas or the lowering of standards to give "preferential treatment" to women and people of color applying for jobs. In establishing affirmative action guidelines for federal contractors (i.e., recipients of federal funding whether in the form of contracts for goods and services, research support, or scholarship assistance), the Office of Federal Contract Compliance within the Department of Labor, however, suggested "numerical objectives" to increase minority employment within specified time frames. These guidelines are sometimes mistakenly confused with court-ordered desegregation as a result of litigation demonstrating patterns of discrimination. In a series of cases involving police forces, fire fighters, and labor unions brought under Title VII of the Civil Rights Act, the Supreme Court imposed hiring quotas as a remedy for ongoing racial discrimination. See, for example, *United States v. Iron Workers Local 86*; *United States v. Hayes International Corporation*; *United States v. United Carpenters and Joiners*.
6 In declaring race a "suspect classification," the court tied the constitutional permissibility of differential treatment on the basis of race to a demonstration that the state has a "compelling interest" in achieving the ends, which the classification is devised to facilitate, and that no alternative, less harmful means are available to achieve the same end. Thus the court established a legal presumption that any use of race by the state was likely to be harmful.
7 After graduating from Stanford Law School, William Rehnquist worked as a law clerk for Justice Robert H. Jackson from 1952 to 1953, during the time that *Brown v. Board of Education* was under consideration. Rehnquist wrote a controversial memo defending the Supreme Court decision in *Plessy v. Ferguson*, arguing that the separate-but-equal approach was constitutionally permissible. Rehnquist later claimed the memo reflected Justice Jackson's views and not his own.
8 At issue in the Bakke case was the constitutional permissibility of a "special admissions" program at the University of California, Davis, Medical School that set aside a small number of seats in each class for students of color. The text of the Bakke decision cited in this paragraph is that printed in *US Law Week*, 46 LW 4896 (June 27, 1978). The page references in the text refer to this version of the decision.
9 In 2015, as 17 Republican presidential hopefuls vied for public attention, appeals to colorblindness took a strange twist. In the first debate organized by FOX news, Ben Carson, an African-American neurosurgeon, was asked what he might do as president to "heal the racial divide." He responded that he prefers not to talk about race. As a neurosurgeon, he "sees" what makes people who they are – their brains. "When I take someone to the operating room, I'm actually operating on the thing that makes them who they are. The skin doesn't make them who they are. The hair doesn't make them

who they are. And it's time for us to move beyond that. Because our strength as a nation comes in our unity. We are the United States of America, not the divided states. And those who want to divide us are trying to divide us, and we shouldn't let them do it." Carson referred to those who draw attention to race as "purveyors of hatred who take every single incident between people of two races and try to make a race war out of it." At the same time that the only Black Republican presidential contender was urging colorblindness, a right-wing faction of the party began deploying a new term, "cuckservative" to express their frustration and contempt for party leaders who cater too much to "minority issues" and were "too soft" on the Obama agenda. According to the Southern Poverty Law Center, the term originated with white nationalists, such as the National Policy Institute, which promotes the preservation and cultivation of white culture in the United States (Rappeport 2015).

10 According to a study of 1 billion votes cast in the United States, voter fraud is almost non-existent in the USA. Examining attempts to cast more than one ballot in the same election, as well as attempts to impersonate a voter, scholars at Loyola University Law School found only 31 credible allegations of fraud in a one billion vote sample (Rutenberg 2015, 38).

11 Section 4b of the Voting Rights Act authorized DOJ preclearance in jurisdictions that, as of November 1964, November 1968, or November 1972, had maintained a prohibited "test or device" as a condition of registering to vote or voting and had a voting-age population of which less than 50 percent either were registered to vote or actually voted in that year's presidential election.

12 Following his graduation from Harvard Law School, John Roberts had worked as a law clerk for Supreme Court Justice William Rehnquist. While working as a Reagan appointee in the Department of Justice, Roberts lobbied against a provision in the 1982 Voting Rights Act that allowed disparate impact on Black voters to stand as proof of discrimination. Suggesting that disparate effect was too lenient a standard, Roberts insisted that proof of discriminatory *intent* should be required to strike down any "colorblind" law. Referring to a state of mind that is not empirically observable, "intent" is notoriously difficult to prove. Roberts was appointed chief justice of the Supreme Court by President G. W. Bush.

13 Political science has failed to predict major political developments such as the collapse of the Soviet system, genocide in the former Yugoslavia and Rwanda, the rise of al-Qaida or ISIS. Tim Luke (1999, 363) has suggested that these failures are integrally related to normalized ways of seeing within the discipline: "the normal science produced by adherents of political science's disciplined normalization has failed to anticipate many major changes, ranging from the end of the welfare state or the implosion of state socialism to the maldevelopment of the second, third, and fourth worlds, or the spread of wild social chaos in many regimes."

14 TVPA was reauthorized in 2003, 2005, 2008, and 2013. In a fascinating example of racialized gendering, the 2008 reauthorization was named the "William Wilberforce Trafficking Victims Protection Act of 2008," celebrating the life of the British abolitionist and linking the abolition of trafficking to the abolition of slavery. For a detailed legislative history of TVPA, see Doonan (2014).

15 "Transactional sex" refers to the provision of some form of economic benefit or subsistence in return for sexual intercourse. Feminist scholars have adopted this term to demonstrate continuities between certain forms of voluntary sex work and traditional forms of cohabitation and common law marriage. Karl Marx and Friedrich Engels were the first to suggest parallels between prostitution and bourgeois marriage in the *Communist Manifesto*.

16 In her ethnographical research on Christian rescue projects in Thailand and China, Elena Shih (2013) has found that nearly all the "victims" rescued from brothels were adult women who had chosen sex work as their highest paying survival strategy.

17 Bergeron (2006, 638) also points out that GNP is a raced-gendered concept. It measures only the "formal economy, thereby rendering some people's – primarily women's – economic activity illegal or unreal ... it elides the centrality of this labor to survival ... an economy that supports 80% of the population is made invisible or worse, backward and in need of change."
18 The claim that Iraq possessed weapons of mass destruction proved to be untrue; the claim concerning Iraq's support for al-Qaida was tenuous.
19 The European Union has recognized LGBT rights since 2000. The Yogyakarta Principles on Application of Human Rights Law in relation to Sexual Orientation and Gender Identity were released 2007; 85 nations produced a joint statement in support of these principles in 2011. Yet, some states, most notably Russia, Namibia, and Uganda, have escalated their "traditionalist defense of gender and nation" in the past decade. And in contrast to any simple division of the world in terms of gay rights, homophobia circulates widely in the global North and South.
20 This report was published in August 2009, scarcely eight months after the end of the G. W. Bush Administration. Its retrospective focus has the ironic effect of positioning the Bush Administration as a defender of LGBT rights, a gross distortion of their record.

6

REVISIONING POWER, RECLAIMING POLITICS

> The imposition of scientific reason's dichotomy between the subject and object on hierarchical relations of race, gender, class, and nationality has deep and abiding consequences for the structuring of privilege and oppression.
>
> (Iris Young 1991, 127)

Although ways of seeing embedded in mainstream political science and in contemporary political culture in the United States drive embodied power below the threshold of visibility, some scholars have worked intensively over the past four decades to document the pervasive operations of race, gender, and sexuality in politics. Scholars of gender, race and ethnicity, for example, have documented that racism and sexism can be potent forces in electoral politics. "Both in-group loyalties and out-group antipathies are apparent in American electoral politics ... There is ample evidence that racially-negative whites are reluctant to support black candidates ... white bias against black candidates may be especially pronounced for candidates perceived or known to be liberal ideologically or supportive of pro-black policies ... Thus black candidates who are proponents of race-based policies likely elicit greater opposition from whites than do black candidates who hold a moderate record and avoid racially-charged issues" (Huddy and Carey 2009, 81, 84). Indeed, as Leonie Huddy and Tony Carey (2009, 94) have documented, sizable minorities of whites in the South and elsewhere (e.g., the swing states of Ohio and Pennsylvania) refused to vote for Obama on explicitly racial grounds. Feminist scholars have provided sophisticated analyses of the operations of gender and race in the historic presidential election of 2008 – the first time a white woman and a Black man vied for a major party's nomination for the presidency (Carroll 2009; Hancock 2009; Junn 2009). Critical race scholars and feminist scholars have launched multifaceted investigations of "collective identity, the relation between stigma and group membership, the role of social networks in political mobilization, and the effects of sociohistorical context ... to move us closer to understanding how marginalization and privilege affect individuals' and groups' life experiences and life chances" (Garcia Bedolla 2007, 238). Intersectionality theorists have demonstrated how conceptual practices of power create categories that reflect prevailing hierarchies of racialized gender and sustain causal claims that are deeply distorted, yet circulate widely informing institutional practices of governance that advantage some while seriously disadvantaging others. Although embodied power typically operates covertly to consolidate systems of privilege and disadvantage, feminist political economists have also demonstrated that strategic racialization and gendering have played key roles in national and international economic policies both in the past and in the present (Peterson 2003; Sassen 2010; Marchand and Runyon 2011).

For those who see the discipline of political science as an expansive and unwieldy aggregate of subfields containing manifold sub-specializations, it may seem adequate to treat the study of race, gender, and sexuality as content specializations. Within such a large and fragmented intellectual field, it may appear sufficient that some scholars accept the challenge of investigating embodied power; the topic need not occupy the discipline at large. Yet, such an intellectual division of labor perpetuates the mystification of disembodied politics. It masks the possibility that political science itself contributes to the normalization of racialized gendering and shores up exclusions grounded on race, sex, and sexuality. As long as the discipline insists that race and sex are epistemically irrelevant to the study of politics *per se*, it fosters the myth of neutrality in relation to perception, state action, social outcomes, political access, and structures of power. And as argued in the foregoing chapters, the myth of neutrality renders racist and sexist exclusions invisible, preferring to blame systemic inequalities on those who suffer most from their effects.

In discussing the epistemology of ignorance, Nancy Tuana (2008, 131) suggests that those involved in scientific knowledge production must "account for conditions that explain the acceptance of belief, whether true or false." She emphasizes that an "appeal to reality" cannot suffice because other factors are always at work in theory-laden perception. Precisely because cognitive authority influences doubt, trust, silencing and uncertainty, academic disciplines have a particular responsibility to examine the role of power in construction of the known. When political science asserts that the institutional operations that produce and conceal unwarranted and unjustifiable harm to human beings through racialized gendering are of no relevance to the discipline at large, it accredits a kind of ignorance that is destructive to the possibility of political equality. Tim Luke (1999, 346) has suggested that by "express[ing] an implicit system of rules, which exert a normalizing effect upon thought and action ... political science provides some ontological stability for a larger social order":

> Political science is implicated in the reproduction of existing systems of social control ... Rational choice theorists illustrate the irrationality of voting, the coalitional strangulation of public goods provision, and the inefficiency of democratic decisionmaking. Voting behavior specialists reshape the public into psychodemographic niche markets ... to produce voting outcomes. Public opinion analysts demonstrate how to generate apathy or outrage. Postmodern normative theorists tear up foundationalist ethics...leaving almost everyone unsure of how to behave ... The inherent conservatism of most political scientists and much of political science becomes an ontological stabilizer shoring up the belief that capitalist democracy is the best of all possible worlds.
>
> (Luke 1999, 346–47)

The social order that political science reinforces also institutionalizes white androcentrism. By perpetuating mistaken notions of perceptual and policy neutrality and proclaiming the irrelevance of race and gender to the discipline as a whole, political science gives free play to embodied power and all the harms that flow from it.

As the academic field that claims to investigate power in all of its varied manifestations, political science has a vested interest in mapping the full scope of its subject matter, including the *microphysics of power* – processes of exclusion, marginalization written on the bodies and minds of those relegated beyond or outside the community and *micropolitics* – the mobilizations of the excluded to contest imposed identities, deform conventional modes of intelligibility, and struggle to survive economically, socially, politically (Shapiro 2006). Toward that end, intersectionality as an analytical tool is essential – and the approach to intersectionality that must be embedded in the discipline is one keenly attuned to the mutual constitution of race-gender-class-sexuality-nationality.

Contrary to the ideal of the "autonomy" of science, which posits a logic of discovery completely insulated from social values, Helen Longino (1990) demonstrated long ago that social norms and values permeate every aspect of scientific investigation, framing research questions, characterizing the objects of inquiry, accrediting forms of explanation, demarcating credible evidence, structuring modes of argumentation, and warranting adequate tests of hypotheses, and enabling certain dominant paradigms to withstand falsification. In a race-evasive culture like the United States, which insists upon the moral irrelevance of race even as it produces racial identities and rationalizes relations of raced-gendered domination and subordination, an academic discipline that refuses to acknowledge the centrality and pervasiveness of embodied power simply reproduces hierarchies of raced-gendered difference.

If political science is to move beyond the stabilization of white male power, standard disciplinary frames, analytic categories, and methods must be reconsidered. This chapter explores the transformational potential of intersectionality. It begins by showing how certain analytical tools central to political science are incompatible with intersectional analyses and identifies alternative analytics that can overcome these limitations. It considers how naturalized notions of race and sex sustain contorted causal claims that span diverse disciplinary frames and contrasts these problematic accounts with more sophisticated modes of explanation afforded by intersectional analysis. The chapter concludes with a discussion of intersectionality's capacity to expand the parameters of politics and deepen contemporary understandings of embodied power.

Intersectionality as an Analytical Frame

Over the past few decades, research informed by intersectional analyses has proliferated across multiple disciplines including American studies, art history, cultural studies, ethnic studies, gender and sexuality studies, history, legal studies, literary criticism, feminist philosophy, political science, psychology, and sociology. The richness and diversity of these studies has motivated Kimberlé Crenshaw, who coined the term intersectionality, to refer to the plurality of intersectional analytic frames as a burgeoning field of intersectionality studies rather than as a single analytical approach (Cho et al. 2013, 785). Despite the hazards associated with oversimplification, it is important to identify key features of intersectional analysis that are essential to the demystification of disembodied politics.

Recognizing Racialized-Gendering

As noted in Chapter 1, critical race feminism, postcolonial theory, and postoccidental theory concur that racialization and the sexualization of women have been hallmarks of modernity, the contradictory twin of Enlightenment thinking. As modernity articulated idealized principles of liberty, equality, and fraternity, it simultaneously insisted on the irrelevance of ascriptive categories such as race and sex, even as it produced new systems of raced-gendered domination and subordination. As a tool for the demystification of disembodied politics, then, intersectional analysis requires recognition that racialization and gendering are co-constitutive processes that create and sustain hierarchical relations of power in the contemporary world.[1] Although they manifest differently in particular contexts and their specification requires empirical investigation, racialized gendering and gendered racialization are features of modernity and contemporary social and political life, not an anomaly, an aberration, or an exception from ordinary politics.

Within political science, raced-gendered state institutions, policies, and categories of citizenship have been primary mechanisms for the production and preservation of systemic inequalities. Far from descriptive classifications, state constructions of race and gender involve scripted practices of subordination that consolidate the power of elite white men. Intersectionality offers multiple methods for the investigation of racialized gendering, ranging from the theorization of embodied power and discursive analysis of representational practices to empirical examination of structures of domination and subordination and their policy manifestations and effects. As Hae Yoon Choo and Myra Marx Ferree (2010, 136) have noted, "attention to these [contingent] interacting forces generates more sophisticated analyses of processes of inclusion and exclusion within the operating dynamics of institutions ... and tightens connections among power relations, institutional contexts, and lived experience."

Displacing White Androcentrism as the Unmarked Norm

Intersectional analysis challenges research presuppositions that position elite white heterosexual men as the unmarked norm against which "difference" is measured. Raced-gendered political discourses that affirm and normalize white heteromasculinity surface in manifold contexts. They underlie norms that validate white men as leaders and position women as emblems of the nation to be defended rather than as equal citizens. They sustain constructions of heterosexual families, which imply that in the absence of a "father" in the home, African Americans have "deviant" family formations and "lack" family values. They inform policy stances that construct the working poor as welfare dependents, thereby rendering invisible how hard the poor work, along with the structural forces that keep low-waged workers clustered in jobs with no security or benefits. Whether interrogating locutions such as "majority" and "minority" that misrepresent national and global demographics or the "grammars of whiteness" that obscure embodied power, intersectional analysis seeks to illuminate non-static vectors of power, and non-additive processes of domination and subordination. Acknowledging that inequalities are socially produced, multiply determined and intertwined, intersectional analysis contests basic methodological norms in the social sciences (Choo and Ferree 2010).

Choo and Ferree (2010, 140) have identified two interrelated analytic problems that arise when gender, race, and class are treated as separate variables in efforts to identify which has the "biggest effect":

1. When the "main effects" of race, gender, and class are studied as essentially unaffected by each other, the interaction among them is not apparent as a process.
2. The effects of class, race, and gender are primarily seen in the experiences of those in the subordinated or "marked" category.

Defining race, class, and gender as independent and separate limits the visibility of dynamic intersections of these processes – making it near impossible to see how whites engage in practices that preserve racial hierarchies and remain invested in race *qua* whiteness even as they proclaim that they are not racist. Seeing race as something that minorities have, whites engage in practices such as living in segregated neighborhoods and sending their children to private schools that reproduce advantage, creating and maintaining segregated spaces and experiences, while never being aware that they are enacting racial logics and producing racialized effects.

In the context of quantitative studies of race, gender, and class, the typical methodological approach is akin to titration – an effort to distil the pure effect of race or class or gender. Toward that end, researchers attempt to isolate the effects of gender by controlling for race, isolate the effects of race by controlling for gender, and isolate the effects of class by controlling for race and gender. Such an approach renders invisible mutual constitution. The best it can achieve is an examination of "interaction effects" – an additive model, which presupposes that distinct forces come together to interact (Choo and Ferree 2010, 131).

As Mustafa Emirbayer (1997, 287) points out: "One of the problems with standard statistical models in social science is that they employ an inter-action framework, conceptualizing independent variables as remaining fixed and unchanging as they bounce off one another within a particular model. The independent variable is assumed to act upon the dependent variable, but not to be changed or affected by that interaction." By contrast, intersectional analysis recognizes that racialized gendering is a process of complex mutual constitution. To treat dimensions of co-constitution as if each is independent is to mis-characterize them for no dimension can be understood as "given" or as existing in isolation.

De-naturalizing Difference

Lisa Garcia Bedolla (2007) has noted that intersectional research requires constant questioning of existing categories and a refusal to accept any social grouping as "natural." The social construction of categories of difference is a political process. Individuals are recruited to categories and positioned within certain vectors of power; yet as human agents, individuals have various options in the "subject positions" they adopt. Thus intersectional analysis investigates the formation of political subjects as a contested process of self-determination in a field of power relations (Yuval-Davis 2006). Toward that end, intersectional research designs are attuned to power, contingency, and unintended consequences, exploring how norms of embodiment, behavior, and thought are created, circulated, resisted and trans-formed (Spade and Willse 2016). Probing the complex nexus of coercion and consent, intersectional analysis captures the dynamic relationships that link indivi-duals, groups, social context, and political practices in complex webs of privilege and disadvantage.

Bodies are not the only phenomena that can be naturalized. Behaviors, emo-tions, aspirations, and hierarchical social relations have been characterized as "natural" in ways that mask the operation of power. Since the U.S. Civil War, for example, the separation of the races was deemed an altogether natural process – even as it was mandated by segregation orders and enforced by state and vigilante violence. Although the brutality of *de jure* segregation has ended, *de facto* segregation remains the norm, "forced upon inferiors by superiors" (Malcolm X, 1963). Yet these coercive forces have been naturalized through claims about ethnic enclaves and individual preferences and choices. Intersectional analysis denaturalizes these discourses by investigating interrelated processes that produce white gated communities and Black ghettos. Processes of urban marginalization must be studied in relation to suburban migration, urban "renewal" and gentrification, which entail construction of highways and public housing, as well as the creation and reclamation of brown fields. Only by examining the interrelation of these policy processes and conducting audits of the raced-gendered effects of the allocation of local, state, and federal resources is it possible to flesh out the intricate operations of embodied power. The cultural logics that enable affluent urban enclaves to coexist with – but remain untouched by – the dispossession of the poor are often naturalized. Intersectional analysis investigates public policies and structural forces intricately involved in the creation of distinctive ways of life hierarchically organized along vectors of class, race, and gender privilege. By disturbing the naturalness of existing social arrangements, intersectional analysis "excavates the power relations that have brought the 'normal' into being" (Choo and Ferree 2010, 139–40).

Disciplinary norms that emphasize parsimonious explanatory models work against seeing or seeking complexity. To achieve simplicity, formal models tend toward reductionist accounts. By contrast, proponents of intersectionality seek to engage messy complexity. Investigating social context, specific relations that bind marked and unmarked categories, particular processes that produce racialized-gendered hierarchies, intersectional analysis denaturalizes hegemonic accounts that mask privilege and power. Rejecting the biological determinism that structures modern discourses on race, sex, and sexuality, intersectionality reconceptualizes power relations that inform the construction of center and margins, and metropole and periphery in national and international orders.

Investigating Processes

As a process-centered approach, intersectionality analyzes the mutual constitution of race, class, gender, sexuality, nationality as these are transformed over time within specific social and political contexts. As an analytic technique, intersectionality explores "dynamic processes: racialization rather than races, economic exploitation rather than classes, gendering and gender performance rather than genders ... Excavating how power operates across particular institutional fields ... the approach emphasizes change over time as well as between sites and institutions" (Choo and Ferree 2010, 134). In contrast to the quest for universal laws, proponents of intersectionality explore processes that vary over time and place. Racialized gendering has been integral to colonization, for example, but the particular dynamics of racialized gendering have differed significantly in North and South America, and in various regions of Africa and Asia, according to the vision of specific colonizing powers and the technologies available to them. Investigating these complex dynamics, intersectionality illuminates embodied processes – both in relation to the particular people who orchestrate the practices that set racialization, exploitation, and gendering into motion – and in relation to the groups and individuals produced through these processes. Attuned to social, geographical and historical context, intersectionality encourages comparative analysis to investigate how the interplay among structures of domination varies across time and space. By examining material and cultural relations of power in diverse historical and geographical contexts, comparative intersectional analysis can reveal structural processes organizing power (Choo and Ferree 2010, 134).

Engaging Multi-level Analysis

Choo and Ferree note that the methodological demands of a process model have a correlate: multi-level analysis. "Attention to explicit comparison, dynamic processes, and variation by context ... calls for data that are multilevel, capturing the agency of individuals in making the world they inhabit, and the enabling and constraining forces of the world as it has been produced" (Choo and Ferree 2010, 134). Toward that end, intersectional analysis challenges categorization schemes within the social sciences that associate gender with micro-level group or individual social psychological processes, race with meso-level structures of social organization such as exclusion, segregation, and group conflict, and class with macro-level processes of societal development and differentiation. Racialized gendering occurs in and across all these sites. Consider, for example, the characterization of "whiteness" by Lake and Reynolds (2008, 3) as a transnational form of racial identification that was at once global in its power and personal in its meaning, the basis of geopolitical alliances and a subjective sense of self. Lake and Reynolds's detailed investigation of "the emergence of 'white men's countries'" from the 1870s through World War II traces the development of an idea of racial commonality that linked Europe with white settler societies in Australia, New Zealand, South Africa and the United States. The perception of a shared "whiteness" forged a sense of "fellow feeling" that was both grounded in and productive of a notion of superiority to "the black and yellow races." And that growing sense of superiority influenced domestic and foreign policies of individual nations, as well as international alliances. An adequate analysis of whiteness, then, must involve multi-level analysis ranging from internalized norms and individual beliefs and attitudes to social practices, governmental programs and policies, international alliances and their effects.

Rather than assuming that one dimension of inequality can be explained in isolation at a single site, intersectional analysis investigates "how each dimension of inequality is itself subdivided and crisscrossed with other axes of power and exclusion in ways that often escape detection" (Choo and Ferree 2010, 135). Intersectionality emphasizes the mutual constitution of raced-sexed relations of privilege and subordination. Rather than "adding more groups to test an initial hypothesis, or separating primary and secondary contradictions, or attempting to control the effects of particular variables," intersectional analysis requires comparative contextualization, attention to similarities and differences in all their messy complexity (Choo and Ferree 2010, 135). Methodologically, then, "intersectional analysis demands attention to mutually constitutive processes of racialization, gendering, sexualization, and economic exploitation that affect the mainstream as well as the marginalized other," thereby illuminating the flow of knowledge and power across levels of social organization rather than assuming nested hierarchies of stratification (Choo and Ferree 2010, 146).

Intersectionality's Methodological Precepts

As an analytical frame for the social sciences, intersectionality challenges scholars to shift their way of seeing, changing the questions they ask, the evidence they seek, and the methods they deploy to examine the world. Focusing specifically on the discipline of political science, Ange-Marie Hancock (2007b) has suggested that intersectionality has six key methodological precepts that help keep complexity in play and avoid reductionist accounts:

- More than one category of difference is involved in every political issue or process.
- The relationship among categories of difference is an open empirical question; and intersections of these categories are more than the sum of their parts.
- Categories of difference are dynamic productions that operate at both individual and institutional levels, created and contested in complex ways.
- There is always variation within a category; intragroup diversity may shed light on the way we think about groups as actors in politics and the potential outcomes of particular political interventions.
- Intersectional research involves both individual level and institutional investigation; integrative analysis captures the interaction between institutions and individuals.
- Intersectional investigations attend to theoretical and empirical aspects of research that span ontological and epistemological assumptions, research design (framing the research question, selecting relevant concepts, and developing categories capable of capturing mutual constitution), and implementation (operationalizing and measuring processes and analyzing results).

(Hancock 2007b, 251)

For those trained in a discipline steeped in methodological individualism and methodological nationalism, who have been taught to understand classification as the creation of mutually exclusive categories, and whose research objectives have been defined in terms of a quest for universal laws, intersectional thinking and analysis go against the grain. Intersectionality problematizes mainstream methodological assumptions, as well as common-sense demarcations of the natural from the social. It demands the investigation of complex modes of embodied power that remain invisible within accredited ways of seeing. And it seeks to divest the unmarked norm of its standard-setting role. In return for such a radical reorientation, intersectional research offers a sophisticated understanding of causal complexity at great remove from abstract universalism. Within an intersectional framework, parsimonious explanation is supplanted by recognition that multiple factors can contribute to a particular outcome; various processes may promote similar outcomes; multiple means may produce the same end; and the same means may produce different ends in various circumstances (Marchand and Runyon 2011). Yet, in acknowledging the messiness of complexity, intersectional analysis promises to enhance the discipline's understanding of power and to generate sophisticated accounts of the production of inequality.

Whiteness: From Historical Artefact to Discursive Formation

Intersectionality scholars attempt to displace whiteness as modernity's unmarked norm by demonstrating that whiteness is a racial formation, which has had manifold manifestations over the past five centuries. Whiteness has shaped scientific discourses on "race," colonial practices of conquest, labor exploitation and resource extraction, as well as property allocations that enriched European settlers in the new world, while dispossessing and causing the death of Indigenous populations. Whiteness was integral to the trans-Atlantic slave trade that fueled the growth of affluence for some while reducing others to the subhuman status of chattel property. Whiteness has also forged political solidarity among the leaders of certain Anglo-European nations and shaped countless public policies from marriage and citizenship to immigration restrictions, segregation, and mass incarceration. Rather than treating these diverse manifestations as an artefact of the past, intersectionality scholars suggest that there are profound continuities linking past practices to contemporary ways of seeing.

To explicate these linkages, Charles Mills (2008) conceptualized whiteness as an epistemology – a system of knowing – that can shape perceptions, public memories, and imaginative possibilities around what is sayable, doable, and thinkable. Mills emphasizes that in addition to enabling certain kinds of knowledge such as the "natural" superiority of the Anglo-European, whiteness also produces structured "nonknowings" (Mills 2008, 234). The lens of whiteness structures perception in ways that strategically exclude certain kinds of evidence and experience from white consciousness (e.g., evidence of the violence associated with colonization and enslavement or the factors that might explain lower crime rates yet higher incarceration rates for Black youth).

Building upon Mills's analysis, Rebecca Clark-Mane (2012) analyzed whiteness as a discursive formation that produces, secures, and maintains material inequalities. Through an examination of dozens of contemporary texts, Clark-Mane identified several "tropes of whiteness" – rhetorical strategies and structures of thought that reproduce whiteness as a naturalized and unspoken set of relations. As a way of organizing perception, these tropes seem "innocent" or "natural," yet they make ongoing racialized gendering invisible, thereby masking pervasive inequalities. By fostering certain kinds of ignorance, the tropes of whiteness undermine efforts to explain growing inequalities, along with transformative efforts to eliminate injustice.

Clark-Mane suggests that the grammar of whiteness is embedded in the everyday organization of social and cultural relations in ways that systemically advantage whites even when they are not aware of these cultural logics. By replicating these tropes, well-meaning whites who believe themselves to be antiracist can nonetheless entrench white privilege. Clark-Mane's astute observations offer important insights into whiteness as a discursive formation, identifying certain tropes that surface regularly in political science discourses and in popular media. Clark-Mane's first trope of whiteness involves a temporal framing that always situates racism and racial injustice in the past. In this way, raced-gendered inequities are accorded validity in an earlier historical period, but positioned as issues that have already been resolved. Not only are raced-gendered injustices cast into the past, so too are mobilizations to demand rectification. Incorporating modernity's emphasis on progress, this trope of whiteness implies that oncelegitimate issues of inequality can now be laid to rest because they have been redressed at some point in the indefinite past. By stripping away specificity, racedgendered harms are decontextualized and removed from the domain of pressing contemporary issues. The conflation of racial injustice with slavery or the equation of state-sponsored racism with *de jure* segregation, for example, acknowledge significant racism in U.S. history, but suggest that those problems no longer exist. Absolving contemporary generations of any responsibility for past injustices, this trope diverts attention away from contemporary racial inequities such as growing economic inequality, ongoing discrimination, voter suppression, hyper-surveillance of Black neighborhoods, and disparate incarceration rates. By assigning the problem of racial and gender injustice to the past, this trope reinforces the mistaken notion that the problem of racism no longer exists.

A second trope of whiteness involves another form of de-contextualization that promotes fallacious claims of equivalence. By ignoring the specific material conditions of racialized harm, a false equivalence is created between disparate experiences. For example, claims of "reverse discrimination" suggest that one white student's failure to win admission to a law school or a medical school is equivalent to centuries of enslavement, dispossession, labor exploitation, disenfranchisement, segregation, substandard schooling, marginalization, and exclusion imposed on African Americans as a collective. Through such faulty equivalence, the sovereign citizens movement, which claim not to recognize the authority of federal and local government":

> Since 9/11, an average of nine American Muslims per year have been involved in an average of six terrorist related plots against targets in the US. Most were disrupted, but the 20 plots that were carried out accounted for 50 fatalities over the past 13.5 years. In contrast, right wing extremists averaged 337 attacks per year in the decade after September 11, causing a total of 254 fatalities according to the US Military Academy's Combating Terrorism Center. The toll has increased since this study's release in 2012 … Other data sets, using different definitions of political violence, tell comparable stories. The Global Terrorism Database maintained by the Start Center at the University of Maryland includes 65 attacks in the United States associated with right wing ideologies and 24 by Muslim extremists since 9/11. The International Security Program at the New America Foundation identifies 39 fatalities from "non-jihadist" homegrown extremists and 26 fatalities from "jihadist" extremists … Meanwhile terrorism of all forms has accounted for a tiny proportion of violence in America. There have been more than 215,000 murders in the US since 9/11. For every person killed by Muslim extremists, there have been 4,300 homicides from other threats.
> (Kurzman and David Schanzer 2015, A27)

Racialized gendering of the "Muslim threat" misdirects attention, fostering mistrust of "others" and unwarranted trust of armed white men. Whether construed as seductive fellow feeling, homophilous social network, or discursive formation, whiteness filters perceptions, generating flawed accounts of danger and of safety.

Class and race segregation can exacerbate perceptions of social distance and concomitant levels of distrust. As Emma Seery and Ana Caistro Arencar (2014, 50) have noted: "When the wealthy physically separate themselves from the less well-off, fear and distrust tend to grow, something consistently demonstrated in global opinion surveys. The World Values Survey asks random samples of the population in numerous countries whether or not they agree with the statement: 'Most people can be trusted.' The differences between countries are large, with a clear correlation between lack of trust and high levels of economic inequality." High levels of distrust can also have a potent impact on social provision. Both Martin Gilens (1995, 1996) and Rodney Hero (1998) have documented a strong correlation between level of racial diversity within a state and diminished social programs and policies provided by the state. More homogeneous states have more generous social policies.

U.S. public opinion polls repeatedly document that whites see the world in starkly different terms than those who have experienced subordinating mechanisms of racialized gendering. Consider, for example, a Wall Street/NBC poll conducted in late April, 2015, which tapped public sentiment about recent riots in the city of Baltimore. Following more than a year of highly publicized police slayings of unarmed Black men, which gave rise to the "Black Lives Matter" campaign across the nation, Freddie Gray, a 25-year-old Black resident of Baltimore, who had been arrested for possession of a switchblade, died from injuries to his spinal cord sustained while in police custody. Riots broke out in Baltimore in the immediate aftermath of his death. Although African-American activists linked the civil unrest to the pervasiveness of police brutality, the hyper-surveillance of Black communities, and escalation of police violence in Baltimore, 58 percent of whites surveyed in the Wall Street/NBC poll reported that the riots in Baltimore were the result of "people seeking an excuse to engage in looting and violence" (Kristof 2015, A25). The depth of this misperception requires explanation, especially in a period when local and national news were accurately reporting recurrent episodes of police violence in the context of mobilizations organized by Black Lives Matter activists.

Social science discourse on ethnicity provides one frame in which to analyze white constructions of urban riots as an "excuse to loot." Both Ian Haney-Lopez (2014) and Edmund Fong (2015) suggest that pluralist accounts of ethnicity are deeply connected to racialization projects. According to Haney-Lopez (2014, 94), the "concept of ethnicity originated in early twentieth century … as a means to erase racial differences among whites." University of Chicago sociologist Robert Park advanced a notion of cultural pluralism, which suggested that all ethnic groups followed the same trajectory toward assimilation – from exclusion, clannishness, and poverty to eventual full inclusion, assimilation, and material success. Although Park's research focused on groups of European descent, his conceptualization of ethnicity seemed neutral and inclusive – describing processes of assimilation open to all. In mapping the gradual assimilation of Irish, German, Italian, and Jewish immigrants, social science research suggested that the boundaries of belonging in the U.S. were flexible; equal citizenship was fluid, voluntary, and non-exclusionary. Yet this characterization obscured the processes of racialization that marked certain people of color (African Americans, Asian Americans, Mexican Americans) as unassimilable. In conceptualizing ethnicity in relation to growing assimilation of white ethnics, social science research also laid the foundation for an account of certain "cultures" that failed to take advantage of opportunities for assimilation.

Ethnicity established a commonsense causal framework in which it became possible to discuss "dysfunctional cultures" whose members suffer through their own refusal to improve their condition. In *Beyond the Melting Pot*, Nathan Glazer and Daniel Patrick Moynihan (1963) drew out the racializing implications of the ethnicity frame, blaming the Black home and Black community for "failure" to assimilate. Adopting an approach that W. E. B. Du Bois (1903) had castigated in *Souls of Black Folk*, Glazer and Moynihan not only constructed African Americans as a "problem," but claimed they were a self-generating problem. Depicting Black women as the perverse inversion of America's "self-made man," Glazer and

Moynihan suggested that Black women were responsible for their own poverty, the crisis of Black masculinity, the dissolution of the Black family, rising crime rates in urban neighborhoods, and untold miseries of their own children. In short, Black women lay at the heart of a "culture of pathology." According to Glazer and Moynihan (1963, 49–50), "the serious obstacles to the ability to make use of a free educational system to advance into higher occupations, and to eliminate the massive problems that afflict colored Americans in the city … must be found in the [Black] home and family and community." In 1966, Moynihan expanded on this theme in recommending a "Family Policy for the Nation." Attributing racial inequality to Black cultural pathology, Moynihan suggested that government intervention could not provide a remedy for self-inflicted wounds. "A community that allows a large number of young men to grow up in broken families, dominated by women, never acquiring any stable relationship to male authority, never acquiring any set of rational expectations about the future – that community asks for and gets chaos. Crime, violence, unrest, disorder… that is not only to be expected … but they are very near to inevitable. And it is richly deserved" (cited in Rainwater and Yancey 1967, 385, 393).

An account of ethnic assimilation based on the experience of white European immigrants thus became the foundation for a cultural deficit model of inequality when applied to the "unassimilable." The dimensions of racialization within this frame are complex. White ethnicity is associated with self-making and self-determination, a capacity to use the resources made available by the state to achieve upward mobility. Presuming that the same public resources are available to Blacks, the only explanation for the failure of Blacks to assimilate is their own refusal to excel. But this presumption itself is at odds with all the historical evidence of racist policies that denied equal opportunity to Black citizens and other citizens of color (recounted in earlier chapters). A certain kind of sanctioned ignorance, then, sustains white misperception of Black experience. Appeals to a culture of pathology render centuries of state racism invisible, exculpate white citizens from any responsibility for Black marginalization and impoverishment, and place remedies for current inequities beyond the reach of the state, while blaming African Americans for their plight. Between the 1960s and the early 21st century, cultural pathology accounts were supplemented by "laissez-faire racism" (Bobo et al. 1997), which attributes the putative cultural deficits of the Black community to the moral character of Black citizens, contending that Blacks "do not try hard enough to overcome the difficulties they face; that they take what they have not earned" (Haney-Lopez 2014, 101). It is a very short step from assumptions about cultural pathology and deficits in moral character to claims that riots are an excuse to loot.

By privileging racialized notions of culture, community and identity, these accounts mask the structural forces that cause socio-economic disadvantage. And they sustain modes of gendered racialization that grossly distort the experiences of African Americans. Consider, for example, the contorted causality of blaming

Black women for economic dislocation in U.S. cities. Contrary to the noxious representations of Black women articulated by Glazer and Moynihan and widely circulated since, Black women are not "lazy" and indifferent to work; they work more hours each week than the average American. Far from being wanton and licentious procreators, Black women bear fewer children than the national average of 2.2 children per family; indeed, child-bearing among African-American women has now fallen below replacement level. Working more jobs and more hours than white Americans, Black women are not the cause of poverty for they do not set minimum wages at levels that fall far below the poverty line. They are not responsible for the 34 percent decline in income in poor households over the past four decades as wages have failed to keep up with living costs. They are not responsible for the 43 percent drop in the value of welfare benefits during the last quarter of the twentieth century. They are not responsible for the racialized "War on Crime" that treats crack cocaine more punitively than more expensive powdered versions (Jordan-Zachery 2009). White perceptual filters get the world wrong – with profoundly destructive consequences for social policy.

Some intersectionality theorists have advocated comparative analysis as one means to illuminate central dynamics of gendered racialization. When considering the potent association of violence and Black masculinity, comparative investigation of the United Kingdom and the United States reveals recurrent patterns in explanatory frames. As Claire Alexander (2010, 275) has demonstrated, in Britain and the USA there are stark parallels in the proliferation of "discourses around an externalized masculine aggression and criminality linked to social deprivation and exclusion on the one hand and to culture conflict and identity on the other." In the United Kingdom:

> ... these two paradigms [social exclusion and culture conflict] underpinned the notion of "the Muslim underclass" and the focus on Asian/Muslim "gangs", in which religio-cultural difference intersected with racial alienation and socio-economic neglect in a potent image of a hypermasculine threat. As with Black young men from the 1970s, Muslim young men were seen as "in crisis" – caught between an anachronistic parental culture and a holistic wider society, failing in mainstream masculine social roles as breadwinner, and turning to crime and violence to compensate for this. As the 1990s wore on, this spectre of threat was compounded by the fear of rising religiosity and fundamentalist ideologies ... With emergence of social unrest (riots), explanations fell into two camps: those focusing on structural issues of socio-economic marginalization and neglect in a situation of post-industrial decline; and those stressing cultural dysfunction, crime, and law and order ... however, these two strands were increasingly indistinguishable, with poverty and unemployment being increasingly explained through the lens of "culture" and "choice", and with the Muslim underclass standing at the crossroad of religious, cultural, and class failure – the cultural deficit model of inequality.
>
> *(Alexander 2010, 275)*

As Alexander's analysis makes clear, in the U.K. as in the U.S., cultural deficit and character deficit accounts remain widely popular in explaining the behavior of minority youth. In both nations, the problem of inequality is individualized as markedly unequal social conditions are attributed to bad choices or pathological cultures. These popular explanatory accounts legitimize state practices of "surveillance, arrests, detentions, interrogations, searches and shootings – all in name of community cohesion" (Alexander 2010, 276). Yet these explanations are markedly defective. Whether circulating in popular culture or within academic scholarship, cultural deficit and character deficit accounts reflect what Nancy Burns (2007, 107) has called "the morselization of experience." As Burns notes, the morselization of experience "enables people – scholars and the individuals they study – to explain any individual outcome as the product of individual and idiosyncratic circumstances and not as a consequence of large-scale structural discrimination" (Burns 2007, 107). Yet this very morselization, which often affects research design and questions investigated, renders structural disadvantage and the cumulative effects of racialized harm invisible. Thus, Burns suggests that the inability to perceive systemic advantage and disadvantage may be methodologically driven – an artifact of methodological individualism operating to mask racialized gendering.

Proponents of intersectional analysis emphasize that cultural deficit and character deficit frames mask both state practices of embodied power and sustained mobilization against these abusive practices. The eruption of urban unrest appears inexplicable, precisely because decades of state violence against poor people of color remain invisible. Unequal schools, dilapidated housing, police harassment and brutality remain below the threshold of visibility, thus the link between abusive state racialization and anomic resistance goes unnoticed.

Edmund Fong (2015) has suggested that several conceptual frameworks circulating within contemporary political science work against recognition of the potent effects of racialized gendering. Multiculturalism, cultural pluralism, and cosmopolitanism in various ways fail to understand the relationship between state racialization and its corollary effects – the development of a sense of collective identity, linked fate, and determined resistance among those who have been racialized and subordinated. Multiculturalism and cultural pluralism are heirs to social science conceptualizations of ethnicity, which posit groups as fluid, voluntary, and non-exclusionary (Fong 2015, 38). Convinced that race as a biological category is wrong-headed, proponents of multiculturalism and cultural pluralism seek to offer an "escape" from the ascriptive, stigmatizing and segregating elements of "black identity," so Blacks can come to resemble other Americans (Fong 2015, 38). According to Fong, multiculturalism treats race as a kind of ethnicity, a variant of hyphenated identity that is both voluntary and symbolic. Cultural pluralism casts the language of race as too corrupted to be positively recuperated, suggesting that any appeal to race invites unacceptable essentialism on the part of dominant and minority groups. Working within an assimilationist logic, "both approaches insist on the declining significance of race," and endorse the transcendence of this fictive and invidious distinction (Fong 2015, 24). Where multiculturalism and cultural pluralism situate race and ethnicity within the nation-state, cosmopolitanism aspires to transcend the boundaries of the nation-state as too restrictive a horizon in this era of globalization. Attempting to transcend "absolutist and exclusive forms of identification, cosmopolitanism casts identity politics as a dead-end akin to ethnoreligious nationalism" (Fong 2015, 29). Yet cosmopolitanism also assumes that "identity is largely voluntary: individuals may choose to retain or reject ethnic identification" (Fong 2015, 29).

By failing to understand the embodied effects of prolonged racialization, multiculturalism, cultural pluralism, and cosmopolitanism "deprive racialized individuals and groups of any kind of normative recognition as other than victims" (Fong 2015, 24). Yet, in "refusing" to move toward assimilation and cast off outmoded racial identities, these "victims" are perceived to be suffering from self-inflicted wounds. Like cultural deficit and character deficit accounts, multiculturalists, cultural pluralists, and cosmopolitans fail to acknowledge historical and continuing practices of state racialization that preclude the possibility of assimilation for those deemed unassimilable. At the social policy level, these intellectual stances are far from progressive. They deny the racialized any legitimate claim on society for redress, such as affirmative action. They depoliticize race by eviscerating inquiries into its causes. They delegitimize collective mobilizations for racial justice. And they reprivatize raced-gendered identities. Indeed, Fong argues that multiculturalism, cultural pluralism, and cosmopolitanism entail a "retreat from race," which erodes the "will to address structural inequities defined by race ... as the enormity of those inequities continues to grow" (Fong 2015, 22).

Intersectionality theorists emphasize that cultural deficit and character deficit explanations not only misdiagnose the causes of inequality, but they seriously misunderstand the relation between oppression and resistance. Because they fail to see state policies and practices that subordinate, marginalize, and exclude racialized-gendered groups, while affirming, privileging, and securing the dominance of whites, these accounts fail to understand that sustained oppression provokes violent and nonviolent forms of resistance. As Fanon (1962) so graphically depicted in *Wretched of the Earth*, domination produces subordination, but it also has corollary effects. It can produce ties of loyalty and a sense of belonging among the subordinated. It can foster modes of collective identification and a perception of linked fate. It can engender group resistance and *identity politics* – forms of oppositional politics organized by the oppressed to overcome marginalization. As a form of social justice activism, identity politics seeks to transform political culture and political institutions to achieve equal recognition, equal respect, and equal citizenship. As the mobilization of the oppressed to make injustices encoded in law, custom, and tradition visible and actionable, identity politics can manifest in violence as well as nonviolence.

Kathleen Staudt (2011) has noted that political scientists far too frequently miss the connection between racialized oppression and violent resistance – whether in the form of riots, armed insurrection, or struggles for national independence:

> The exertion of power in anything but an open vacuum produces resistance. Political scientists were slow to develop this insight, tied as the mainstream discipline was to the study of formal institutions and easily countable proactive individual behavior. Moreover, mainstream political scientists studied phenomena that functioned to support whole political systems, rather than undermine or transform them.
>
> *(Staudt 2011, 345)*

In *Weapons of the Weak*, James Scott (1985) analyzed the complex relationship between domination and resistance in the context of peasant societies, emphasizing the manifold forms that resistance can take – from sabotage, playing ignorant, and willful noncooperation to armed insurrection. Yet, as Staudt (2011, 345) points out "less attentive political scientists fail to see" the connection between injustice and escalating resistance. Or worse, they attribute violent resistance to the "barbaric" nature of racialized others or their pathological cultures.

Questions of causality are notoriously fraught in the social and natural sciences. Whether qualitative or quantitative methods are involved, it is exceptionally difficult to identify the necessary and sufficient conditions for specific political phenomena. It would be a mistake to assume that all anomic violence and organized conflict can be understood as a mobilization against state practices of embodied power. The conditions under which raced-gendered subordination engenders violent or lesser forms of resistance are sorely in need of empirical investigation. But it is also a mistake to ignore racialized gendering and gendered racialization as possible explanatory hypotheses in political life. When mainstream political scientists refuse to read the scholarship on race, gender, and sexuality, opting for a division of labor that cordons off this research as a content specialization of interest only to those in a particular subfield, they effectively condemn the discipline to disembodied politics. In so doing, they insulate many contorted causal claims from interrogation and refutation.

Expanding the Contours of the Political

In offering explanations of sanctioned ignorance, systemic misperception, and distorted causal claims, intersectionality scholarship expands the understandings of political life. A central theme of this book has been the *politics of embodiment*. Far from being a natural phenomenon, racialized-gendered bodies are produced. Although multiple social and cultural forces are at play in circumscribing embodied experience, the role of the state is by no means negligible. Designated on birth and death certificates, driver's licenses and marriage licenses, enumerated in census documents, and deemed a legal requirement to qualify for a host of government programs and benefits, race, gender, and sexuality are related to the state in ways that are too seldom recognized. Forms of physical embodiment that are taken as natural are often the product of oppression, the result of hyper-stimulation of certain capabilities (e.g., musculature, sexuality) and forced repression of others (e.g., intellect, creativity). States have been intricately involved in the raced-gendered allocation of particular types of education, labor, and military training, the organization of domestic responsibilities, the cultivation of structures of servility, and the segregation of public and private spaces – in ways that profoundly affect racialized-gendered embodiment. The politics of embodiment within and across nations is thus a rich field for investigation across a host of policy domains.

By excavating specific points at which gendered racialization has barred subordinated groups from political life, intersectional analysis offers insights into the *politics of exclusion*, another topic seldom addressed in mainstream political studies. By situating continuing efforts to gain political inclusion in relation to an overt politics of exclusion and complex modes of resistance, intersectional analysis illuminates racialized gendering as a political issue in need of redress and as a phenomenon in need of systematic study.

Additional dimensions of political life become visible when diverse women and men are the subjects of inquiry. Universal claims become suspect once it is clear that those marked as racialized genders do not experience the world on the same terms as the unmarked white male norm. Whether investigating the official institutions of state, social movements, stratified political participation, distribution of burdens and benefits, or transnational forces and global flows, the *politics of diversity* remains in need of detailed study.

Intersectionality scholars have emphasized that official institutions of governance are only one site of political action; politics pervades what is often depicted as "the private sphere," a sphere supposedly free from intrusion by the state. In contrast to liberal notions about negative liberty, modern states – like their ancient precursors – have played key roles in constituting families, regulating marriage and sexuality, and controlling reproduction – whether by creating incentives for childbearing through pro-natalist policies, coercing women to bear children by prohibiting access to contraception and abortion, or restricting childbearing by dictating family size or sterilizing women in accordance with racialized population control policies. In contrast to the notion that relations within the private sphere lie beyond the reach of the state, intersectional analysis provides concrete examples of state interference with the most intimate decisions and actions an individual can make. Thus intersectionality studies call attention to the *politics of intimacy*, identifying embodied power dynamics omitted from mainstream accounts of politics.

Drawing evidence from the lives of the subordinated as well as from the dominant, intersectionality theorists have challenged concepts central to theories of liberal democracy: negative liberty (freedom from state interference) and the public/private distinction itself. Rather than demarcating the sphere of state action from the sphere of individual privacy, the concept of negative liberty masks the role of the state in producing inequalities among citizens. In marked contrast to accounts of the laissez-faire state, the "night watchman" state, and the "shrinking" state in a global era, intersectional analysis suggests that democratic and authoritarian states are deeply involved in the embodied politics. Far from being natural, private or pre-political, genders, families, ethnicities, and races are constituted by state action and regulated by law and policy. From laws prohibiting miscegenation, same-sex marriage, and various sexual practices, states intrude on the most intimate decisions citizens make. Moreover, nation-states consistently use racial criteria to fix the boundaries of citizenship – the most basic mode of political belonging (Haney-Lopez 1996; Stevens 1999).

Investigating the lives of diverse women and men suggests that the *politics of identity* is a ubiquitous phenomenon: authoritarian regimes, social democracies, liberal democracies, secular states, and states embroiled in civil conflict are deeply enmeshed in microphysics of power that position men and women of various races and classes differently in the national imaginary, producing raced-gendered modes of national belonging and self-understanding. Nation-states accord full rights, recognition and respect to some members, while subjecting others to stigma, heightened regulation, and control. As male leaders act to secure and protect "the nation," women of particular classes, races, and ethnicities are subjected to regulations of dress, deportment, and reproductive activity that deeply encroach on individual freedom. Far from affecting only what women wear in public or how they conduct their reproductive lives, these raced-gendered regulations position particular states in relation to transnational geopolitics that play out in refugee camps, media campaigns, peace-keeping missions, and litigation taken to the European Court of Justice and the International Criminal Court. When the production of raced-gendered identities is understood as a dimension of state action, then *identity politics* takes on new meaning. As the mobilization of the oppressed to make injustices encoded in law, custom, and tradition visible and actionable, identity politics is neither special interest pleading nor inherently fractious. It is a form of social justice activism.

Intersectionality scholars emphasize that racialization and gendering operate well beyond the boundaries of the nation-state. Raced-gendered patterns of skilling and de-skilling, differences in political rights and economic opportunities, and specific modes of political visibility and invisibility structure transnational and international regimes as well as power within the nation-state. Contrary to depictions of the international as an exclusive interaction among states, international policies and conventions structure human relationships as well as relations among states. Development, for example, has been one of the hallmarks of international policy in the post-World War II era. An intersectional approach illuminates complex racing-gendering in development policies, tracing how policies explicitly designed to foster economic development have devoted significant resources to the control of impoverished women's fertility and how policies intended to improve "quality of life" have adopted birth control and sterilization of women of color as appropriate means to that end (Briggs 2002; Bergeron 2006). In so doing, intersectional analysis demonstrates that international institutions are also intricately involved in the politics of intimacy, contrary to popular beliefs. By investigating women's and men's lives and livelihoods across the globe, intersectional studies of international political economy call attention to increasing poverty, the transnational care economy, and the proliferation of trafficking as racialized-gendered phenomena integrally related to state practices of embodied power in an era of globalization, and to neoliberal structural adjustment programs and austerity regimes imposed by international financial institutions.

Population policies, development policies, disarmament protocols, the law of the sea, peace-keeping missions, refugee policies, anti-poverty initiatives, Millennium goals, human rights protocols, and trade agreements constrain individual action as well as state conduct. Operating through national legislation, moral prohibitions, informal mechanisms of social control, appeals to the conscience of the world community, sexual and racial divisions of labor, and armed peace-keepers, international conventions support and maintain regulatory sexual and racial regimes that undermine the autonomy of certain subjects while shoring up the power of others (Bleiker 2000). Raced-gendered "regimes" or practices of inequality embedded in international institutions and structures enable systems of racial, ethnic, gender, and sexual advantage and disadvantage to operate independently of the will of particular agents (Fierke 1999). Racialization, gendering, and heteronormativity permeate global processes such as the outsourcing of reproductive labor and care economies, converting forms of privilege into rules, routines, practices, policies, institutions, and structures that serve and promote certain interests, creating transnational political opportunity structures that are neither race nor gender neutral (Kronsell 2005).

Processes of racialization operating transnationally need not be tied exclusively to color or "epidermalization" (Fanon 1952). Although hierarchies of difference have been and continue to be constructed along axes of marked physical differences, racializing technologies may also involve more subtle appropriations of sameness and more blatant applications of force. In contrast to practices of racialization and gendering that are written on the body, colonial and neocolonial regimes have also established ethnocultural hierarchies through regulation of domesticity, mobility, migration, and visuality (Raissiguier 1999; Philipose 2007b; Kuokkanen 2008). As the "war on terror" and the U.S. occupation of Iraq have once again made painfully clear, violence and torture are themselves primary instruments of gendered racialization (Philipose 2007b; Richter-Montpetit 2007; Sjoberg 2007; Briggs 2015). When neoliberal globalism weds free trade and antiterrorism under the rubric of democratization, for example, racial profiling justified as a securitization measure mobilizes internal divisions within and across nations that haunt formal and informal economic sectors, voting booths, educational institutions, and civil society organizations.

Intersectional analysis demands multi-level investigation of gendered, raced, and classed politics of embodied power. Offering conceptual and methodological tools that challenge methodological nationalism and methodological individualism, intersectionality investigates the political economy of neocolonial relations and structures in scales that are larger and smaller than the nation-state, examining transnational connections and disjunctures that emerge from households, communities, and bodies, as well as nation-states, international institutions, and transnational actors (Nagar et al. 2002).

The politics of embodiment, the politics of intimacy, the politics of identity, identity politics, and the politics of raced-gendered institutions directly challenge the view that the twenty-first century is a "post-racial," "postfeminist" world. Claims about a post-racial, postfeminist era convey the idea that inequality is no longer a pressing concern, that race, gender, class, and sexuality pose no obstacles to individual or group advancement. By masking systemic inequities, claims that equality has already been achieved encourage the demobilization of social justice activists. In contrast to mistaken claims that equality has been achieved, intersectionality scholarship illuminates significant obstacles to inclusive democracy and social justice. These obstacles include national and international regimes structured by raced-gendered institutions; raced-gendered stereotypes and biases in evaluation that continue to work to the advantage of elite men; the pervasive pressure to assimilate to norms derived from elite men's experience – norms that are too narrow to encompass embodied differences; political frames that mask raced-gendered power; economic practices that heighten inequalities; resistance within existing institutions to policies designed to foster equality; and the mobilization of forces that aspire to further entrench racial and gender subordination. These obstacles indicate the depths of the challenges that the majority of the global population face in the 21st century. Including embodied power on the research agenda is one way to keep these issues in the public eye and to assign them priority status on national and transnational political agendas.

When mainstream political science refuses to engage this array of pressing contemporary issues, the discipline raises questions about the *politics of knowledge*. As this book has demonstrated, discipline-based decisions about what counts as politics, what questions are worthy of sustained investigation, and what explanatory frameworks warrant accreditation are never neutral. Intersectionality theorists suggest that racialized gendering and gendered racialization permeate politics in ways that exceed the boundaries of any and all content specializations within political science. If the discipline is to break the hold of foundational assumptions that shore up white supremacy, methodological individualism, and methodological nationalism, disembodied politics must be demystified and embodied politics recognized and studied.

Conclusion

Intersectionality as an analytical tool demonstrates that the political extends well beyond the official institutions of state, the struggle for power, or the authoritative allocation of values – the dominant conceptions of politics circulating within mainstream political studies in the United States. If political science is to grapple with the intricate and robust forms of power operating in the 21st century, then the discipline needs an enhanced understanding of politics. Both the central concepts and the accredited methodologies within political science must be expanded to address new political questions concerning embodied power – not only in relation to the raced and gendered constitution of subjectivities but also encompassing the state's role in producing racialized and gendered bodies. The scope of racialized gendering and gendered racialization in need of investigation includes the asymmetries of power in public and private spheres; the politics of racialized reproduction; the raced-gendered distributions of types of work; the organization of domestic activity; the divisions of paid and unpaid labor; the structures of the formal, informal, and subsistence economies; the segregation of labor markets; patterns of production and consumption; terms and conditions of labor exchange; racialized and gendered opportunities for education, employment and promotion; the politics of representation; the structures and outcomes of public decision-making; the operating procedures of regulatory and redistributive agencies; the dynamics of diasporas and decolonization; the potent contradictions of globalization, war-making and militarization; and the mobilization of manifold resistances against oppressive forces structuring and constraining life prospects.

Intersectionality studies offer a means to conceptualize the political world anew, identifying and dislodging modes of oppression that mainstream scholarship leaves untouched. Intersectionality theorists suggest that a political commitment to struggle against systems that subordinate and denigrate the majority of the human population can enhance the truth content and deepen the insights of academic accounts of the world. Attuned to ambiguity and indeterminacy and committed to an ethics of freedom, intersectional analysis challenges essentialized racial and gender differences and static models of domination and subordination, calling for investigation of the specificity of particular situations. Troubling both false universals and confining stereotypes, intersectional scholarship tracks complex operations of embodied power by resisting overgeneralization, recognizing the roots of particular judgments, and trying to think against itself by actively engaging multiple theoretical frames and cultural perspectives. Grounded in particularity, attentive to specificity, intersectional inquiry pays tribute to the singularity of events and lives, while investigating possible patterns and cross-case resonances. Intersectional analysis involves reflective comparisons and judgments that illuminate the visible and invisible – modes of embodiment, facets of desire, dynamics of social existence, categories that structure perception and action, intended and unintended consequences of action and inaction, macro, meso and micro structures that constrain. Emanating from specific locales and offering critiques of particular canonical accounts, intersectional analysis is a form of intellectual insurgency designed to open new modes of thinking and create the conditions of possibility for new modes of social, political, and intellectual life.

Notes

1 Whether or not race is an essential vector of power for intersectional analyses has been the subject of heated debate. Some European scholars have argued that problems of race and racialization are unique to the United States; others note that they are also central problematics in Great Britain, but they suggest that race and racialization are relatively absent from continental Europe (see, for example, Davis 2008 and Lykke 2010). For trenchant critiques of this view, see Lewis (2013), Bilge (2013), and Hancock (2016).
2 *Regents of the University of California vs. Bakke* (438 U.S. 265, 1978).
3 For a stark account of the increasingly dire situation of families living on less than $2/day, see Edin and Schaefer (2015).

BIBLIOGRAPHY

Aberbach, Joel and Jack Walker. 1973. *Race in the City*. Boston, MA: Little, Brown.
Alexander, Claire. 2010. "Culturing Poverty? Ethnicity, Religion, Gender, and Social Disadvantage among South Asian Muslim Communities in the United Kingdom." In Sylvia Chant, ed. *The International Handbook of Gender and Poverty*. Cheltenham: Edward Elgar, pp. 272–277.
Alexander, Michelle. 2011. *The New Jim Crow: Mass Incarceration in the Age of Colorblindness*. New York: The New Press.
Alexander-Floyd, Nikol. 2012. "Disappearing Acts: Reclaiming Intersectionality in the Social Sciences in a Post-Black Feminist Era." *Feminist Formations* 24(1): 1–25.
Allen, Anita. 1988. *Uneasy Access: Privacy for Women in a Free Society*. New York: Rowman and Littlefield.
Almond, Gabriel A. 1996. "Political Science: the History of the Discipline." In Robert E. Goodin and Hans-Dieter Klingemann, eds. *A New Handbook of Political Science*. New York: Oxford University Press, pp. 50–90.
American Political Science Association (APSA). 2011. *Report of the Task Force on Political Science in the 21st Century*. Washington, DC: American Political Science Association. Available at: www.apsanet.org/files/Task%20Force%20Reports/TF_21st%20Century_AllPgs_webres90.pdf.
Anderson, Benedict. 1991. *Imagined Communities: Reflections on the Origin and Spread of Nationalism*. London: Verso.
Anderson, Elijah. 1999. *Code of the Street*. New Haven, CT: Yale University Press.
Aoki, Andrew L. and Okiyoshi Takeda. 2004. "Small Spaces for Different Faces: Political Science Scholarship on Asian Americans." *PS: Political Science and Politics* 37(3): 497–500.
Apter Klinghoffer, Judith and Lois Elkis. 1992. "The 'Petticoat Electors': Women's Suffrage in New Jersey, 1776–1807." *Journal of the Early Republic* 12(2): 159–193.
Banton, Michael. 1998. *Racial Theories*. Cambridge: Cambridge University Press.
Bargu, Banu. 2015. "Sovereignty as Erasure: Rethinking Enforced Disappearances." University of Pennsylvania Political Theory Forum, January 29.

Bedford, Kate. 2004. "Gender and Politics." In Mary Hawkesworth and Maurice Kogan, eds. *Encyclopedia of Government and Politics*, 2nd edn, Vol. I. London: Routledge, pp. 603–615.

Berger, John. 1972. *Ways of Seeing*. London: British Broadcasting Corporation and Penguin Books.

Berger, Susan. 2009. "Production and Reproduction of Gender and Sexuality in Legal Discourses of Asylum to the United States." *Signs: Journal of Women in Culture and Society* 34(3): 659–685.

Bergeron, Suzanne. 2006. *Fragments of Development: Nation, Gender, and the Space of Modernity*. Ann Arbor, MI: University of Michigan Press.

Berman, Ari. 2015. *Give Us the Ballot: The Modern Struggle for Voting Rights in America*. New York: Farrar, Straus and Giroux.

Bernstein, Elizabeth. 2007a. "The Sexual Politics of the 'New Abolitionism'." *differences* 18 (3): 128–151.

Bernstein, Elizabeth. 2007b. *Temporarily Yours: Intimacy, Authenticity, and the Commerce of Sex*. Chicago, IL: University of Chicago Press.

Bernstein, Elizabeth. 2010. "Militarized Humanitarianism Meets Carceral Feminism: The Politics of Sex, Rights, and Freedom in Contemporary Anti-Trafficking Campaigns." *Signs: Journal of Women in Culture and Society* 36(1): 45–71.

Bettcher, Talia. 2013. "When Selves Have Sex: What the Phenomenology of Trans Sexuality Can Teach About Sexual Orientation." *Journal of Homosexuality*, December 3.

Bilge, Sirma. 2013. "Intersectionality Undone: Saving Intersectionality from Feminist Intersectionality Studies." *Du Bois Review* 10(2): 405–424.

Bilgín, Pinar and L.H.M. Ling. 2014. "Transcultural Asia: Unlearning Colonial/Imperial Power Relations." *Perceptions: Journal of International Affairs* 19(1): 1–8.

Bleiker, Roland. 2000. "We Don't Need Another Hero." *International Feminist Journal of Politics* 2(1): 30–57.

Bobo, Lawrence, James Kluegel and Ryan Smith. 1997. "Laissez-Faire Racism: The Crystallization of a 'Kinder, Gentler' Anti-Black Ideology." In Steven Tuch and Jack Martin, eds. *Racial Attitudes in the 1990s: Continuity and Change*. Westport, CT: Praeger.

Brennan, Denise. 2008. "Competing Claims of Victimhood? Foreign and Domestic Victims of Trafficking in the United States." *Sexuality Research and Social Policy* 5(4): 45–61.

Briggs, Laura. 2002. *Reproducing Empire: Race, Sex, Science, and U.S. Imperialism in Puerto Rico*. Berkeley, CA: University of California Press.

Briggs, Laura. 2015. "Making Sex, Making Race: Perspectives on Torture." *International Feminist Journal of Politics* 17(1): 20–39.

Briggs, Laura, Gladys McCormick, and J. T. Way. 2008. "Transnationalism: A Category of Analysis." *American Quarterly* 60(3): 625–648.

Brown, Harold. 1977. *Perception, Theory and Commitment: The New Philosophy of Science*. Chicago, IL: Precedent Publishing Company.

Brown, J. Larry. 1995. "Key Welfare Reform Issues: The Empirical Evidence." Center on Hunger, Poverty, and Nutritional Policy. Medford, MA: Tufts University.

Brown, Wendy. 1995. *States of Injury: Power and Freedom in Late Modernity*. Princeton, NJ: Princeton University Press.

Bryce, James. 1888. *The American Commonwealth*, 3 Volumes. New York and London: Macmillan.

Bryce, James. 1902. *The Relations of the Advanced and the Backward Races of Mankind*. London: Clarendon Press.

Buff, Rachel. 2008. "Deportation Terror." *American Quarterly* 60(3): 523–551.

Bump, Philip. 2014. "Is President Obama's Claim to Have Increased Criminal Deportation Accurate?" *The Washington Post*, November 14. Available at: www.washingtonpost.com/blogs/the-fix/wp/2014/11/20/is-president-obamas-claim-to-have-increased-criminal-deportations-accurate/.

Burgess, John W. 1890. *Political Science and Comparative Constitutional Law*. Boston, MA: Gunn and Company.

Burgess, John W. 1902. *Reconstruction and the Constitution, 1866–1876*. Boston, MA: Gunn and Company.

Burke, Edmund. 1790 [1909]. *Reflections on the Revolution in France*. New York: P. F. Collier & Son.

Burns, Nancy. 2007. "Gender in the Aggregate, Gender in the Individual, Gender and Political Action." *Politics & Gender* 3(1): 104–124.

Butterfield, Herbert. 1931. *The Whig Interpretation of History*. London: G. Bell.

Cacho, Lisa Marie. 2012. *Social Death: Racialized Rightlessness and the Criminalization of the Unprotected*. New York and London: New York University Press.

Carbado, Devon. 2013. "Colorblind Intersectionality." *Signs: Journal of Women in Culture and Society* 38(4): 811–845.

Carroll, Susan. 2009. "Reflections on Gender and Hillary Clinton's Presidential Campaign: The Good, the Bad, and the Misogynic." *Politics & Gender* 5(1): 1–20.

Chuang, Janie. 1998. "Redirecting the Debate Over Trafficking in Women: Definitions, Paradigms, and Contexts." *Harvard Human Rights Journal* 11: 65–107.

Chibber, Vivek. 2013. *Postcolonial Theory and the Specter of Capital*. London: Verso.

Children's Bureau. 2012. *Child Welfare Outcomes, 2009–2012: A Report to Congress*. Washington, DC: Department of Health and Human Services. Available at: www.acf.hhs.gov/sites/default/files/cb/cwo09_12.pdf.

Cho, Sumi, Kimberlé Crenshaw and Leslie McCall. 2013. "Toward a Field of Intersectionality Studies: Theories, Applications, Praxis." *Signs: Journal of Women in Culture and Society* 38(4): 785–810.

Choo, Hae Yoon and Myra Marx Ferree. 2010. "Practicing Intersectionality in Sociological Research." *Sociological Theory* 28(2): 129–149.

Ciccariello-Maher, George. 2010. "Jumpstarting the Decolonial Engine: Symbolic Violence from Fanon to Chavez." *Theory and Event* 13(1): 1–19.

Clark, Anna. 1998. "The Chevalier d'Eon and Wilkes: Masculinity and Politics in the Eighteenth Century." *Eighteenth-Century Studies* 32(1): 19–48.

Clark-Mane, Rebecca. 2012. "Transmuting Grammars of Whiteness in Third-Wave Feminism: Interrogating Postrace Histories, Postmodern Abstraction, and the Proliferation of Difference in Third-Wave Texts." *Signs: Journal of Women in Culture and Society* 38(1): 71–98.

Cockburn, Cynthia. 1981. "The Material of Male Power." *Feminist Review* 9 (October): 41–58.

Cohen, Patricia. 2015. "Public-Sector Jobs Vanish, and Blacks Take Blow." *New York Times*, May 25, A1, B5.

Cohen, Simon Baron. 2004. *The Essential Difference*. London: Penguin.

Cole, David. 2003. *Enemy Aliens: Double Standards and Constitutional Freedoms in the War on Terrorism*. New York and London: The New Press.

Condit, Celeste and John Lucaites. 1993. *Crafting Equality: America's Anglo-African Word*. Chicago, IL: University of Chicago Press.

Connell, R.W. 1987. *Gender and Power*. Stanford, CA: Stanford University Press.

Constitution Project. 2004. *Report on Post 9/11 Detentions*. Washington, DC: Georgetown University Public Policy Institute.

Coontz, Stephanie. 2013. "Why Gender Equality Stalled." *New York Times*, February 17, Sunday Review, 1, 6–7.

Cooper, Brittney. 2016. "Intersectionality." In Lisa Disch and Mary Hawkesworth, eds. *Oxford Handbook of Feminist Theory*. Oxford and New York: Oxford University Press.

Corrigan, Rose. 2013. *Up Against the Wall: Rape Reform and the Failure of Success*. New York: New York University Press.

Cott, Nancy. 1998. "Marriage and Women's Citizenship in the United States, 1830–1934." *American Historical Review* 103(5): 1440–1474.

Cott, Nancy. 2000. *Public Vows: A History of Marriage and the Nation*. Cambridge, MA: Harvard University Press.

Courtney, Mark, Amy Dworsky, Adam Brown, Colleen Cary, Kara Love and Vanessa Vorhies. 2011. *Midwest Evaluation of the Adult Functioning of Former Foster Youth: Outcomes at Age 26*. Chicago, IL: Chapin Hall at the University of Chicago.

Crenshaw, Kimberlé Williams. 1989. "Demarginalizing the Intersection of Race and Sex: A Black Feminist Critique of Antidiscrimination Doctrine, Feminist Theory, and Antiracist Politics." *University of Chicago Legal Forum* 1989: 139–167.

Crenshaw, Kimberlé Williams. 1991. "Mapping the Margins: Intersectionality, Identity Politics, and Violence against Women of Color." *Stanford Law Review* 43(6): 1241–1299.

Crenshaw, Kimberlé Williams. 2012. "From Private Violence to Mass Incarceration: Thinking Intersectionally About Women, Race, and Social Control." *UCLA Law Review* 59: 1419–1472.

Cryle, Peter. 2009. "Les Choses et les Mots: Missing Words and Blurry Things in the History of Sexuality." *Sexualities* 12(4): 437–450.

Currier, Ashley. 2012. "Decolonization and Gender and Sexual Dissidence in Post-Independence Namibia." *Signs: Journal of Women in Culture and Society* 37(2): 441–467.

Cuvier, Georges. 1817 [1831]. *The Animal Kingdom: Arranged in Conformity with Its Organization*, Translated from the French by H. M. Murtrie. New York: G. C. & H. Carville.

Danchev, Alex. 2008. "Human Rights and Human Intelligence." In Steve Tsang, ed. *Intelligence and Human Rights in the Era of Global Terrorism*. Stanford, CA: Stanford University Press.

Darling, Marsha. 1998. "African American Women in State Elective Office in the South." In Sue Thomas and Clyde Wilcox, eds. *Women and Elective Office*. Oxford and New York: Oxford University Press.

Davidson, Adam. 2013. "Coming to America: Are Illegal Immigrants Actually Detrimental to the U.S. Economy?" *New York Times Magazine*, February 17, 17–18.

Davis, Angela. 1972. "Reflections on the Black Woman's Role in the Community of Slaves." *The Massachusetts Review* 13(1/2): 81–100.

Davis, Angela. 2003. "Racism, Birth Control and Reproductive Rights." In Reina Lewis and Sara Mills eds. *Feminist Post-Colonial Theory: A Reader*. London and New York: Routledge.

Davis, Kathy. 2008. "Intersectionality as Buzzword: A Sociology of Science Perspective on What Makes a Feminist Theory Successful." *Feminist Theory* 9(1): 67–85.

De Tocqueville, Alexis. 1840. *Democracy in America*. New York: Adlard & Saunders.

Delgado, Richard and Jean Stefancic. 2001. *Critical Race Theory*. New York: New York University Press.

Devor, Holly. 1989. *Gender Blending: Confronting the Limits of Duality*. Bloomington, IN: Indiana University Press.

Disch, Lisa. 2016. "Representation." In Lisa Disch and Mary Hawkesworth, eds. *Oxford Handbook of Feminist Theory*. Oxford and New York: Oxford University Press.

Doonan, Christina. 2014. *The Sexual Politics of Humanitarian Regulation*. PhD thesis, Rutgers University, New Brunswick, New Jersey.

Du Bois, W.E.B. 1903. *The Souls of Black Folks*. Chicago, IL: A.C. McClurg & Company.

Du Bois, W.E.B. 1910. "The Souls of White Folks." *Independent* 69: 339–342, 18 August, Reprinted in *Darkwater: Voices from Within the Veil*. New York: Harcourt Brace and Company. 1920. Available at www.gutenberg.org/files/15210/15210-h/15210-h.htm#Chapter_II.

Du Bois, W.E.B. 1935. *Black Reconstruction in America*. New York: Atheneum.

Douglass, Frederick. 1845. *Narrative of the Life of Frederick Douglass: An American Slave*. Boston, MA: Anti-Slavery Society.

Edin, Kathryn and H. Luke Schaefer. 2015. *$2.00 a Day: Living on Almost Nothing in America*. New York: Houghton Mifflin Harcourt.

Ehrenreich, Barbara and Arlie Russell Hochschild. 2002. *Global Woman: Nannies, Maids, and Sex Workers in the New Economy*. New York: Henry Holt & Company.

Emirbayer, Mustafa. 1997. "Manifesto for a Relational Sociology." *American Journal of Sociology* 103(2): 281–317.

Enloe, C. 2000. *Maneuvers: The International Politics of Militarizing Women's Lives*. Berkeley, CA: University of California Press.

Enloe, C. 2007. *Globalization and Militarism: Feminists Make the Link*. Lanham, MD: Rowman & Littlefield Publishers.

Fanon, Frantz. 1952 [1967]. *Black Skin, White Masks*. New York: Grove Press.

Fanon, Frantz. 1962. *Wretched of the Earth*. New York: Grove Press.

Farr, James. 2004. "The Science of Politics – as Civic Education – Then and Now." *PS: Political Science and Politics* 37(1): 37–40.

Fausto-Sterling, Anne. 1986. *Myths of Gender*. New York: Basic Books.

Fausto-Sterling, Anne. 1993. "The Five Sexes: Why Male and Female Are Not Enough." *The Sciences* (March/April): 20–24.

Fedigan, Linda M. 1992. *Primate Paradigms*. Chicago, IL: University of Chicago Press.

Festinger, Trudy. 1988. Expert Testimony. United States District Court, D. Maryland, L.J. By and Through Darr v. Massinga, decision, Civ. No. JH-84-4409, September 27. F. Supp. 508 (D.Md. 1988).

Fierke, K.M. 1999. "Besting the West: Russia's Macchiavellian Strategy." *International Feminist Journal of Politics* 1(3): 403–434

Finifter, Ada. 1983. *Political Science: The State of the Discipline*. Washington, DC: American Political Science Association.

Finney, Nissa and Ludi Simpson. 2009. *Sleepwalking to Segregation? Challenging Myths about Race and Migration*. Bristol: Policy Press.

Fletcher, Michael. 2014. "Whites Think Discrimination against Whites is a Bigger Problem than Bias against Blacks." *The Washington Post*, October 8. Available at: www.washingtonpost.com/news/wonkblog/wp/2014/10/08/white-people-think-racial-discrimination-in-america-is-basically-over/.

Foner, Eric and John A. Garraty. 1991. *The Reader's Companion to American History*. New York: Houghton Mifflin Harcourt Publishing Company.

Fong, Edmund. 2015. *American Exceptionalism and the Remains of Race: Multicultural Exorcisms*. New York: Routledge.

Fraser, Nancy. 1989. "Women, Welfare, and the Politics of Need Interpretation." *Unruly Practices*. Minneapolis, MN: University of Minnesota Press.

Gallop Poll. 2014. "Black and White Differences in Views on Race." December 12. Available at: www.gallup.com/poll/180107/gallup-review-black-white-differences-views-race.aspx.

Garcia Bedolla, Lisa. 2007. "Intersections of Inequality: Understanding Marginalization and Privilege in the Post-Civil Rights Era." *Politics & Gender* 3(2): 232–248.

Gerson, Kathleen. 2010. *The Unfinished Revolution: Coming of Age in a New Era of Gender, Work, and Family*. Oxford and New York: Oxford University Press.

Gilens, Martin. 1995. "Racial Attitudes and the Opposition to Welfare." *Journal of Politics* 57(November): 994–1014.

Gilens, Martin. 1996. "Race Coding and White Opposition to Welfare," *American Political Science Review* 90(September): 593–604.

Glazer, Nathan and Daniel Patrick Moynihan. 1963. *Beyond the Melting Pot: The Negroes, Puerto Ricans, Jews, Italians and Irish of New York City*. Cambridge, MA: MIT Press.

Goldberg, David Theo. 1993. *Racist Culture: Philosophy and the Politics of Meaning*. Oxford: Blackwell Publishers.

Goodin, Robert and Hans Dieter Klingemann. 1996. *A New Handbook of Political Science*. Oxford: Oxford University Press.

Gould, Stephen J. 1980. "Sociobiology and the Theory of Natural Selection." In G. W. Barlow and J. Silverberg, eds. *Sociobiology: Beyond Nature/Nurture*. Boulder, CO: Westview Press, pp. 257–269.

Green, Kristen. 2015. *Something Must Be Done About Prince Edward County: A Family, a Town, a Civil Rights Battle*. New York: Harper & Row.

Greenstein, Fred and Nelson Polsby. 1975. *Handbook of Political Science*, vols. I–VII. Reading, MA: Addison-Wesley.

Gutierrez, David and Pierette Hondagneu-Sotelo. 2008. "Introduction: Nation and Migration." *American Quarterly* 60(3): 503–521.

Hajer, Maarten. 2006. "Doing Discourse Analysis: Coalitions, Practices, Meanings." In M. van den Brink and T. Metze, eds. *Words Matter in Policy and Planning: Discourse Theory and Method in the Social Sciences*. Utrecht: Netherlands Geographical Studies, pp. 65–74.

Hajer, Maarten and David Laws. 2006. "Ordering through Discourse." In M. Moran, M. Rein, and R. Goodin, eds. *The Oxford Handbook of Public Policy*. Oxford: Oxford University Press.

Hamilton, Charles. 1977. "De-racialization: Examination of a Political Strategy." *First World* (March–April): 3–5.

Hancock, Ange-Marie. 2004. *The Politics of Disgust: The Public Identity of the Welfare Queen*. New York: New York University Press.

Hancock, Ange-Marie. 2007a. "Intersectionality as a Normative and Empirical Paradigm." *Politics & Gender* 3(2): 248–254.

Hancock, Ange-Marie. 2007b. "When Multiplication Doesn't Equal Quick Addition: Examining Intersectionality as a Research Paradigm." *Perspectives on Politics* 5(1): 63–79.

Hancock, Ange-Marie. 2009. "An Untraditional Intersectional Analysis of the 2008 Election." *Politics & Gender* 5(1): 96–105.

Hancock, Ange-Marie. 2011. *Solidarity Politics for Millennials: A Guide to Ending the Oppression Olympics*. New York: Palgrave Macmillan.

Hancock, Ange-Marie. 2016. *Intersectionality: An Intellectual History*. Oxford and New York: Oxford University Press.

Haney-Lopez, Ian. 2014. *Dog Whistle Politics: How Coded Racial Appeals Have Reinvented Racism and Wrecked the Middle Class*. Oxford and New York: Oxford University Press.

Haney, Lynne. 2010. "Working through Mass Incarceration: Gender and the Politics of Prison Labor from East to West." *Signs: Journal of Women in Culture and Society* 36(1): 73–97.

Haney, Lynne. 2013. "Motherhood as Punishment: The Case of Parenting in Prison." *Signs: Journal of Women in Culture and Society* 39(1): 105–130.

Haney-Lopez, Ian. 1996. *White by Law: The Legal Construction of Race*. New York: New York University Press.

Harris, Frederick. 2012. "The Price of a Black President." *The New York Times*, October 27.

Harvey, David. 2004. *A Brief History of Neoliberalism*. Oxford: Oxford University Press.

Hawkesworth, Mary. 2003. "Congressional Enactments of Race-Gender: Toward a Theory of Raced-Gendered Institutions." *American Political Science Review* 97(4): 529–550.

Hawkesworth, Mary. 2006. *Feminist Inquiry: From Political Conviction to Methodological Innovation*. New Brunswick, NJ: Rutgers University Press.

Hawkesworth, Mary. 2012. *Political Worlds of Women: Activism, Advocacy and Governance in the 21st Century*. Boulder, CO: Westview Press.

Hennessy-Fiske, Molly. 2015. "Immigrants Sue Texas over State's Denial of Birth Certificates for U.S.-born Children." *Los Angeles Times*, July 18. Available at: www.latimes.com/nation/immigration/la-na-texas-immigrant-birth-20150718-story.html#page=1.

Hegel, Georg Wilhelm Friedrich. 1807. *Phänomenologie des Geistes* [*The Phenomenology of Spirit* or *The Phenomenology of Mind*]. Bamberg and Wurzburg.

Herbert, Bob. 2010. The Shame of New York. Op-Ed. *The New York Times*. Available at: www.nytimes.com/2010/10/30/opinion/30herbert.html?_r=0.

Hero, Rodney. 1998. *Faces of Inequality: Social Diversity in American Politics*. Oxford: Oxford University Press.

Holland, Catherine. 2001. *The Body Politic: Foundings, Citizenship and Difference in the American Political Imagination*. New York: Routledge.

Horsman, Reginald. 1981. *Race and Manifest Destiny: The Origins of American Racial Anglo-Saxonism*. Cambridge, MA: Harvard University Press.

Hsu, Madeline Y. 2003. "Unwrapping Orientalist Constraints: Restoring Homosocial Normativity to Chinese American History." *Amerasia Journal* 29(2): 230–253.

Huddy, Leonie and Tony Carey. 2009. "Group Politics Redux: Race and Gender in the 2008 Democratic Presidential Primaries." *Politics & Gender* 5(1): 81–96.

Huntington, Samuel. 1996. *The Clash of Civilizations and the Remaking of World Order*. New York: Simon and Schuster.

Huntington, Samuel. 2004. "The Hispanic Challenge." *Foreign Policy* (March–April): 30–45.

Isaac, Jeffrey. 2003. "Conceptions of Power." In Mary Hawkesworth and Maurice Kogan, eds. *Encyclopedia of Government and Politics*, 2nd edn. London: Routledge.

International Labor Organization (ILO). 2010. *International Labor Migration: A Rights-Based Approach*. Geneva: ILO.

Jordan-Young, Rebecca. 2010. *Brain Storm: The Flaws in the Science of Sex Differences*. Cambridge, MA: Harvard University Press.

Jordan-Zachery, Julia. 2007. "Am I a Black Woman or a Woman who is Black: A Few Thoughts on the Meaning of Intersectionality." *Politics & Gender* 3(2): 254–263.

Jordan-Zachery, Julia. 2008. "Policy Interaction: The Mixing of Fatherhood, Crime and Urban Policies." *Journal of Social Policy* 37(1): 81–102.

Jordan-Zachery, Julia. 2009. *Black Women, Cultural Images, and Social Policy*. New York: Routledge.

Jordanova, Ludmilla. 1989. *Sexual Visions: Images of Gender in Science and Medicine between the 18th and 20th Centuries*. Madison, WI: University of Wisconsin Press.
Junn, Jane. 2007. "Square Pegs and Round Holes: Challenges of Fitting Individual-level Analysis to a Theory of Politicized Context of Gender." *Politics & Gender* 3(1): 124–134.
Junn, Jane. 2009. "Making Room for Women of Color: Race and Gender Categories in the 2008 U.S. Presidential Election." *Politics & Gender* 5(1): 105–110.
Kain, John F. 1968. "Housing Segregation, Negro Employment, and Metropolitan Decentralization." *Quarterly Journal of Economics* 82(2): 175–197.
Kane, Nazneen. 2007. "Frantz Fanon's Theory of Racialization." *Human Architecture: Journal of the Sociology of Self-Knowledge* 5(Summer): 353–362.
Kaufman-Osborn, Timothy. 2005. "Gender Trouble at Abu Ghraib." *Gender & Politics* 1(4): 597–619.
Kessler, Suzanne and Wendy McKenna. 1978. *Gender: An Ethnomethodological Approach*. New York: John Wiley.
King, Deborah. 1988. "Multiple Jeopardy, Multiple Consciousness: The Context of Black Feminist Ideology." *Signs: Journal of Women in Culture and Society* 14(1): 42–72.
King, Desmond and Rogers Smith. 2011. "On Race, The Silence is Bipartisan." *New York Times*, September 2.
Kitch, Sally. 2009. *The Specter of Sex*. Albany, NY: State University of New York Press.
Knott, Theresa and Kirsten Donovan. 2010. "Disproportionate Representation of African-American Children in Foster Care: Secondary Analysis of the National Child Abuse and Neglect Data System." *Children and Youth Services Review* 32(5): 679–684.
Kretsedemas, Philip. 2008. "Immigration Enforcement and the Complication of National Sovereignty: Understanding Local Enforcement as an Exercise in Neoliberal Governance." *American Quarterly* 60(3): 553–573.
Kristof, Nicholas. 2015. "Malachi's World." *New York Times*, June 18, A25.
Kronsell, Annica. 2005. "Gendered Practices in Institutions of Hegemonic Masculinity." *International Feminist Journal of Politics* 7(2): 280–298.
Krumholtz, Norman. 1997. "Urban Planning, Equity Planning, and Racial Justice." In June Manning Thomas and Marsha Ritzdorf, eds. *Urban Planning and the African American Community*. Thousand Oaks, CA: Sage, pp. 109–125.
Kuokkanen, Rauna. 2008. "Globalization as Racialized, Sexualized Violence: The Case of Indigenous Women." *International Feminist Journal of Politics* 10(2): 216–234.
Kurzman, Charles and David Schanzer. 2015. "The Other Terrorist Threat." *New York Times*, June 16, A27.
Lakatos, Imre. 1970. "Falsification and the Methodology of Scientific Research Programs." In Imre Lakatos and Alan Musgrave (eds.), *Criticism and the Growth of Knowledge*. Cambridge, MA: Cambridge University Press, pp. 91–195.
Lake, Marilyn and Henry Reynolds. 2008. *Drawing the Global Colour Line: White Men's Countries and the International Challenge of Racial Equality*. Cambridge: Cambridge University Press.
Landes, Joan. 1988. *Women and the Public Sphere in the Age of the French Revolution*. Ithaca, NY: Cornell University Press.
Landes, Joan. 1998. *Feminism, the Public and the Private*. New York: Oxford University Press.
Laqueur, Thomas. 1990. *Making Sex: Body and Gender from Greeks to Freud*. Cambridge, MA: Harvard University Press.
Laqueur, Thomas. 2009. "Sexualities and the Transformation of Culture: The Longue Durée." *Sexualities* 12(4): 418–436.

Laqueur, Thomas. 2012. "The Rise of Sex in the Eighteenth Century: Historical Context and Historiographical Implications." *Signs: Journal of Women in Culture and Society* 37(4): 802–813.

Latour, Bruno. 1988. *The Pasteurization of France*. Translated by Alan Sheridan and John Law. Cambridge, MA: Harvard University Press.

Lavariega Monforti, Jessica and Adam McGlynn. 2010. "Aquí Estamos? A Survey of Latino Portrayal in Introductory U.S. Government and Politics Textbooks," *PS: Political Science and Politics* 43(2): 309–316.

Lawless, Jennifer. 2009. "Sexism and Gender Bias in Election 2008: A More Complex Path for Women in Politics." *Politics & Gender* 5(1): 70–80.

Le Doeuff, Michele. 2007. *Hipparchia's Choice: An Essay Concerning, Women, Philosophy, etc.* Trans. Trista Selous. New York: Columbia University Press.

Levi-Strauss, Claude. 1969. *The Elementary Structures of Kinship*. Boston, MA: Beacon Press.

Levi-Strauss, Claude. 1971. "The Family." In H. Shapire, ed. *Man, Culture and Society*. London: Oxford University Press.

Lewis, Gail. 2013. "Unsafe Travel: Experiencing Intersectionality and Feminist Displacements." *Signs: Journal of Women in Culture and Society* 38(4): 869–892.

Lewis, Michael. 1978. *The Culture of Inequality*. Amherst, MA: University of Massachusetts Press.

Lezra, Esther. 2015. *The Colonial Art of Demonizing Others*. London and New York: Routledge.

Lieberman, Robert C. 1995. "Race and the Organization of Welfare Policy." In Paul E. Peterson, ed. *Classifying by Race*, pp. 157–187. Princeton, NJ: Princeton University Press.

Lipsitz, George. 2011. *How Racism Takes Place*. Philadelphia, PA: Temple University Press.

Long, Scott and Rasha Moumneh. 2009. *"They Want Us Exterminated": Murder, Torture, Sexual Orientation and Gender in Iraq*. New York: Human Rights Watch. Available at: https://www.hrw.org/report/2009/08/17/they-want-us-exterminated/murder-torture-sexual-orientation-and-gender-iraq.

Longino, Helen. 1990. *Science as Social Knowledge*. Princeton, NJ: Princeton University Press.

Lovejoy, Arthur O. 1936. *The Great Chain of Being: A Study of the History of an Idea*. Cambridge, MA: Harvard University Press.

Lovenduski, Joni. 2000. *Feminism and Politics*. Monograph Collection. London: Matt–Pseudo.

Lugones, Maria. 2007. "Heterosexualism and the Colonial Modern Gender System." *Hypatia* 22(1): 186–209.

Lugones, Maria. 2010. "Towards a Decolonial Feminism." *Hypatia* 25(4): 742–759.

Luke, Timothy. 1987. "Methodological Individualism: The Essential Ellipsis of Rational Choice Theory." *Philosophy of the Social Sciences* 17(3): 341–355.

Luke, Timothy. 1999. "The Discipline as Disciplinary Normalization: Networks of Research." *New Political Science* 21(3): 345–363.

Lukes, Stephen. 1973. *Individualism*. New York: Harper and Row.

Lutz, Catherine. 2001. *Homefront: A Military City and the American Twentieth Century*. Boston, MA: Beacon Press.

Lutz, Catherine. 2006. "Empire is in the Details." *American Ethnologist* 33(4): 593–611.

Lykke, Nina. 2010. *Feminist Theory: A Guide to Intersectional Theory, Methodology, and Writing*. London: Routledge.

Marchand, Marianne and Anne Sisson Runyon. 2011. *Gender and Global Restructuring*, 2nd edn. New York: Routledge.

Markowitz, Sally. 2001. "Pelvic Politics: Sexual Dimorphism and Racial Difference." *Signs: Journal of Women in Culture and Society* 26(2): 389–414.

Marks, Jonathan. 2009. *Why I Am Not a Scientist*. Berkeley, CA: University of California Press.

McLafferty, Sara and Valerie Preston. 1992. "Spatial Mismatch and Labor Market Segmentation for African American and Latina Women." *Economic Geography* 68(4): 406–431.

McWilliams, Carey. 1968. *North from Mexico: The Spanish-Speaking People of the United States*. New York: Greenwood Press.

Mendoza, Breny. 2014. "La cuestión de la colonialidad de género." In Breny Mendoza, *Feminismo y Colonialidad del Poder. Ensayos de Crítica Feminista en Nuestra América*. Mexico: Editorial Herder.

Mendoza, Breny. 2016. "Coloniality of Gender and Power: From Postcoloniality to Decoloniality." In Lisa Disch and Mary Hawkesworth, eds. *Oxford Handbook of Feminist Theory*. Oxford and New York: Oxford University Press.

Mettler, Suzanne. 2000. "States' Rights, Women's Obligations: Contemporary Welfare Reform in Historical Perspective." *Women and Politics* 21(1): 1–34.

Meyers, Jan. 1993. *Congressional Record*, 103rd Cong., 1st Sess., pH1084, March 10.

Mignolo, Walter. 2000. *Local Histories/Global Designs: Coloniality, Subaltern Knowledges, and Border Thinking*. Princeton, NJ: Princeton University Press.

Millhiser, Ian. 2015. "Federal Appeals Court Strikes Down Texas Voter ID Law." *Think Progress*. August 5. Available at: http://thinkprogress.org/justice/2015/08/05/3688384/breaking-federal-appeals-court-strikes-down-texass-voter-id-law/.

Mills, Charles. 2008. "White Ignorance." In Robert Proctor and Londa Schiebinger, eds. *Agnotology: The Making and Unmaking of Ignorance*, pp. 230–249. Stanford, CA: Stanford University Press.

Mills, Charles W. 2015. "Decolonizing Western Political Philosophy." *New Political Science* 37(1): 1–24.

Mills, Charles and Carole Pateman. 2007. *Contract and Domination*. Cambridge, MA: Polity Press.

Mink, Gwendolyn. 1995. *The Wages of Motherhood: Inequality in the Welfare State*. Ithaca, NY: Cornell University.

Molony, Barbara. 2010. "Crossing Boundaries: Transnational Feminisms in Twentieth-Century Japan." In Mina Roces and Louise Edwards, eds. *Women's Movements in Asia: Feminisms and Transnational Activism*. New York: Routledge.

Monroe, Kristen. 2005. *Perestroika! The Raucous Rebellion in Political Science*. New Haven, CT: Yale University Press.

Morgan, Jennifer. 1997. "'Some Could Suckle Over Their Shoulder': Male Travelers, Female Bodies, and the Gendering of Racial Ideology, 1500–1770." *The William and Mary Quarterly*, 3rd Series, LIV: 167–192.

Morgan, Jennifer. 2004. *Laboring Women: Reproduction and Labor in New World Slavery*. Philadelphia, PA: University of Pennsylvania Press.

Moses, Claire. 1984. *French Feminism in the Nineteenth Century*. Albany, NY: State University of New York Press.

Mouffe, Chantal. 1996. "Democracy, Power and the Political." In Seyla Benhabib, ed. *Democracy and Difference: Contesting the Boundaries of the Political*. Princeton, NJ: Princeton University Press, pp. 245–256.

Mounmeh, Rasha. 2015. "What is a Gay Refugee? Producing Wartime Queerness between Iraq, Syria, and Lebanon." Department of Women's and Gender Studies Convivial Conversations. Rutgers University, New Brunswick. February 16.

Muñoz, José Esteban. 1996. "Ephemera as Evidence: Introductory Notes to Queer Acts." *Women and Performance: A Journal of Feminist Theory* 8(2): 5–16.

Murray, Thomas. 1983. "Partial Knowledge." In Daniel Callahan and Bruce Jennings, eds. *Ethics, the Social Sciences, and Policy Analysis.* New York: Plenum Press, pp. 305–334.

Nagar, Richa, Victoria Lawson, Linda McDowell and Susan Hanson. 2002. "Locating Globalization: Feminist (Re)Readings of the Subjects and Spaces of Globalization." *Economic Geography* 78(3): 257–284.

National Advisory Commission on Civil Disorders (NACCD). 1968. *Report of the National Advisory Commission on Civil Disorders.* Washington, DC: National Institute of Justice, U.S. Department of Justice.

National Coalition for Child Protection Reform. 2011. "Who Is in 'The System' – and Why." Issue Paper No. 5. Alexandria, VA: National Coalition for Child Protection Reform. Available at: www.nccpr.org/reports/05SYSTEM.pdf.

Ngai, Mae. 2004. *Impossible Subjects.* Princeton, NJ: Princeton University Press.

Norton, Michael and Samuel Sommers. 2011. "Whites See Racism as a Zero-Sum Game That They Are Now Losing." *Perspectives on Psychological Science* 6(3): 215–218.

Nova, Carlos and Nikolas Rose. 2000. "Genetic Risk and the Birth of the Somatic Individual." *Economy and Society* 29(4): 485–513.

Novkov, Julie, and Scott Barclay. 2010. "Lesbians, Gays, Bisexuals, and the Transgendered in Political Science: Report on a Discipline-Wide Survey." *PS: Political Science & Politics* 43(1): 95–106.

Offen, Karen. 2000. *European Feminisms, 1700–1950.* Stanford, CA: Stanford University Press.

Okonjo, Kamene. 1994. "Women and the Evolution of a Ghanian Political Synthesis." In Barbara Nelson and Najma Chowdhury, eds., *Women and Politics Worldwide.* New Haven, CT: Yale University Press, pp. 285–297.

Okuma, Marquis Shigenobu. 1921. "Illusions of the White Race." *Asian Review,* January. Reprinted in Kyoshi Kawakami, ed., *What Japan Thinks.* New York: Macmillan, pp. 160–170.

Olson, Joel. 2000. "The Du Boisian Alternative to the Politics of Recognition." Paper presented at the Annual Meeting of the Western Political Science Association. San Jose, CA, March 24–26.

O'Malley, Pat. 2000. "Uncertain Subjects: Risks, Liberalism, Contract." *Economy and Society* 29(4): 460–484.

Omi, Michael and Howard Winant. 1986. *Racial Formation in the United States: From the 1960s to the 1980s.* New York: Routledge.

Open Society Foundation. 2013. *Globalizing Torture: CIA Secret Detention and Extraordinary Rendition.* New York: Open Society Justice Initiative. Available at: www.opensocietyfoundations.org/sites/default/files/globalizing-torture-20120205.pdf.

Orr, Marion and Valerie C. Johnson. 2007. "Race and the City: the View from Two Political Science Journals." In Wilbur Rich, ed., *African American Perspectives on Political Science.* Philadelphia, PA: Temple University Press, pp. 308–324.

Osborne, Thomas and Nikolas Rose. 1999. "Do the Social Sciences Create Phenomena? The Example of Public Opinion Research." *British Journal of Sociology* 50(3): 367–396.

Oyewumi, Oyeronke. 1997. *The Invention of Women: Making an African Sense of Western Gender Discourses.* Minneapolis, MN: University of Minnesota Press.

Pateman, Carole. 1998. "The Patriarchal Welfare State." In Joan Landes, ed. *Feminism, the Public and the Private.* New York: Oxford University Press.

Pearson, Charles H. 1893. *National Life and Character: A Forecast*. London: Macmillan.
Pease, Donald. 2009. *The New American Exceptionalism*. Minneapolis, MN: University of Minnesota Press.
Peterson, V. Spike. 2003. *A Critical Rewriting of Global Political Economy: Integrating Reproductive, Productive, and Virtual Economies*. London: Routledge.
Philipose, Elizabeth. 2007a. "Decolonizing Political Theory." *Radical Pedagogy* 9(1) Winter. Available at http://radicalpedagogy.icaap.org/content/issue9_1/philipose.html.
Philipose, Liz. 2007b. "The Politics of Pain and the Uses of Torture." *Signs: Journal of Women in Culture and Society* 32(4): 1047–1071.
Pinker, Steven. 2002. *The Blank Slate: The Modern Denial of Human Nature*. New York: Viking.
Poovey, Mary. 1988. *Uneven Developments*. Chicago, IL: University of Chicago Press.
Popper, Karl. 1959. *The Logic of Scientific Discovery*. New York: Basic Books.
Popper, Karl. 1972a. *Conjectures and Refutations: The Growth of Scientific Knowledge*, 4th edn. London: Routledge & Kegan Paul.
Popper, Karl. 1972b. *Objective Knowledge: An Evolutionary Approach*. Oxford: Clarendon Press.
Proctor, Robert. 2008. "Agnotology: A Missing Term to Describe the Cultural Production of Ignorance (and its Study)." In Robert Proctor and Londa Schiebinger, eds. *Agnotology: The Making and Unmaking of Ignorance*. Stanford, CA: Stanford University Press, pp. 1–33.
Proctor, Robert and Londa Schiebinger, eds. *Agnotology: The Making and Unmaking of Ignorance*. Stanford, CA: Stanford University Press.
Puar, Jasbir 2007. *Terrorist Assemblage: Homonationalism in Queer Times*. Durham, NC: Duke University Press.
Pynchon, Thomas. 1984. *Slow Learner*. Boston, MA: Little, Brown and Company.
Quadagno, Jill. 1994. *The Color of Welfare: How Racism Undermined the War on Poverty*. New York: Oxford University Press.
Quijano, Anibal. 2000. "Coloniality of Power, Eurocentrism, and Latin America." *Nepantla: Views from South* 1(3): 533–580.
Rabin, Yale. 1997. "The Persistence of Racial Isolation: The Role of Government Action and Inaction." In June Manning Thomas and Marsha Ritzdorf, eds. *Urban Planning and the African American Community*. Thousand Oaks, CA: Sage, pp. 93–108.
Rabinow, Paul and Nikolas Rose. 2003. "Thoughts on the Concept of Biopower Today." Paper presented at Conference on Vital Politics: Health, Medicine, and Bioeconomics into the 21st Century. London School of Economics, September 5–7.
Rainwater, Lee and William Yancey. 1967. *The Moynihan Report and the Politics of Controversy*. Cambridge, MA: MIT Press.
Raissiguier, Catherine. 1999. "Gender, Race, and Exclusion: A New Look at the French Republican Tradition." *International Feminist Journal of Politics* 1(3): 435–459.
Rappeport, Alan. 2015. "From the Right: A New Slur for G.O.P. Candidates." *New York Times*, August 13, A13.
Rawls, John. 1971. *A Theory of Justice*. Cambridge, MA: Belknap Press.
Reich, Robert B. 1991. "Secession of the Successful." *New York Times Magazine*, January 20. Available at www.nytimes.com/1991/01/20/magazine/secession-of-the-successful.html?pagewanted=1.
Richardson, Sara. 2012. "Sexing the X: How the X Became the 'Female Chromosome'." *Signs: Journal of Women in Culture and Society* 37(4): 909–933.
Richter-Montpetit, Melanie. 2007. "Empire, Desire, and Violence: A Queer Transnational Feminist Reading of the Prisoner 'Abuse' in Abu Ghraib and the Question of Gender Equality." *International Feminist Journal of Politics* 9(1): 38–59.

Rivera Cusicanqui, Silvia. (2004) "La noción de 'derecho' o las paradojas de la modernidad postcolonial: indígenas y mujeres en Bolivia." *Ecuador: Revista Aportes Andinos* October: 1–9.

Roberts, Dorothy. 1999. *Killing the Black Body: Race, Reproduction, and the Meaning of Liberty.* New York: Vintage.

Roberts, Dorothy. 2011. *Fatal Invention: How Science, Politics and Big Business Re-create Race in the 21st Century.* New York: The New Press.

Rorty, Richard. 1979. *Philosophy and the Mirror of Nature.* Princeton, NJ: Princeton University Press.

Rose, Nikolas. 1996. "Power and Subjectivity: Critical History and Psychology." In C.F. Graumann and K.J. Gergen, eds. *Historical Dimensions of Psychological Discourse.* Cambridge, MA: Cambridge University Press.

Rose, Nikolas. 2001. "The Politics of Life Itself." *Theory, Culture, and Society* 18(1): 1–30.

Rose, Nikolas and Peter Miller. 1992. "Political Power beyond the State: Problematics of Government." *British Journal of Sociology* 43(2): 172–205.

Rose, Tricia. 2013. "Public Tales Wag the Dog: Telling Stories about Structural Racism in the Post-Civil Rights Era." *Du Bois Review* 10(2): 447–469.

Roshanravan, Shireen. 2014. "Motivating Coalition: Women of Color and Epistemic Disobedience." *Hypatia* 29(1): 41–58.

Roosevelt, Theodore. 1897. "National Life and Character." In *American Ideals and Other Essays Social and Political.* New York: Putnam & Sons, pp. 293–294.

Roosevelt, Theodore. 1902. *Strenuous Life: Essays and Addresses.* London: Grant Richards.

Ross, Edward A. 1901. "The Causes of Race Superiority." *Annals of the American Academy of Political and Social Science,* 18 July.

Rousseau, Jean Jacques. 1758 [1960]. *Politics and Arts: Letter to M. D'Alembert on the Theatre.* Allan Bloom, Trans. Ithaca, NY: Cornell University Press.

Rousseau, Jean Jacques. 1762 [1950]. *The Social Contract.* G.D.H. Cole trans. New York: E. P. Dutton & Company.

Rubin, Gayle. 1975. "The Traffic in Women: Notes on the Political Economy of Sex." In Rayner Reiter, ed. *Toward an Anthropology of Women.* New York: Monthly Review Press.

Rutenberg, Jim. 2015. "A Dream Undone: Inside the Fifty Year Campaign to Roll Back the Voting Rights Act." *New York Times Magazine.* August 2, pp. 32–39, 46–48.

Sadowski-Smith, Claudia. 2008. "Unskilled Labor Migration and the Illegality Spiral: Chinese, European, and Mexican Indocumentados in the United States, 1882–2007." *American Quarterly* 60(3): 779–804.

Said, Edward. 1977. *Orientalism.* London: Penguin.

Sampaio, Anna. 2015. *Terrorizing Latino/a Immigrants.* Philadelphia, PA: Temple University Press.

Samuelson, Meg. 2007. "The Disfigured Body of the Female Guerrilla: (De)militarization, Sexual Violence, and Redomestication in Zoe Wicomb's David's Story." *Signs: Journal of Women in Culture and Society* 32(4): 833–856.

Santos, Boaventura de Sousa. 2014. *Epistemologies of the South: Justice against Epistemicide.* Boulder, CO: Paradigm Publishers.

Sassen, Saskia. 2001. "The Excesses of Globalisation and the Feminisation of Survival." *Parallax* 7(1): 100–110.

Sassen, Saskia. 2002. "Global Cities and Survival Circuits." In Barbara Ehrenreich and Arlie Russell Hochschild, eds., *Global Woman: Nannies, Maids, and Sex Workers in the New Economy.* New York: Metropolitan Books/Henry Holt, pp. 254–274.

Sassen, Saskia. 2010. "Strategic Gendering: One Factor in the Constituting of Novel Political Economies." In Sylvia Chant, ed. *The International Handbook of Gender and Poverty*. Cheltenham: Edward Elgar Publishing, pp. 35–40.

Schram, Sanford F. and Brian Caterino, 2006. *Making Political Science Matter: Debating Knowledge, Research, and Method*. New York: New York University Press.

Scott, James. 1985. *Weapons of the Weak: Everyday Forms of Peasant Resistance*. New Haven, CT: Yale University Press.

Scott, James. 1998. *Seeing Like a State: How Certain Schemes to Improve the Human Condition Have Failed*. New Haven, CT: Yale University Press.

Scott, Joan. 1996. *Only Paradoxes to Offer: French Feminists and the Rights of Man*. Cambridge, MA: Harvard University Press.

Seery, Emma and Ana Caistro Arendar. 2014. *Even It Up: Time to End Extreme Inequality*. Oxford: Oxfam. Available at: https://www.oxfam.org/sites/www.oxfam.org/files/file_attachments/cr-even-it-up-extreme-inequality-291014-en.pdf.

Segato, Rita. 2001. "The Factor of Gender in the Yoruba Transnational Religious World." Departamento de Antropologia, Universidade de Brasília. Série Antropologia #289. Brasília, Distrito Federal, Brazil.

Segato, Rita. 2011. "Género y colonialidad: en busca de claves delectura y de un vocabulario estratégico descolonial." In Karina Bidaseca y Vanesa Vazquez Laba, eds. *Feminismos y poscolonialidad. Descolonizando el feminismo desde y en América Latina*. Buenos Aires: Godot.

Sehgal, Parul. 2015. "Power Play." *The New York Times Magazine*, July 19, 11–13.

Seidelman, Raymond and Edward Harpham. 1985. *Disenchanted Realists: Political Science and the American Crisis, 1884–1984*. Albany, NY: SUNY Press.

Shapiro, Michael J. 2006. *Deforming American Political Thought: Ethnicity, Facticity, and Genre*. Lexington, KY: University of Kentucky Press.

Sheftall, Beverly Guy. 1995. *Words of Fire*. New York: The New Press.

Shelby, Tommie. 2007. "Justice, Deviance and the Dark Ghetto." *Philosophy & Public Affairs* 35(2): 126–160.

Shih, Elena. 2013. "After-Trafficking Work: Moral, Ethical and Vocational Rehabilitation." In Sallie Yea and Pattana Kitiarsa, eds. *Forcing Issues: Rethinking and Rescaling Human Trafficking in the Asia-Pacific Region*. London and New York: Routledge.

Simien, Evelyn. 2007. "Doing Intersectionality Research: From Conceptual Issues to Practical Examples." *Politics and Gender* 3(2): 264–271.

Siu, Paul C.P. 1987. *The Chinese Laundryman: A Study of Social Isolation*. New York: New York University Press.

Sjoberg, Laura. 2007. "Agency, Militarized Femininity, and Enemy Others: Observations from the War in Iraq." *International Feminist Journal of Politics* 9(1): 82–102.

Smart, Carol. 1992. "The Woman of Legal Discourse." *Social Legal Studies* 1(1): 29–44.

Smith, Rogers. 2004. "The Puzzling Place of Race in American Political Science." *PS: Political Science and Politics* 37(1): 41–50.

Smith, Steven G. 1992. *Gender Thinking*. Philadelphia, PA: Temple University Press

Somit, Albert and Joseph Tanenhaus. 1967. *The Development of American Political Science*. Boston, MA: Allyn and Bacon.

Spade, Dean and Craig Willse. 2016. "Norms and Normalization." In Lisa Disch and Mary Hawkesworth, eds. *Oxford Handbook of Feminist Theory*. Oxford and New York: Oxford University Press.

Sperling, Valerie. 2009. *Sex, Politics, and Putin: Political Legitimacy in Russia*. Oxford: Oxford University Press.

Spillers, Hortense. 1987. "Mama's Baby, Papa's Maybe: An American Grammar Book." *Diacritics: A Review of Contemporary Criticism* 17(2): 65–81.

Squires, Judith. 1999. *Gender in Political Theory*. Cambridge: Polity Press.

Srivastava, Sarita. 2005. "'You're calling me a racist?' The Moral and Emotional Regulation of Antiracism and Feminism." *Signs: Journal of Women in Culture and Society* 31(1): 29–62.

Staudt, Kathleen. 2011. "Globalization and Gender at Border Sites: Femicide and Domestic Violence in Ciudad Juárez." In Marianne Marchand and Anne Sisson Runyon, eds. *Gender and Global Restructuring*, 2nd edn. New York: Routledge, pp. 187–200.

Stevens, Jacquelyn. 1998. "Race and the State: Male Order Brides and the Geographies of Race." *Theory & Event* 2(3) Fall.

Stevens, Jacquelyn. 1999. *Reproducing the State*. Princeton, NJ: Princeton University Press.

Stuurman, Siep. 2000. "François Bernier and the Invention of Racial Classification." *History Workshop Journal* 50 (Autumn): 1–21.

Suchland, Jennifer. 2015. *Economies of Violence: Transnational Feminism, Postsocialism, and the Politics of Sex Trafficking*. Durham, NC: Duke University Press.

Sullivan, Laura, Tatjana Meschede, Lars Dietrich, Thomas Shapiro, Amy Traub, Catherine Ruetschlin, and Tamara Draut. 2015. *The Racial Wealth Gap: Why Policy Matters*. New York: Demos. Available at: www.demos.org/sites/default/files/publications/RacialWealthGap_1.pdf.

Sullivan, Shannon and Nancy Tuana. 2007. *Race and Epistemologies of Ignorance*. Albany, NY: State University of New York Press.

Swain, Carol. 1993. *Black Faces, Black Interests*. Cambridge, MA: Harvard University Press.

Taibbi, Matt. 2014. *The Divide: American Injustice in the Age of the Wealth Gap*. New York: Spiegel and Grau.

Tang-Martinez, Zuleyma. 1997. "The Curious Courtship of Sociobiology and Feminism: A Case of Irreconcilable Differences." In Patricia Adair Gawaty, ed. *Feminism and Evolutionary Biology*. New York: Chapman Hall, pp. 116–150.

Threadcraft, Shatema. 2014. "Intimate Injustice, Political Obligation, and the Dark Ghetto." *Signs: Journal of Women in Culture and Society* 39(3): 735–760.

Thompson, Krissah. 2010. "Arrest of Harvard's Henry Louis Gates Jr. Was Avoidable, Report Says." *Washington Post*, June 30. Available at: www.washingtonpost.com/wp-dyn/content/article/2010/06/30/AR2010063001356.html.

Ting, Jennifer. 1995. "Bachelor Society: Deviant Heterosexuality and Asian American Historiography." In Gary Okihiro et al. eds. *Privileging Positions: The Sites of Asian American Studies*. Pullman: Washington State University Press.

Titus, Jill Ogline. 2014. *Brown's Battleground: Students, Segregationists, and the Struggle for Justice in Prince Edward County, Virginia*. Chapel Hill, NC: University of North Carolina Press.

Towns, Anne. 2009. "The Status of Women as a Standard of 'Civilization'." *European Journal of International Relations* 15(4): 681–706.

True, Jacqui and Michael Mintrom. 2001. "Transnational Networks and Policy Diffusion: The Case of Gender Mainstreaming." *International Studies Quarterly* 45(1): 27–57.

Tuana, Nancy 2008. "Coming to Understand: Orgasm and the Epistemology of Ignorance." In Robert Proctor and Londra Schiebinger, eds. *Agnotology*. Stanford, CA: Stanford University Press, pp. 108–145.

Tulloch, Hugh. 1988. *James Bryce's American Commonwealth: The Anglo-American Background*. Rochester, NY: The Boydell Press.

Vivas, E. 1960. "Science and the Studies of Man." In H. Schoek and J. Wiggans, eds. *Scientism and Values*. Princeton, NJ: D. van Nostrand Company.

Wacquant, Loïc. 2002. "Deadly Symbiosis: Rethinking Race and Imprisonment in Twenty-First-Century America." *Boston Review* (April/May). Available at: http://bostonreview.net/BR27.2/wacquant.html.

Wacquant, Loïc. 2008. "The Body, the Ghetto, and the Penal State." *Qualitative Sociology* 32(1): 101–129.

Wallace, Sherri L., and Marcus D. Allen. 2008. "Survey of African American Portrayal in Introductory Textbooks in American Government/Politics: A Report of the APSA Standing Committee on the Status of Blacks in the Profession." *PS: Political Science and Politics* 41(1): 153–160.

Walton, Hanes, Jr, Cheryl M. Miller, and Joseph P. McCormick II. 1995. "Race and Political Science: The Dual Traditions of Race Relations Politics and African-American Politics." In James Farr, John S. Dryzek, and Stephen T. Leonard, eds. *Political Science in History: Research Programs and Political Traditions*. New York: Cambridge University Press, pp. 145–174.

Weiser, Wendy and Erik Opsal. 2014. *The State of Voting, 2014*. New York: Brennan Center for Justice, New York University Law School. Available at: www.brennancenter.org/analysis/state-voting-2014.

White, Ruth Anne and Debra Rog. 2004. "Introduction." *Child Welfare* 83(5): 389–392.

Williams, Bernard. 1985. *Ethics and the Limits of Philosophy*. Cambridge, MA: Harvard University Press.

Willoughby, Westel. 1900. *Social Justice: A Critical Essay*. New York: Macmillan.

Wilson, Edward O. 1975. *Sociobiology: The New Synthesis*. Cambridge, MA: Harvard University Press.

Wilson, Edward O. 1978. *On Human Nature*. Cambridge, MA: Harvard University Press.

Wilson, William Julius. 1980. *The Declining Significance of Race*. Chicago, IL: University of Chicago Press.

Wimmer, Andreas and Nina Glick Schiller. 2003. "Methodological Nationalism, Social Sciences, and the Study of Migration: An Essay in Historical Epistemology." *International Migration Review* 37(3): 576–610.

Wood, Ellen. 1972. *Mind and Politics*. Berkeley, CA: University of California Press.

X, Malcolm. 1963. "The Race Problem." African Students Association and NAACP Campus Chapter. Michigan State University, East Lansing, Michigan. January 23. Available at: http://ccnmtl.columbia.edu/projects/mmt/mxp/speeches/mxt14.html.

Young, Iris Marion. 1991. *Justice and the Politics of Difference*. Princeton, NJ: Princeton University Press.

Yuval-Davis, Nira. 2006. "Belonging and the Politics of Belonging." *Patterns of Prejudice* 40 (3): 197–214.

INDEX

abstract universalism 18, 41, 45–6, 149
Abu Ghraib 3, 99
academic disciplines 11, 33, 41, 141–2
AFDC (Aid to Families with Dependent Children) 1, 95
affirmative action 119–21, 137n5, 158
Afghanistan 80, 97, 99–100, 106, 109n25
African Americans: Agassiz on 72n1; Burgess on 39; DNA samples from 71; enfranchisement of 34, 36–7, 45, 122; as failing to assimilate 154–5; families of 144; fear of 91; incarceration of 90–1; legal subordination of 57, 75, 105; and national origins 83; and the police 116; in political science 35; racial profiling of 89; urban poor communities of 86–8; white beliefs about 118, 132, 154; *see also* Black men; Black women
African slave trade 3, 16, 57
African women 12, 76
agency, equal 43
agnotology 5
alien absconders 103
Almond, Gabriel 29–30
American Exceptionalism 27, 45–6, 49n11
Americanization courses 131
American political science: critical history of 17–18, 33–4, 38, 41; as hegemonic approach 47–8; methodological nationalism in 128; as replicating hierarchies 142

American Political Science Association (APSA) 17, 25, 28–31, 48n10
Anglo-Saxon civilization 36, 38, 40, 44, 48n8, 77
anti-colonial theory 10–11
APSR (*American Political Science Review*) 35
Arabs 1, 98–9, 101, 108n23, 152
Aristotle 58–9, 136n1
Arizona, anti-migrant laws in 81, 104
arms, bearing 56
Ashcroft, John 102, 108n23
Asian Americans 83, 113, 120, 154
Asians, as racial category 3, 20, 53, 69, 75, 80–1
axiological individualism 124

"backward races" 11–12, 18, 34, 36–7, 39–42, 48, 51
behavioral revolution 17, 30
Berger, John 110–11, 136
Bernier, François 53
biological determinism: historical development of 18–19, 50–2, 64; and individuality 17; and intersectionality 7, 146; resurrection of 66–8, 72; and sexual dimorphism 14
biologism 19, 52, 72, 98
biologization 50, 52, 54–5, 62, 72–3
birth certificates, denial of 105, 109n32
birth control 162
birthright citizenship 46, 77, 79, 105
Black Lives Matter 154

Black men: criminalization of 4; and violence 155–6
Blacks, as homogenized identity 11–12, 14, 17
black sites 2, 97, 99
Black Skin, White Masks 3, 11
Black women: excluded from "woman" 42; hypervisibility of 4; invisibility of 7–8; legal personhood of 75; as responsible for own poverty 154–6; sterilizations of 108n19; and welfare policy 95–6, 151
Blumenbach, J. F. 55
body: inequality written on the 3; racialized-gendered 72, 159–60
Bosnia 127
brain, sex differences in 67
Brown, Michael 2
Bryce, James 17, 36–9
Burgess, John W. 17, 35, 37–9, 48n7, 56
Bush, George W.: invasion of Iraq 132–3; and LGBT rights 139n20; and methodological nationalism 22; and Supreme Court 138n12; war on terrorism 97–9; and workfare 108n18
Bush v. Gore 1

California: Asian migration to 38, 48n9, 79–81; DNA database in 92; prison labor in 93; racial laws in 81–3
care economies 126–7, 162
Carson, Ben 137–8n9
categorization 7, 42–3, 51, 147
causality, contorting 6, 37, 135, 141, 143, 152, 155, 159
center-periphery frame 129
character deficit accounts 157–8
Cherokee nation 77
Chertoff, Michael 102
Chicago School 30
childbearing, state control of 160
child care 114
children: channeling through education systems 131; removal from parents 95–6, 108n20
Chinese Americans 38, 79–80
Christianity: and coloniality 12–13; and sex trafficking laws 125; and slavery 53
citizenship: boundaries of 74, 96, 161; homogenous 10; in settler colonies 56; US racial restrictions on 77–9, 85, 106n4; *see also* equal citizenship
civic education 34, 130
civilizations, clash of 46, 97, 101

civilized/barbaric binary 4, 11, 13
civilizing mission 13–14, 34, 39, 72
Civil Rights Act 119, 137n5
class: with race and gender 144–5; segregation by 153
classification: as conceptual practice of power 41–2; disciplinary norms on 18; rejection of racial 27
CODIS (Combined DNA Index System) 92
colonial hierarchies 62
colonialism 3, 10, 15, 133
colonization: and sex-segregation 64; unknowing about 19
color-blindness: in 2016 Republican presidential race 137n9; and affirmative action 120–2; as presupposition 21, 112, 117–19, 135; and racialized gendering 85; strategic 46
comparative analysis 147, 156
complementarity 15, 68
complexity, messiness of 23, 42, 146, 148–9
CompStat 92
corporations, as people 107n5
cosmopolitanism 23, 157–8
Crenshaw, Kimberlé 7, 143
crime, war on 156
critical history 17, 33–4
critical race studies 51, 74, 106n1
critical reflexivity 29, 31
"cuckservative" 138n9
cultural deficit models 21, 119, 154–8
cultural literacy 130
cultural pluralism 23, 154, 157–8
Cuvier, Georges 55

de-colonial theory 10, 13, 15, 18
decorporealization 6
defense, national 22, 132, 135
de-gendering 16
degeneration 55, 57
de Gouges, Olympe 62
dehumanization, gendered 76
democracy: American mission to protect 22; racial and gender exclusions in 17, 34, 36–8, 40–1
Department of Justice (DOJ) 2, 98–100, 102–3, 108n23, 109n24, 122–3
deportation 20, 85, 101–5, 130
de-racialization 121
despotism, healthy 38
detainees, abuse of 1, 97–101, 106, 109n27
development policies 161–2

DHS (Department of Homeland Security) 101–2, 104
difference: de-naturalizing 145–6; embodied 44, 74, 163; flattening of 23, 151; hierarchies of 19, 21, 48n3, 72–3, 162
disembodied politics: in American political science 34; assumptions of 2–3; conceptual practices of power in 18; demystification of 143
DNA profiles 92–3, 107n13
Du Bois, W. E. B. 75, 106n2, 154
Dunning, W. A. 37

economic crisis of 2008 87–8
economic migration 103
education, and political participation 32
embodied power: analytical tools making visible 17, 136, 140–1; and anti-terrorism 97; and biological determinism 19; double-binds resulting from 114; and intersectionality 8, 10, 149, 163; and mass mobilization 4; and nation building 131; overlapping dynamics of 73; rendering invisible 5–6, 17–18, 21, 32, 135; science and politics in 51; state practices of 2–3, 23, 43, 73–4; tropes of whiteness as 151; in United States 1–2, 19–20, 85, 105–6; use of term 3
embodied processes 147
embodiment: biological accounts of 51–2, 68, 73; de-politicization of 6; "one sex" model of 59; politics of 24, 159–60, 163
empiricism 29, 110–11, 136n1
"enemy combatants" 20, 97–8, 106
enslaved women 16, 56, 64, 75–6
epidermalization 11, 162
epistemic authority, withholding 5
epistemological individualism 123
equal citizenship: assumption of 2, 113; and democracy 38; denying 62; and ethnicity 154; formal guarantees of 20, 85, 105
equality, formal 21, 43–4, 73–4, 113–14, 116
Equality Clause 107, 119
equivalence, false 150–1
essentialism 27
ethnicity, social science discourse on 154–5, 157
eugenics 7, 68, 108n19
Eurocentrism 10–11, 13–14, 26
European epistemic regimes 7
European women 14, 16, 52

evolutionary psychology 19, 66
exclusion, politics of 160
ex-convicts, exclusion of 90–1
experience: assumptions behind 111–12; morselization of 157
extraordinary rendition 99, 109n25

failed states 4
Fanon, Frantz 3, 11, 158
fathers, absence of 94, 144
femininity 14, 51, 65–6, 68, 98, 100
feminism, and de-colonial theory 15
feminization: homophobia as defense against 134; of indigenous men 15; of migration 126; rape as 76; of terror suspects 2–3, 98–100
Ferguson, Missouri 2, 89
feudal hierarchies 50, 60–3
Filipinos 40, 85
foreclosures 87–8
Fourth Amendment 97

Gates, Henry Louis 115–16
gender, as dichotomous variable 27
gender differences: multiple hierarchies of 16; philosophical approaches to 58–9; in political science 27; racialized concept of 14–15, 51–2, 64; in republican politics 60–3; in social science 65, 67–8; state complicity in 44
gendered racialization see racialization and gendering
gendering: and colonization 15–16; and interrogation techniques 20, 100; of the market 126
gender segregation 82
genetic surveillance 92–3
Geneva Convention 98, 106
genocide 4, 68, 138n13
genomics 69–71
gentrification programs 20, 87, 146
ghettoes 80, 86–8, 146
Ginsberg, Ruth Bader 122
globalization 47, 158, 162, 164
global South: in political investigation 32; scholarship from 10, 26; seen as backwards 129; silencing of 14; and structural adjustment processes 126
GNP (gross national product) 129, 139n17
Gray, Freddie 154
great chain of being 53–4, 58
group membership 3, 43, 113, 115, 141
Guantánamo 3, 97, 99

habeas corpus 20, 85, 97, 106
Harlan, John Marshall 115, 117
Hegel, G. W. F. 10, 38, 40
heteronormativity 23, 116, 162
Homeland Security Act 101
homogeneity 14, 38, 44
homogenization 12, 17
homonationalism 134
Human Genome Project 58, 69–70
Human Rights Watch 22, 133–5
Hussein, Saddam 22, 133
hyper-surveillance 88, 150, 154
hypervisibility 4

ICE (Immigration and Customs Enforcement) 103–4, 109n28
identity: articulations of 9; imposed 4; in political science 28; politics of 161, 163
identity politics 24, 158, 161, 163
ignorance: epistemology of 141; geography of 5; sanctioned 155, 159
imagined communities 85, 107n7, 129
imperial expansion 17, 40–1
income inequality, and gender 32
indentured servants 13–14, 56
'Indians,' as homogenized identity 3, 11–12, 14, 17; *see also* Native Americans
indigenous peoples: and colonialism 3, 12–14; and gendering 15–16; invisibility of 6; racializing of 20, 57; suppression of knowledges 10; and women's authority 64
individual irresponsibility 21, 119
individualism: dialectical and metaphysical 136n3; and essentialism 27; as presupposition 21, 112–17, 135
industrialization 72, 129
inequality: cultural deficit model of 155–7; dimensions of 147–8; and international institutions 162; role of state in 43, 161
inferiority: internalization of 3, 11; state production of 6, 12, 19
injustice, and escalating resistance 159
Innocence Project 93
interaction effects 145
intermarriage 57, 76, 79, 106n3
internalized stereotypes 116
international institutions 124–6, 162–3
internment camps 85
interracial sex 57
interrogation techniques: enhanced 99–100; gendering 20
intersectional asymmetries 74

intersectionality: as analytical frame 143–4, 164–5; and deficit analyses 157–8; denaturalizing discourses 145–6; on dichotomous variables 42; framework of 6–10, 23; and gender dichotomy 16; interrogating tropes of whiteness 152; investigating processes 146–7; methodological precepts of 148–9; and multiple structures of oppression 47; in political science 18, 24, 142–3; on race and sex 51; and sites of politics 160–1
intersexuals 65
intimacy, politics of 24, 160, 162–3
intra-group differences 27
invisibility, modes of 4
Iraq 22, 99–100, 106, 132–5, 139n18, 162

Jackson, Andrew 77
Japan, and US racial laws 81–2, 107n6
Japanese Americans 20, 80–1, 85
Jefferson, Thomas 76
Jim Crow 37, 94
Johnson-Reed Immigration Act 83–4

King, Martin Luther 117
knowledge, politics of 163
knowledge production: and acceptance of belief 141; embodied power in 41, 47; and epistemic location 9; racialization and gendering in 17; scientific transformation of 30; segregation in 35; suppression of indigenous 12

labor: domestic 76, 114; gendered divisions of 63–4, 66; intellectual division of 141, 159; reproductive 15, 76, 162; sexualization of women's 126–7; undocumented workers in division of 103
Latin American Modernity/Coloniality Group 10
Latinos: fear of 91–2; home ownership by 88; racial profiling of 20, 88–91, 101, 103–5
laws, fair 113
League of Nations 82
legislative assemblies 56
lending, predatory 87
LGBT (lesbian, gay, bisexual, transgender) 133–5, 139nn19–20
liberation groups 116
liberty, negative 73–4, 106, 160–1
Linnaeus, Carl 54–5

literacy, criminalization of 57
literacy tests 37, 48n5, 97
Lodge, Henry Cabot 35
lower races *see* "backward races"

Mahdi Army 22, 134–5
Manifest Destiny 78, 82
Maple Heights 89
marketization 125–6
marriage: and race 57; same-sex 133, 161; social science on 65
Martin, Trayvon 2, 9
masculinity: in feudal and republican regimes 63; psychological inventories of 65; and race 14
Merriam, Charles 30
Mestizos 11–12
methodological individualism: as conceptual practice of power 43; and embodied power 5, 21; masking systemic disadvantage 157; in political science 18, 21–2, 27, 41; as presupposition 112, 123–4, 135; and TVPA 128; and white androcentrism 46
methodological nationalism: as conceptual practice of power 44; and embodied power 21; and NGOs 133–5; in political science 18, 22, 41; as presupposition 112, 128–32, 135
Mexican Americans 78, 85, 154
Mexico, US border with 102
microphysics of power 116, 142, 161
micropolitics 142
Middle Passage 7, 12
Middletown studies 30–1
minorities, classification as 26
Minute Men 2, 97
miscegenation 57, 70, 161
modernity: and coloniality 7, 10, 13; neoliberal capitalism as 42; as post-racial 150; racialization and gendering as features of 23, 59, 68, 143; and temporality 72
monarchy, women blamed for 60–2
motherhood: and paid work 114–15; republican 61, 63–4; responsible 94
mothers: single 96, 108n17; teenaged 94–5
multiculturalism 23, 157–8
multi-level analysis 147–8, 163
multiple jeopardy 7
Muslims: detention of 1, 98; expulsion from European countries 14; and gang violence 156; in Iraq 133

Muslim terrorists 20, 98, 152–3
Muslim women, 'rescuing' 101
mystification 14, 33, 40, 141

NACCD (National Advisory Commission on Civil Disorders) 87
NAFTA (North American Free Trade Agreement) 87
Napoleonic Code 62
national identity 44, 104, 131, 135
national interest 124, 132–3, 135–6
Nationality Act 77–9, 106n4
national origin 83–4, 108
nation-states: in American political science 34–5, 38–41, 128; historical origins of 130; and Indigenous communities 15; and methodological nationalism 22; naturalizing 5, 42, 44, 135; producing populations of 130–1, 161; and racialization 3, 13–14, 17; ranking 129
Native Americans 69, 75–8, 108n21, 120
natural hierarchies 11, 52–3
naturalized citizenship 77, 80
"natural kinds" 57, 64–5, 69
natural order 18, 56, 117
neocolonial relations 163
neoliberalism 22, 42, 85, 87, 125–6, 162
New Deal 84
non-average events 31–2

Oath Keepers 2, 97
Obama, Barack 104, 122
observations, controlled 111
ontological individualism 123
Operation Community Shield 102–4
Operation Return to Sender 103
Operation Tarmac 102–3, 109n29
Operation Wagon Train 102–3
oppression: internalized 11; simultaneity of 7–8

patriarchy, in Indigenous and enslaved communities 15
PATRIOT Act 97, 99, 101, 108n22, 109n24
Pearson, Charles H. 48n8
perception: common modes of 131; presuppositions of 110–11, 135–6; theory-laden 141
personal responsibility 85, 94, 108n16
Plessy v. Ferguson 117, 119 , 137n7

police: incentive systems for 92; in inner-city neighborhoods 88–9; respecting authority of 116
political homophobia 133–4
political objects 40–1
political outcomes, prediction of 124
political science: APSA taskforce on 30–2; biologism in 19; conceptual practices of power within 17, 32–3, 41–7; embodied power in 2, 5, 17–18, 25–8, 164; and epidermalization 11; implicated in social control 141–2; lack of self-critique 28–9; mainstream 23, 24n1; observations and facts in 111–12; and state practices 35–6, 74
political sphere, inequality in 32, 113
political subjects 43, 145
politics: disembodied concepts of 26; of diversity 160; of embodiment 24, 159–60, 163; of exclusion 160; of identity 160,163; of knowledge 163; use of term 25
polygenesis 55, 72n1
Popper, Karl 111
postcolonial theory 6, 10, 13, 143
post-occidental theory 47, 143
post-racialism 122
post-socialist states 125–6
Powell, Lewis 120–1
power: conceptual practices of 18, 25–49, 141; in political science 25, 142; rendering invisible 32
power relations 8–9, 32–3, 43, 72, 144–7
precarity 126
preference maximization 124
presuppositions: on gender 68; in political research 21, 111–12; on race 70
prison labor 93, 107–8n15
prison population 20, 90–3
private sphere: and Black women 95; gendering of 15–16, 64; in liberal political theory 73, 113–14; politics in 160
professional occupations, exclusion from 64, 83
pro-natalism 39–40, 160
property: right to own 19, 56, 130; as voting qualification 37
prostitution 125, 127–8, 138n15
PRWORA (Personal Responsibility and Work Opportunity Reconciliation Act) 94–5, 108n16
psychological individualism 124

public housing 91, 146
public opinion, shaped by presuppositions 112
public schools 86, 107n8
PUC (person under control) 100
Puerto Rico 84, 108n19

al-Qaida 97, 132, 138n13, 139n18
quantitative approaches 27, 31, 42, 48n2, 93
Quijano, Anibal 10–14, 110, 119
Quota Board 84

race: behavioral stereotypes of 115; biologization of 18, 52–8, 68–71; Bryce on 36–8; Burgess on 39; contradictory claims about 151; in critical race theory 51; debate over essentiality of 165n1; depoliticizing 24, 158; and DNA samples 93; du Bois on 106n2; in political science 25–8, 34–5, 157–8; as suspect classification 137n6; theorizations of 18
race and sex: biological deterministic accounts of 7, 16, 18–19, 26; and group membership 3; as identity 28; naturalization of 73; as political 50, 52, 141, 143; quantitative studies of 144–5; restricting jobs by 137n5
raced-gendered institutions 24, 143, 163
race-evasive culture 142, 152
race/gender hierarchies: in American political science 35; and colonization 16; and immigration laws 78; practices preserving 144, 146; scientific taxonomy of 55; and slavery 75; state creation of 22, 124; and war-making 4
race-neutrality 45, 84, 122
racial bias 92, 94
racial categories, variations in 74–5, 83
racial difference: and American culture 27; in colonial division of labor 12; and genomic thinking 69; and labor stratification 12; naturalization of 54
racial discrimination, as ongoing problem 119–22, 137n5
racial exclusions 37, 80, 84
racial formation 75, 83, 149
racial inequality 32, 71, 88, 117–19, 121–2, 155
racialization: colonial 11–12; continuing state practices of 22, 135, 157–8; ethnocultural hierarchies of 162; and race neutrality 83–5; temporality of 13;

transnational politics of 81–3; violent resistance to 159; and war-making 3–4
racialization and gendering: beyond the nation-state 161; colonial 10, 14–16; and embodied power 2–3; intersectionality and 7, 143–5, 152; invisibility of 21, 23, 41, 72, 114, 122; and low-income communities 88; normalization of 6, 141; and perceptions of crime 90–1; in political science 47, 157, 164; processes of 5, 19–20, 52, 101, 146–7; and sex trafficking 128; in state practices 3–5, 18, 74, 105–6, 160; violence and torture in 162; in war on terror 97–8, 100–1; in welfare policy 94–6
racial profiling: Holder's guidelines against 107n10; and immigration 104; and intersectionality 9; in race-neutral language 105; in war on terror 20, 89–90, 162
racing-gendering 74
racism: laissez-faire 155; temporal framing of 150
rape 4, 76, 99, 134, 152
rational choice model 41, 46, 48n2, 123, 142
Rawls, John 113, 137n4
Reconstruction 34, 36–7, 39, 48n6
recurrent histories 33, 46
Regents of the University of California vs. Bakke 120–1, 137n8
Rehnquist, William 120–1, 137n7, 138n12
republics, liberal 14, 62
research heuristics, fundamental 41, 44, 46
research questions, framing 29, 41, 142
residential segregation 85–6, 107n9, 145, 152
reverse discrimination: Supreme Court rulings on 21, 120; as trope of whiteness 150–1; use of notions of 23; and white androcentrism 46
rights of Man 16–17
riots 22–3, 87, 130, 153–6, 159
Roberts, John 138n12
Roosevelt, Theodore 17, 35, 37–40, 42, 48n8, 80–1
Ross, Edward 17, 40, 48n9
Rousseau, Jean-Jacques 14, 61
Royal Africa Company 56
Rumsfeld, Donald 99

al-Sadr, Moqtada 22, 134
Said, Edward 152

school segregation 80–1, 85–6, 119
science, authority of 45, 51
scientific discourses 18, 33, 52, 149
scientific investigations 111, 142
scientific language 50–1
Secured Communities program 103
securitization measures: as embodied power 98–9; and Latino/a communities 2, 20, 101–2; racialization and gendering in 3–4, 89, 97, 152; and sex work 127
self-determination 17, 83, 113, 130, 145, 155
self-governance, fitness for 6, 18–19, 38, 40–1, 43, 56
self-making 46, 154
self-protection 56, 90, 113
self-understanding 4, 12, 22, 74, 116, 124, 161
separate spheres 62
September 11, 2001 attacks 1, 89, 97, 102
servility, performances of 3
settler societies 6, 14, 40, 58, 77, 130, 147
sex: biologization of 58, 64–5; in feminist theory 51; 'opposite' 18, 59; *see also* race and sex
sex/gender, base/superstructure model of 68; *see also* gender
sex/gender dimorphism: as achievement of civilization 14, 51; and cultural traits 18; and evolutionary psychology 66; as imposed 65–6; and politics of modernity 59–60; presumption of 7
sex trafficking 22, 124–8
sexual differences *see* gender differences
sexual hierarchies 15, 72, 113
sexual humiliation 79, 99–101
sexualization, processes of 6
sex work 125–8, 138n16
Shelby County vs. Holder 122
silencing 5, 141
single axis analysis 7, 27
slavery: chattel 3, 45–6, 52–3, 56; and Indigenous patriarchy 15; and marriage 57; as Other of wage labor 72; and race 12–13, 75–6
social control 107n14, 142, 162
social justice activism 158, 161, 163
social networks 141, 152–3
social norms 142
social sciences: causality in 159; constituting their own object 40–1; explanatory frames in 23; methodological nationalism in 128; methodological norms of 7,

144–5; and natural kinds 65; phenomenological bases of 28
social security cards 102–3
social values 110, 142
sociobiology 19, 67
the South, epistemologies of 10
sovereign citizens 2
Spanish-American War 40
Stalin, Joseph 49n11
statistical analysis 29, 42, 46
sterilizations 42, 108n19, 162
strip searches 1, 20, 98–9
Subaltern Studies Group 10
subordination, scripted practices of 3, 58, 98
subsistence economies 126, 129, 164
Supreme Court: in 2000 election 1; and anti-Chinese laws 79–80; color-blind discourse of 21, 120, 122, 151; on corporations as persons 107n5; and internment of Japanese-Americans 85; on racial profiling 99, 104; on segregation 86, 115, 117, 119; on women 78

TANF (Temporary Assistance to Needy Families) 1, 95, 108n18, 115, 151
Tea Party 151
teen pregnancy *see* mothers, teenaged
temporality 13, 23
terrorism: accounts of origins of 31–2; DHS operations against 101–2; and invasion of Iraq 132–3; and racial profiling 1, 89, 97–8
theoretical presuppositions 21, 111
Thomas, Clarence 121
tokenism 114
torture 20, 22, 99, 101, 162
Tourgée, Albion 117
Trail of Tears 77
transactional sex 125–6, 138n15
Trans 72n4

ummah 135
unassimilability 23, 44, 75, 78, 80–1, 101, 131, 158
underground economy 127
undocumented migrants 102–4, 109n30
UNESCO (United Nations Educational, Scientific, and Cultural Organization) 68–9
United Kingdom, ethnicity and violence in 156
United Nations, on terrorism 132–3

United States: building national identity in 22, 131–2; electoral politics in 140–1; history of racism in 145–6, 150; and homonationalism 133–5; immigration laws in 80–1, 83–4, 96–7, 130; legal enactment of racing-gendering 73–4, 77; Manifest Destiny policy 78; mass incarceration in 90–3, 107n14; mass migration to 37–8; political science in *see* American political science; and sex trafficking 124–6; welfare policy in 94–5, 115, 151; white beliefs on racism in 118–19; white extremist terrorism in 152–3; white male privilege in 26–7
universal claims 16, 20, 54, 67, 160
"unknowing" 19, 21, 72
"unseeing" 21
urban marginalization 146

value-neutrality 9
Victims of Trafficking and Violence Protection Act (TVPA) 22, 124–5, 127–8, 138n14
vigilantes 2, 79
violence: epistemic 10, 13–14; by police 91, 119, 154; political 44, 135, 153; revolutionary 11; state 157
voter fraud 105, 122, 138n10
voting rights: exclusion of ex-convicts from 91; racialized attacks on 104–5; Supreme Court decisions on 21
Voting Rights Act (VRA) 94, 105, 119, 122–3, 138n11–12

"war on drugs" 20, 88, 90
"War on Terror" 3, 20, 104, 162
"ways of seeing" 21–2, 110, 112, 136, 140
weapons of mass destruction 132, 139n18
welfare dependency 4, 94, 144
welfare queens 151
Westernization, in Iraq 134–5
white androcentrism: as conceptual practice of power 45–6; displacing 23, 144; in political science 18, 41, 142
white men: as focus of political science 31; invisibility of 4; as modal category 43; in settler societies 56; as ungendered 45
whiteness: Anglo-American identity of 20; as discursive formation 149–52; du Bois on 106n2; globalization of 81, 147, 149; grammars of 23, 144, 150

whites: legal definitions of 75, 77; people of color acting like 114; racialization of 44; as self-making 155; as unraced 45, 144–5

white supremacy: in American history 27, 37, 106n1, 131; Japanese reaction to 82; in public policy 74; science and politics fostering 72

Wilson, Woodrow 35, 37, 82

women: acting like men 114; in American political science 34; Aristotle on 58–9; Chinese 79–80; enfranchisement of 78; exclusion from Columbia University 48n7; exclusion from political rights 40, 60–4, 78, 82; incarceration of 93–4; in labor force 114–15; and natalism 39; state regulation of 161; and Westernization 134–5; work on 45

women of color 8–10, 74, 93–4, 115, 162; *see also* Black women

Yorubas 12, 15

Lightning Source UK Ltd.
Milton Keynes UK
UKHW020300220219
337666UK00020B/619/P

9 781138 667310